AMINTAPHIL: The Philosophical Foundations of Law and Justice

Volume 12

The *AMINTAPHIL book series* considers the philosophical foundations of law and justice from the perspectives of academic philosophy, practical political science and applied legal studies. The American Section of the International Association for the Philosophy of Law and Social Philosophy ("AMINTAPHIL") supervises the series, which dedicates each volume to the most pressing contemporary problems in legal theory and social justice. AMINTAPHIL holds biennial meetings of leading scholars in philosophy, law, and politics to discuss the philosophical basis of vital questions. The AMINTAPHIL volumes present the ultimate results of these discussions.

Gordon Albert Babst • Renée Nicole Souris
Joan McGregor
Editors

Liberal Constitutionalism and its Contemporary Challenges

Springer

AMINTAPHIL

Editors
Gordon Albert Babst
Chapman University
Orange, CA, USA

Renée Nicole Souris
Florida Institute of Technology
Melbourne, FL, USA

Joan McGregor
Arizona State University
Tempe, TX, USA

ISSN 1873-877X ISSN 2351-9851 (electronic)
AMINTAPHIL: The Philosophical Foundations of Law and Justice
ISBN 978-3-031-53601-4 ISBN 978-3-031-53602-1 (eBook)
https://doi.org/10.1007/978-3-031-53602-1

This Springer imprint is published by the registered company Springer Nature Switzerland AG
The registered company address is: Gewerbestrasse 11, 6330 Cham, Switzerland

Contents

Introduction

Gordon A. Babst

Abstract Liberal Constitutionalism refers to a political regime governed by a constitution that establishes the rule of law, reflects liberal principles, and is supported by a society whose people can be said to reasonably understand and value those principles as well as the rule of law enshrined in it or in a well-settled understanding if unwritten. As society evolves, so too does its self-understanding of what those principles mean, and how its constitution should be interpreted so as to maintain its relevancy and vibrancy. This evolution in self-understanding and constitutional interpretation guides the regime to enrich the ideals it stands for, such as equality before the law, individual liberty, democracy, tolerance of differences, and the like. Liberal constitutionalism, then, involves a reasonable concord, though not unanimity surrounding political organization and principles. The meanings and applications of documents and principles may be contested and change over time. Nevertheless, though disputes about the meaning and application of liberal principles are to be expected their resolutions are supposed to be amiable even when there is great diversity in the citizenry.

For some years now the liberal constitutional order enshrined within the American political regime has increasingly found itself under a stress test, and the American people are divided as ever since the Civil War, not only politically, but on a variety of social issues about which their polarized opinions are deeply entrenched. A noticeable portion of the electorate is losing faith in our liberal democracy, encouraged by election deniers and those who want to undermine our political principles, or has expressed unease at the fragility of our political institutions. Perhaps most distressing, the rule of law has been questioned by some who seem to have a more personalist take on political authority.

America enjoys a liberal constitutional order that has had the greatest longevity among its peers, but it is nevertheless being challenged to its core to see whether the rule of law can persist and whether the example of its democratic institutions will

G. A. Babst (✉)
Chapman University, Orange, CA, USA
e-mail: gbabst@chapman.edu

G. A. Babst et al. (eds.), *Liberal Constitutionalism and its Contemporary Challenges*, AMINTAPHIL: The Philosophical Foundations of Law and Justice 12, https://doi.org/10.1007/978-3-031-53602-1_1

endure. The role of education and some curricular matters have also become highly contested in the political arena, especially at the local level, though there is also strategic coordination to reshape the civic education of future generations at the national level. Economically, the disparity between the total wealth of the richest as compared to the poorest has been rising, and with this growing economic divide and the increasing role of money in politics there is a corrupting influence of oligarchic leanings among some politically active donors and influencers of politicians and policymakers. All-in-all, the current condition of American politics raises questions about the ability of liberal constitutional regimes to weather the assaults against them.

The array of challenges not only to America but to other modern liberal constitutional states is both broad in scope and alarming, and it may require us to re-think assumptions about how government performs and the expectations of civility we may take for granted. For example, under the administration of former President Donald Trump, we observed that some of the norms that we expected would corral abuses of power in the executive branch were mere conventions, not laws that any branch of government could enforce either directly or via an oversight function. In addition, we saw that the momentum of progress in civil rights, tolerance of differences, and greater income equality for all could actually be set back.[1]

Public verbal attacks by our highest officeholders on formerly disfavored groups, such as racial minorities, women, immigrants, and members of the LGBTQ+ community, ramped up and, worse, were reflected in the condonation and even episodic celebration of acts of aggression carried out against members of such groups. Anti-immigrant sentiment, the Muslim ban, anti-Asian sentiment, and an emerging but no less worrisome anti-science view specifically as regards the covid pandemic received an affirmation by some of the nation's highest leaders. Moreover, extremist groups with minority views—many of whom were amply armed—emerged from America's backwaters as they did similarly in other countries such as Poland and Hungary. Perhaps of greatest concern, white supremacists began to enjoy a long sought-after day in the sun, their perspective normalized through social media amplification of their messages and greater sophistication in fundraising.

The connective tissue that links these groups and the followers of the ideological perspectives they tender in American society is a rejection of the democratic process wherein each citizen is equal with the same full rights to vote and have their votes counted. These folks reject the pluralism of American society, and seek to adjust electoral mechanisms and influence elections office-holders to prioritize their voices, setting fire to our democratic order and not for good reason. The fascist leanings of certain loud voices in social media, combined with the faux news coverage provided by some major television and cable networks, undermine the social contract by challenging the liberal principles upon which our regime rests.

[1] For an accessible discussion of the points made in this paragraph, see "America is Headed Toward Collapse" by Peter Turchin in the June 2, 2023 issue of *The Atlantic*.

Volumes have been and continue to be written on the maladies that affect our liberal constitutional order.[2] In this volume we present cogent analyses of select challenges, some more focused on the foundations and health of our political regime. The first chapter in Part I asks whether the United States is in fact a democracy, or perhaps more of an oligarchy. Identifying aspects of political rule in all three branches of government that are oligarchic in nature, Laurence Houlgate argues that the country has become a mixture of democratic and oligarchic rule, and this is a most unwelcome development. Joshua Kassner probes the extent to which political legitimacy rests not merely on proceduralist accounts, but fundamentally on truth understood as factual accuracy and rational assessments of the available data, that is, on information we can share. The current state of post-truth politics undermines the achievement of common understandings and our ability to make sound decisions that are not only procedurally correct, but what is equally important, also politically legitimate.

The next two chapters in Part I take on different approaches to understanding the U.S. Constitution and using its tools to respond vigorously to contemporary challenges. These chapters critically examine recent proposals that risk hampering our constitutional principles rather than helping to advance them. The third chapter probes the weaknesses in approaching the Constitution as though it were limited by its late eighteenth-century roots, by meanings that prevailed back then. Wade Robison argues that language does not work that way, as simply and definitively as originalists would have us believe, and so we should not attempt to freeze the language and how we use it so that we can continue to achieve liberal purposes within the constitutional framework. Renée Nicole Souris challenges a contemporary approach to constitutional arrangements, called "common good constitutionalism" and its repurposing of Ronald Dworkin's judge-centered theory of law. Common good constitutionalism, Souris argues, pays insufficient attention to the vices of politicians who are supposed to legislate on morality in ways acceptable to the majority of Americans and thus cannot secure the conclusion it aims to establish, which is that judges should defer to legislators' visions of the common good. Souris argues that there is no sound basis for thinking that American legislators cultivate the virtue of prudence in the course of their official roles, such that common good constitutionalism needs a new basis for judicial deference to the legislative branch, especially with respect to constitutional law.

The final two chapters in this section concern Ronald Dworkin's notion of a 'protestant attitude' in interpreting constitutional provisions. Win-chiat Lee's chapter challenges the propriety of adopting Dworkin's suggestion to adopt the

[2] Examples include Yascha Mounk's The Great Experiment: Why Diverse Democracies Fall Apart and How They Can Endure, *How Democracies Die* by Steven Leyitsky and Daniel Ziblatt, *The Fifth Risk: Undoing Democracy* by Michael Lewis, *Political Argument in a Polarized Age: Reason and Democratic Life* by Scott F. Aikin and Robert B. Talisse, *Freedom's Dominion: A Saga of White Resistance to Federal Power* by Jefferson Cowie, *Left is Not Woke* by Susan Neiman, and *The Paradox of Democracy: Free Speech, Open Media, and Perilous Persuasion* by Zac Gershberg and Sean Illing.

protestant attitude, given that doing so may have the effect not of settling but of unsettling established law to the detriment of our liberal democracy and any notion as to what a final word on the law might be. Lee draws on the recent *Dobbs* decision that set the legal right to abortion adrift, making it depend on preferences within each state in developing this argument. Imer Flores offers an additional interpretation of Dworkin's work, finding it useful for a constructive interpretation of the constitution and a partnership conception of democracy.

Turning now to some important specific issue areas, the first two chapters in Part II focus attention on education in a liberal democracy. Joan McGregor evaluates the woeful lack of Black, Latino/-a, and Native American students in higher education, a concern made all the more relevant in the light of the Court's recently announced decision in *Students for Fair Admissions, Inc. v. President and Fellows of Harvard College* (2023). McGregor argues that the core political issue at stake in a liberal constitutional democracy is that all citizens should be standing in relations of equality to one another, yet persisting inequality in higher education is likely only to perpetuate worrisome disparities in access to resources and economic achievement, redounding in social hierarchy if not oppression against minorities. At the same time, the presumption of free speech and academic freedom, which are prerequisites to truth-seeking and dissemination of knowledge, are under attack on our college and university campuses. Eric Smaw addresses the baleful, menacing wave of intolerance promoted by and on behalf of some white constituencies through legislation and executive actions. Unfortunately, he argues, faculty can no longer rely on the courts to secure their rights to teach and publish free of ideological constraints. These two developments—the continued lack of diversity in higher education and attacks on diversity itself, coupled with ideologically motivated legal restrictions on faculty speech and what students may be exposed to—are profound challenges to liberal democracy insofar as this kind of regime relies upon an educated citizenry that can apprehend facts and discern the truth.

The next two chapters each address voting and the apparatus of elections, expressing concerns that the basic mechanics of democratic decision-making may work against democratic outcomes that reflect the considered will of the people. Alistair Macleod notes the centrality of the vote to a well-functioning democracy, and offers that its purpose is to assure that citizens individually and collectively participate in deciding the overall framework for their self-governance. But, an electoral system structured on the basis of first past the post—where voters choose a single candidate and the one with the most votes wins—actually hampers achievement of that purpose. Co-authors Robbie Robinette and Nicolaus Tideman promote Condorcet consistent voting rules and consensus voting—where votes are cast for a plurality of candidates—because this approach to electoral design dampens polarization by partisan extremes and promotes the centrist-leaning outcomes that the voters actually want.

Our final chapter, by Emily R. Gill, takes on the increasingly more complicated threat to liberal constitutionalism posed by the free exercise of religion, in light of the recent rise of Christian nationalism in the public domain. She argues that groups that seek to elevate Christianity to a place of legally and politically recognized privilege threatens the pluralism of the country and, in addition, that religious exemptions for Christian nationalists might pave a path away from the liberal commitment to equal access, especially for the non-religious.

Ultimately, the chapters in this volume take on a variety of critical challenges to liberal constitutional states and attempt to propose some solutions. We largely focus attention on the United States, but our interests and conclusions extend beyond our geographical boundaries to speak to liberal democratic regimes around the world. The principles that undergird our public order such as the rule of law, equality, liberty, democracy, tolerance of differences, can be undermined by flames of intolerance, conspiracy mongering baseless distrust in free and fair elections inflamed by unscrupulous social media, and religious nationalism, among other things. Select reforms to corral the reach of recent challenges would do our liberal constitutional order tremendous good and present citizens with an awareness of both the panoply of contemporary challenges, and how responses might be crafted to meet them.

Gordon A. Babst Associate Professor of Political Science at Chapman University, teaches political philosophy and has published on liberal political theory and in the areas of religion and politics, tolerance, and diversity.

Part I

Is the American Form of Government a Democracy? Signs of Systemic Oligarchy in a Constitutional Democracy

Laurence D. Houlgate

Remember Democracy never lasts long. It soon wastes, exhausts and murders itself. There never was a Democracy Yet, that did not commit suicide.—John Adams (Letter to John Taylor 1814)

Abstract This paper is an exercise in political philosophy with an emphasis on political concepts used to describe various forms of government, for example 'democracy,' 'oligarchy,' and 'aristocracy,' and political concepts used to describe lawful activities or strategies within forms of government, for example, 'filibuster,' 'presidential veto', 'representation,' and 'elector'. The main question in the paper is about the logical consistency of these concepts and the concept of democracy.

Section 1 of the paper is about key concepts that give more detail about types of democracy, for example, 'direct' and 'representative' democracy, and the distinction between democracy and oligarchy. Section 2 describes several instances of oligarchic rule in all branches of the United States government, including a novel rule that the author refers to as 'the rule of a shifting minority.' Assuming that these instances of oligarchic rule in a government. are defects, then Sect. 3 offers several recommendations for repairing or removing them. It is left up to the reader to decide whether the instances of oligarchic rule in American government are either defects or non-defective strategies borrowed from oligarchy to prevent what John Adams calls the 'suicide' of American democracy.

L. D. Houlgate (✉)
California Polytechnic State University, San Luis Obispo, CA, USA

G. A. Babst et al. (eds.), *Liberal Constitutionalism and its Contemporary Challenges*, AMINTAPHIL: The Philosophical Foundations of Law and Justice 12, https://doi.org/10.1007/978-3-031-53602-1_2

1 Introduction

Americans proudly call their form of government a *democracy*. Politicians like to brag about this, reminding other countries that the United States is "the oldest continuous democracy in the world" (Barksdale 2018). But after the shocking mob attack on the U.S. Capitol on January 6, 2021, there has been much talk about the "fragility" of American democracy and constant warnings that the long continuity of our old and cherished system of government might soon be over (Powell 2022).

I agree that there is much to like about our government and there are good reasons to fear a future overthrow, but the *form* of government that is bragged about by politicians is *not* a true democracy. There are many features in the U.S. system similar to those found in oligarchies and aristocracy. Hence, the first task is to clarify concepts and show how they are instantiated in the government of the United States of America.

Democracy is a form of government in which *the power to legislate is either held directly by a simple majority of the people or by representatives who have been elected by the people.*[1] It is the only system of government in which (in theory) all citizens have *equal* power (rights) to either legislate or give their power of legislating to others of their choosing. The former system is called *direct or true democracy*. The latter is called *representative democracy.* Whether democracy is either direct or representative, the agreement of a simple majority of the whole people *or* their elected representatives is necessary before a law canbe created or changed. Finally, the democracy of the United States of America is *constitutional*. The government is based on a Constitution that is "supreme" in the sense that it "not only provides the framework for how the federal and state governments are structured, but also places significant limits on their powers." (U.S. Govt. Embassy)

In a democracy, if a law is proposed that (for example) mandates citizens to wear face masks during a pandemic, then the proposal becomes law only if there is a simple majority of legislators who approve. The proposal fails if there are one or more votes less than a simple majority. Any system of rule that allows a minority to pass a law would violate majority rule as a central principle of democracy. If more than a simple majority is required to create or change laws, then the minority has been granted the power to block legislation. This requirement dissolves democracy and replaces it with another form of government that John Locke refers to as

[1] I am aware of the distinction that some scholars make between the words "democracy" and "republic." In *The Federalist*, James Madison (n.d.) defined a 'pure democracy' as "a society consisting of a small number of citizens, who assemble and administer the government in person," and a republic as "a government in which the scheme of representation takes place." In Madison's words, "The two great points of difference between a democracy and a republic, are: first, the delegation of the government, in the latter, to a small number of citizens elected by the rest; secondly, the greater the number of citizens, and greater sphere of country, over which the latter may be extended." In short, for Madison, *democracy* meant direct democracy, and *republic* meant representative government. In this paper, I am dropping the word 'republic' and replacing it with 'representative democracy'.

oligarchy,[2] and Jean- Jacques Rousseau and other philosophers call *aristocracy*.[3] What oligarchy and aristocracy have in common is that legislative power is given to "the few." The governing few are often corrupt or have inherited their power to legislate by birth. But this is irrelevant. What makes oligarchy a threat to democracy is not *how* the minority got their power or *what* they do with their power, but that a minority *has* the power to create, change or prevent legislation.[4]

Signs of oligarchy in governance will be discussed in Sect. 2. Repairs of the defects of oligarchy in the current American government will be explained in Sect. 3.

2 Signs of Oligarchy in Governance

2.1 *The Oligarchy of the Filibuster*

The *filibuster* is a tactic frequently used in the United States Senate. It is a perfect example of the political power of a shifting oligarchy. The number of oligarchs or aristocrats who rule in a commonwealth is historically small and *permanent.* When we think of an oligarchy, we usually imagine a system of government that has only a few individuals with the power to create or change laws and have this power for a lifetime. But suppose there is a country or state with a rule of governance that places legislative power in the hands of a *temporary* minority by requiring laws that can *only* be created or changed by the vote of a *supermajority*. Thus, any minority group of legislators can block laws proposed by a majority if the majority fails to meet a certain threshold, for example, sixty percent of the total number of voting legislators. If a majority of 100 legislators is 51 and it takes 60 to pass a law, then we can refer to this system of rule as *a shifting oligarchy.* It is an oligarchy because it is a minority with the power to block legislation. It is 'shifting' because the *makeup* of

[2] I am using John Locke's (1996) definition of the word "oligarchy" to mean "government by the few," although I recognize that "oligarchy" is often used to mean that the governing few exercise control "for corrupt and selfish purposes." (Second Treatise, chapter 10).

[3] The word "aristocracy" is usually taken to mean "government by the best" (nobility, intellect, wealth) but it is also used to simply mean "government by the few." (Merriam Webster). Thomas Jefferson separated those who are naturally best (based on virtue and talent) from the artificial best (based on wealth and birth). He was convinced that that the country would be much healthier if the aristocrats who govern it were of the class who are naturally best. But our question is not "What kind of aristocracy is the best?" but "What form of government, democracy or aristocracy, do we now have in America?"

[4] A system of government in which only one person has the power to legislate is called a monarchy or autocracy. The monarch (autocrat) may have inherited the power to legislate by birth or was directly elected by the people for a few years or for a lifetime. It is the placement on one person of the power to legislate, not how a person acquires the placement that defines the meaning of monarch and autocrat.

the minority group that is doing the blocking is temporary. A later minority group might be composed of a different group of legislators.

Filibusters are actions allowed in a legislature (such as a prolonged speech) that obstruct progress in passing a bill while not technically contravening the required procedures. Although filibusters can be overridden by the vote of a supermajority of senators (60 instead of 50 in a group of 100), this rarely happens, especially if there is an equal number of senators on both sides of an issue. In most cases, the filibuster succeeds because a supermajority to override the filibuster cannot be found, and a simple majority of senators are thereby prevented from passing the desired bill or law. The minority who opposed the law get what they want, but only because the system of rule has been transformed by the filibuster from a democracy into a shifting oligarchy.

The argument for keeping the filibuster was repeated many times by Democratic senators Joe Manchin (West Virginia) and Krysten Sinema (Arizona) in 2021–2022. They claimed that the filibuster justifiably forces senators from both parties to seek a bipartisan solution. It was more important to Manchin and Sinema that a bill had bipartisan support than passing a bill proposed by a simple majority of senators of one party. In other words, for these senators, using the filibuster to *prevent* a simple majority of senators from one party from passing a bill is more important than adherence to the rule of the majority as a foundational rule of democracy.

The will of the people is expressed only through a majority, not through a minority that has its own agenda to promote. There is no requirement in the U.S. Constitution that a majority must be composed of members of contending factions.

2.2 The Oligarchy of the Electoral College

The Electoral College is an oligarchical system for electing the president and vice president because the popular vote of the whole people is actually a vote for a slate of electors who have previously been appointed by the political parties in their state.

The Electoral College is composed of a group of presidential electors required by the U.S. Constitution to meet every 4 years. Their only purpose is to elect the president and vice president. Each state has as many 'electors' in the Electoral College as it has Representatives and Senators in the United States Congress (the District of Columbia has three electors). When voters go to the polls in a presidential election, they are voting for a slate of electors who have vowed to cast their ballots for the winning ticket in the Electoral College. Most voters ae not aware that when they go to the polls to cast their ballot they are not directly voting for a particular president or vice president. For those who know about and understand the process, they cast their vote *hoping* that the ticket that wins the popular vote will also be the ticket that the electors vote for when the Electoral College meets in Washington, D.C. two months after the election. Although the Constitution does not require electors in each state to cast their vote for the president and vice president that the people chose by popular vote, most electors will do so.[5]

The source of inequality is to be found in the distribution of electors in each state. The distribution is not proportionate to the number of eligible voters. For example, the voting population of the state of California is over 22 million and the number of California electors is 55. Wyoming has 269,000 voters and 3 electors. If the number of electors was proportionate to the voting population of these states, California *would have 245 electors,* not 55.

The implication of this is that the three electors from Wyoming have much more power than the 55 electors representing California. Each Wyoming elector represents 90,000 voters but each California elector represents 400,000 voters, making each Wyoming voter *4.4 times more powerful* than each California voter when the final electoral votes are cast.

In their effort to give small states like Wyoming, Vermont, and Delaware more power in presidential and vice-presidential elections than they would have if electors were appointed in numbers proportionate to the voting population, the founding fathers ignored the principle of equality. If this moral principle had been employed when the Constitution was ratified, each vote would count for one, and *no vote would count for more than one*. A voting system that gives more power to voters who live in one state than those who live in another state violates this foundational principle of democracy.

2.3 The Oligarchy of the United States Senate

The composition of the United States Senate is undemocratic for the same reason that the Electoral College is undemocratic. The Constitution of the United States gives each state two senators, regardless of the number of registered voters in the state. For example, the legislative power of the people in the state of Vermont who elect their two senators to represent them in the Senate is much greater than the legislative power of the two senators who represent the state of New York.[6]

> Vermont's 625,000 residents have two United States senators, and so do New York's 19 million. That means that a Vermonter has 30 times the voting power in the Senate of a New Yorker just over the state line — the biggest inequality between two adjacent states. The nation's largest gap, between Wyoming and California, is more than double that… The difference in the fortunes of Rutland (Vermont) and Washington (New York) Counties reflects the growing disparity in their citizens' voting power, and it is not an anomaly. The Constitution has always given residents of states with small populations a lift, but the size and importance of the gap has grown markedly in recent decades, in ways the framers

[5] In a unanimous 2020 decision, the U.S. Supreme Court upheld as constitutional "faithless elector laws" in several states. These are laws that penalize or remove presidential electors who fail to vote for the candidate they have pledged to support (Howe 2020).

[6] It was not always this way. In the early years of the new country, there were only 13 states and each state had approximately the same population.

probably never anticipated. It affects the political dynamic of issues as varied as gun control, immigration, and campaign finance (Liptak 2013).

The principle of voter equality is expressed in the sentence, "Each person should have one vote and no person should have more than one vote." Although it is the moral bedrock of democracy, it is violated in the extreme by the constitutional delegation of U.S. Senators (Article I, Section 3), mirroring the delegation of the eighteenth-century aristocratic British House of Lords. Although U.S. senators are elected by the people, not appointed as "lifetime peers" by a king,[7] the disproportionate legislative power held by both the U.S. senators and the eighteenth century House of Lords is the same.

A popular justification for granting each state, small and large, the same number of senators is the "stability argument." The Framers were worried that a majority of the House of Representatives, empowered by their constituents, might pass legislation as tyrannical as the legislation they had experienced and endured under British rule. This would divide the country in ways that would make the new government unstable. The Framers' solution, "…as reflected in Article I, Section 3, [was to design] the Senate, like they had other fixtures within the Constitution, such as the Electoral College and the judiciary, to be counter-majoritarian" (Calabresi and Gerhardt 2023). The Framers hoped that this pro-minority design would bring stability to the government and the country.

The stability argument makes two assumptions. First, it assumes that a government by the people and their representatives will create legislation so tyrannical that the country will be dissolved. Second, the argument also assumes that the only solution is to grant each state two senators, no matter what the difference in the population of each state might be in the future.

Both assumptions are questionable. There are other ways to prevent tyrannical legislation, as was proved in the passage of the first ten amendments to the Constitution (Bill of Rights). And granting each state, small and large, the same number of senators, has little or nothing to do with the effort to prevent the passage of bad laws. The Senate's power to override bills passed by the House lies not in the equal distribution of senators but in the constitutional power granted to the whole body in Article I, Part 3.

Another argument for the two-senator per-state distribution is that this mitigates the political power of states with much larger populations. This wrongly assumes that the political power of the state is more important than the political power of the individual citizens. The smaller states get this power at the cost of the diminished effectiveness of senators in the larger states to pass legislation that will benefit their

---

[7] Lifetime peerage still exists in Great Britain, although significantly diminished. "In The House of Lords Act of 1999 all but 92 hereditaries were dismissed, then numbering 750, breaking a 700-year-old right for all peers to sit on and vote from the red benches. The remaining 92 were elected by all the previous hereditary peers in the House grouped by party affiliation – 42 Conservatives, 28 Crossbenchers, three Lib Dems, two Labour and 17 others.

These numbers are set – when one Conservative resigns, a new Conservative is elected" (Scolari 2021).

constituents. Of more importance, this dilution of power violates the moral principle of equality. It is *oligarchic injustice* that the Vermonter's voting power in the U.S. Senate is now 30 times greater than the New Yorker's voting power.

2.4 The Oligarchy of the Presidential Veto

The power of *presidential veto* in Article I, section 7 of the Constitution is undemocratic because it grants one person, the President of the United States, the authority to veto legislation passed by Congress. Congress can override a presidential veto but only if both the House of Representatives and the Senate can muster two-thirds of its members to approve an override.

Although the veto power of the president was approved by the Framers to diminish the legislative power of Congress and thereby achieve a balance of power between the legislative, executive, and judicial branches, the use of the veto is a clear assault on democracy. Congress can override a veto, but it takes a supermajority of the members to do so. This requirement is sufficient to categorize this article of the Constitution as another endorsement of oligarchy (minority rule) that is inconsistent with the concept of democracy and majority rule.

The objection to this is that the President will use the veto power "to prevent the misuse or abuse" of legislative power. Examples of misuse or abuse are measures that the President "finds unconstitutional, unjust, or unwise" (National Archives). My reply is that only the Supreme Court can find a legislative measure to be unconstitutional and a finding by a single person (the President) that a measure is unjust or unwise should not negate a different finding by Congress. The President is not a philosopher king blessed with special insight.

2.5 The Oligarchy of Representation

The eighteenth century Genevan philosopher Jean-Jacques Rousseau famously argued that most governments that call themselves democracies do not qualify as such because the only true democracy is direct democracy. When a proposed bill or law comes up for a vote, the only persons who should be allowed to cast a vote for or against the proposed law are *the citizens themselves*. The majority vote determines the general will (that is, the common good) and since legitimate laws are based only on the general will of the citizens, the minority in obeying the law after the vote is counted, are now obeying themselves as members of an organic political community.

Those who claim that they are a representative of a group of citizens and are voting "on the behalf of others" should not be allowed to join the assembly of voters. They can cast their single vote as a citizen but cannot cast a vote for other citizens. (*The Social Contract* II.6). To give one's vote to another is equivalent to not voting at all. When citizens go to the polls and vote for candidate X as their representative, they alienate their right to legislate by giving the power of their vote to X. Once X is sworn in office, those who voted for X will have no control over how X votes until the next election. For the next 2, 4, or 6 years the votes cast by the representatives are *their* votes, not the votes of the citizens that they represent.

If the *only* legitimate votes for new laws are the votes of representatives and not the votes of the people, then the assembly of elected representatives in the U.S. House of Representatives is no different than an assembly of elected aristocrats who have been given legislative power. In the spirit of Rousseau's words, an assembly of representatives, no matter how they came to power, is not an instantiation of democratic rule. Democracy exists only when the whole people rule. The 'whole people' is a simple majority of citizen voters. Only the vote of a majority can express the general will.

2.6 *The Oligarchy of Judicial Review*

On September 28, 1820, Thomas Jefferson wrote a letter to William Jarvis complaining about what Jefferson believed was a serious omission in the Constitution:

> Nothing in the Constitution has given them (judges) a right to decide for the Executive, more than to the Executive to decide for them … You seem … to consider the judges as the ultimate arbiters of all constitutional questions; a very dangerous doctrine indeed, and one which would place us under the DESPOTISM of an oligarchy.

Jefferson was right about the claim that there is nothing in the Constitution that gives the Supreme Court the power to make the final interpretation of the content of the Constitution. And I should add, the framers of the Constitution left no instructions about how it should be interpreted by the judges. This gives the Supreme Court free rein to impose their interpretations, with the advice but not the command of lower courts, the president, or the legislature.

If you put these two observations together, then Jefferson's warning is that the United States is under the rule of an oligarchy composed of a few Supreme Court judges who, in an early court decision (*Marbury v Madison,* 1803) gave themselves the sole right to decide what is and is not constitutional for all three branches of government.[8]

---

[8] "With John Marshall as chief justice, the Supreme Court greatly expanded its powers, prestige, and independence. When Marshall took office, in the last days of John Adams's administration in 1801, the Court met in the basement of the Capitol and was rarely in session for more than six weeks a year. Since its creation in 1789, the Court had only decided 100 cases. In a series of critical decisions, the Supreme Court greatly expanded its authority. Marbury v. Madison (1803) established the Supreme Court as the final arbiter of the Constitution and its power to declare acts of Congress unconstitutional. Fletcher v. Peck (1810) declared the Court's power to void state laws. Martin v. Hunter's Lessee (1816) gave the Court the power to review decisions by state courts." (Digital History 2021).

Another anti-democratic sign of the Supreme Court's power is that the justices of the Supreme Court who exercise this power are not elected by the people. They are appointed by the president on the approval of a majority of the Senate. Justices of the court have never had to face an election by the very people who must obey their rulings. Moreover, an appointment to the Supreme Court is for a life-long term.[9] By way of contrast, the president of the United States is elected by the people through the Electoral College for a 4-year term and can only be re-elected once.

"*The combination of judicial review with a judiciary that is not electorally accountable is what is antidemocratic*" (Altman 2001, p. 85). But is Jefferson right when he said that this combination is "*a dangerous doctrine*" that "*place(s) us under the despotism of an oligarchy*"?

An oligarchy is the rule of a minority in which only the few can make law. If Supreme Court decisions are *acts of legislation* then objectors could *ipso facto* declare that the rulings of the judicial branch of government are the rules of a few judges who together constitute an oligarchy. Laws are being made or changed, not by the people or their representatives but by an ever-shifting majority of Supreme Court judges.

One response to this charge is to deny that the Supreme Court is legislating when they decide cases that are on the docket. Judgments of the court are usually *interpretations* of the constitution, not acts of legislation. For example, when the current court decided to overturn the 1973 *Roe v Wade* decision granting women the constitutional right to abortion, the 2022 court believed that they had a *better* interpretation of the Constitution than the interpretation given in 1973. If the 2022 decision (*Dobbs v Jackson*) was legislation not interpretation, then the same thing could be (and has been) said of the 1973 decision or for that matter, any other contested decision of the Supreme Court.

What manner of interpreting the Constitution is best? When does an interpretation cease being an interpretation and become an act of legislation? These are questions that have yet to be answered to the satisfaction of a majority of philosophers of law (Altman 2001, pp. 94–107). Some philosophers are *originalists*. They believe that provisions of the Constitution should either be taken literally or if difficult passages require some interpretation, they should be limited to what the framers of those passages intended to say (Bassham 1992). Other originalists argue that interpretations of provisions of the Constitution should be determined by how they were understood by the people at the time of the Constitution's adoption (Bork 1990). On the other side of the debate are *non-originalists* who insist that the judges of the Supreme Court should look behind the constitution's provisions in search of "a philosophy of government" that could justify these provisions and precedents (Dworkin 1996).

[9]Article III of the U.S. Constitution states that Supreme Court judges "hold their office during good behavior," which means they have a lifetime appointment, except under very limited circumstances. Article III judges can be removed from office only through impeachment by the House of Representatives and conviction by the Senate.

When these theories are applied, each theorist often comes up with a different interpretation of a provision or amendment of the Constitution and each will often accuse their rivals of legislating, not interpreting the Constitution. This has led to a politicization of the Supreme Court, with appointees of Republican presidents generally siding with originalism and appointees of Democrats siding with non-originalist approaches to constitutional interpretation.

There is no universal support for the claim that the Supreme Court usually makes its own law instead of interpreting existing law when it decides a case. The problem is the *politicization* of the Court of the sort that leads to interpretations of constitutional provisions and decisions of the court that please the president who appointed them and the senators that give their consent.[10] This at least has the appearance of political interference. However, the fact that a president wants and appoints only conservative judges does not imply that appointees will consult with the president before they decide a case that has been brought before the court. If judges did this, they and the president would probably be impeached.

The fact that Supreme Court judges are appointed not elected appears to make the Court an instance of oligarchy. John Locke referred to the judiciary as a part of the executive branch of government. In the United States, the judiciary is a distinct branch of government, not a part of an existing branch. But both agree that it is the charge of the executive to *appoint* not only Supreme Court judges who interpret the law, but also appoint attorneys general who will investigate to determine violations of federal law, lower court federal judges who hear cases to determine guilt or innocence, and jailers who manage federal prisons where the guilty are incarcerated.

In none of the aforementioned cases is the person or persons who occupy these roles elected by the people. They are all appointees of the president. Hence, it should be no surprise that judges of the Supreme Court are appointed, and no appointment made by the executive branch is a feature of oligarchy.[11] The relevant constitutional difference between Supreme Court appointees and other executive appointees is that the former are lifetime appointments authorizing judges to overturn laws forged by Congress.

[10] This was obvious in the recent ruling of the court that abortion is not a constitutional right. The majority decision was made by judges Roberts, Thomas, Alito, Kavanaugh, and Barrett all of whom are both Catholic and have a conservative ideology that is promoted by the Republican Party.

[11] It would be a feature of oligarchy if the Supreme Court were to be caught making new laws under the guise of interpreting existing constitutional laws. But if they were "caught", there is no law that they could be accused of having violated. The United States Constitution provides little guidance as to what offenses constitute grounds for the impeachment of federal judges. As with other government officials, judges may be removed following impeachment and conviction for 'Treason, Bribery, or other high Crimes and Misdemeanors'; otherwise, under Article III, Section 1, judges "shall hold their Offices during good Behaviour" (Brennan Center for Justice).

3 Repairing the Defects

The United States of America is a mix of oligarchy and democracy. If these words are too much to bear, then we can call the American form of government a *flawed democracy.* Parts of the system of government are democratic and other parts are undemocratic. If we are to declare that the U.S. government is a true democracy, then the defective (undemocratic) parts must be removed or repaired.

Is there any way to do this? Here are some recommendations.

3.1 Abolish the Filibuster

The U.S. Senate should abolish the filibuster. The argument that the filibuster is needed to guarantee bipartisanship in the Senate is not a sufficient reason to violate the principle of majority rule and with it the heart of democracy. This justification for the filibuster is equivalent to saying that *no law* should be passed unless it is approved by a supermajority of senators, for example, by 75 out of 100 votes of approval. If it is argued that this would permanently enshrine a *tyranny of the minority* (the 25 senators who disapprove), then the same words can be applied to the use of the filibuster.

3.2 Abolish the Electoral College

The Constitution should be amended to abolish the Electoral College. It is a remnant of aristocratic governments and it has no place in a country of people who are taught to understand and repeat the words "our government is of the people, by the people, and for the people."

3.3 Abolish or Remake the U.S. Senate

The U.S. Senate should be abolished entirely or remade in a way that citizens of each state have equal voting power. "Remaking" means that the number of senators who represent states that have a large number of citizens (for example, California or New York) should be proportionately larger than the number of senators who represent states with much smaller populations (for example, Vermont or Montana). If equal representation is made a requirement, then the total membership of the Senate would be so large that it would rival the membership of the House of Representatives. Stripped of unequal senatorial power for small states, the U.S. Senate would become a redundant legislative body.

3.4 *Abolish the Veto Power of the President*

Veto power should be removed from the presidency. It is obviously in violation of the principle of majority rule. The power of the president should be entirely executive, not legislative, for reasons already cited above. Congress has the power to federalize the vote for president and vice president. At this writing, recent attempts to pass this legislation have failed in the U.S. Senate because Republicans pretend that practices like mail-in ballots and same-day voting will increase the number of fraudulent votes, even though there is no evidence that this happened in the 2020 election.

3.5 *Grant Citizens the Right to Vote for Legislation*

Rousseau's recommendation for direct democracy should be taken seriously Sect. (2.5). At the time that Rousseau wrote *The Social Contract* (1762), there was no practical way for most states to adopt in-person voting for proposed laws. If it is to work at all, Rousseau opined, direct democracy could only work in small states with very small populations in which each citizen could easily travel and assemble at designated polling places.

But times have changed. We now have the technology for people to approve or disapprove proposed laws by ballot. The recent referendum in the state of California is a prime example of direct democracy. 17.8 million residents voted for president, senators, and representatives on November 6, 2020. More than 15 million ballots were cast by mail. But more to the point, Californians also voted for or against 12 proposed measures that would become law if approved by a majority. If millions of Californians can legislate, why can't all Americans do the same in every state of the union?

We should trust the citizens to do more legislating than they are now legally allowed to do. If we allow citizens to vote for their representatives in Congress, then there is no justification for not allowing them to vote for or against proposed federal and state laws. It might be objected that the average voter is not smart enough to vote for proposed laws or they do not have the time to do this. To this, I would answer that if they are smart enough to choose their representatives, then with the help of educators to inform them about the content of proposed laws, they are smart enough to legislate. If some citizens don't have the time to understand complex proposals because of the necessity to work and provide for their families, then a democratic government should make time and give compensation for lost work time. What is important is that we properly educate actual and potential voters so they can say that the laws they have made are truly the will of the people. State requirements for Civics courses in all high schools would be of great benefit to students and to an enlightened community eager to participate in the democratic process of legislation (Shapiro and Brown 2018).

The right to vote granted to all citizens for legislation implies that citizens are free to exercise this fundamental democratic right. Although suppression of the vote is not a sign of oligarchy, the right to vote means little if all they can do with their voting power is to give it away to a representatives every 2, 4 or 6 years. And if the right to vote is expanded to voting for legislation in a direct democracy, there is no guarantee that citizens can exercise this important right unsuppressed by barriers making it difficult for citizens to cast a vote, e.g. by not allowing mail-in ballots (Morgan, B. 2020), and limiting the number of polling places and voting days.

As a first step, Congress should immediately codify the right to vote[12] or put into action the long process of amending the U.S. Constitution to guarantee a right to vote. Codification would be much easier to accomplish than a constitutional amendment, although recent attempts in Congress to codify right-to-vote laws have failed.[13] The long process of constitutional change could be done by amending the First Amendment by inserting these italicized words: "Congress shall make no law…*prohibiting the free exercise of the right to vote.*"

3.6 Dilute Politicization of the Supreme Court

If the politicization of Supreme Court decisions is seen as a way of disguising legislation desired by political factions, then interpretive rulings of the Court are the sign of an oligarchy composed of nine judges.

One solution for reducing the politicization of the Court is to correct what the Framers failed to do when they designed the Constitution. As mentioned earlier Sect. (2.6), the Framers did not leave instructions about how the Constitution and its amendments should be interpreted. They left this up to the Supreme Court. However, instructions for interpretation could be created by a special bipartisan congressional committee composed of originalists, non-originalists, and those who are neutral about the correct way to read and interpret the Constitution. The instructions would set limits about what would constitute a valid interpretation, consistent with the

[12] "The process of codification can involve taking judicial decisions or legislative acts and turning them into codified law. This process does not necessarily create new law; it merely arranges existing law, usually by subject, into a code." (Legal Information Institute 2021).

[13] "The John Lewis Voting Rights Advancement Act, named for the late congressman from Georgia, aims to reverse a 2013 Supreme Court decision that struck down key portions of the Voting Rights Act of 1965. That law required several states with a history of voting rights discrimination, largely in the South, to get preclearance from the Department of Justice for any changes to voting laws. The Lewis act would restore the requirement and update the formula used to determine which states must get preclearance. Other changes to voting laws in any state, such as relocating polling places and imposing strict voter ID requirements, would also be subject to preclearance. The Freedom to Vote Act would make Election Day a national holiday, aimed at making easier for all voters to get to the polls that day; allow states to have early voting for at least two weeks prior to Election Day, including nights and weekends; allow voting by mail with no excuses needed, and voters could put their ballots in drop boxes; require that states make voting more accessible for people with disabilities; require that states that require IDs for voting would have to broaden the types of identification acceptable. States would also have to offer same-day voting registration, online registration and make it easier to register at places like departments of motor vehicles." (Naylor 2022)

ideals of liberty and equality that motivated the work of the Constitutional Convention of 1787. When finished, the instructions should be proposed as an amendment to the Constitution, asserting that the Supreme Court and other federal courts shall not interpret the Constitution in a way that exceeds the limits set by the aforesaid instructions.

The second correction for the federal judiciary is to reduce the years of appointment from a lifetime to a maximum of 12 years of judicial service. There is no good reason why unelected judges should serve more years on the Court than elected senators serve in the Senate.

But there is a good reason why unelected judges should serve no more than elected senators. *This change would dilute the politicization of the Court.* A conservative judge would be replaced by a liberal judge (and vice versa) more frequently than is now the case. Instead of waiting a generation for the Court to flip from majority conservative to majority liberal (and vice versa), as is now the case, reducing the term of appointment to 12 years has a greater chance of changing the impact on the Court of a single political ideology promoted by a shifting court majority.

4 Conclusion

In the epigraph to this paper, I quoted John Adams' depressing remark about the future of democracy: "*Remember, democracy never lasts long. It soon wastes, exhausts, and murders itself. There never was a democracy yet that did not commit suicide*." Unfortunately, Adams did not explain what it is about democracy that "wastes, exhausts and murders itself." Perhaps he was referring to Plato's prediction that direct democracy would eventually devolve into tyranny (Republic, 569c). One response to this grim fate would be to replace direct democracy with representative democracy and add a few features from oligarchy that might help to prevent chaos and death. Another response is to reject oligarchic features entirely.

Whether such radical changes in governance would avoid the suicide of which Adams speaks is an empirical prediction requiring evidence from observation and experience. But prediction is a task of political science not political philosophy. What the philosopher can say is that there is a point at which the *concept* of democracy does not apply to the American form of governance. Perhaps that is all that Adams meant by the 'suicide' of democracy.

References

Adams J (1814) Letter to John Taylor. National Archives: Founders Online. https://founders.archives.gov/documents/Adams/99-02-02-6371

Altman A (2001) Arguing about law, 2nd edn. Wadsworth, Belmont

Barksdale N (2018) What is the world's oldest democracy? History.com. https://www.history.com/news/what-is-the-worlds-oldest-democracy. Accessed 24 Dec 2022

Bassham G (1992) Original intent and the constitution. Rowman and Littlefield, New York

Bork R (1990) The tempting of America. Free Press, New York

Calabresi SG, Gerhardt M (2023) Interpretation of Article I, Section 3. National Constitution Center. https://constitutioncenter.org/the-constitution/articles/article-i/clauses/765

Digital History (2021) Judicial nationalism. https://www.digitalhistory.uh.edu/disp_textbook.cfm?smtID=2&psid=3528

Dobbs v. Jackson Women's Health Organization. 2022. No. 19-1392, 597 U.S. (2022)

Dworkin R (1996) Freedom's law. Harvard University Press, Cambridge

Howe A (2020) Opinion analysis: Court upholds "faithless elector" laws. SCOTUSblog, 6 July 2020. https://www.scotusblog.com/2020/07/opinion-analysis-court-upholds-faithless-elector-laws/

Jefferson T (1820) Thomas Jefferson to William Charles Jarvis, 28 September 1820. Founders Online. National Archives. https://founders.archives.gov/documents/Jefferson/03-16-02-0234 [Original source: The Papers of Thomas Jefferson, Retirement Series, vol. 16, 1 June 1820 to 28 February 1821, ed. J. Jefferson Looney et al. Princeton: Princeton University Press, 2019, pp. 287–289.]

Legal Information Institute (2021) Definition of 'codify'. Cornell Law School. https://www.law.cornell.edu/wex/codify

Liptak A (2013) Smaller states find outsize clout growing in senate. New York Times, 11 March 2013. https://archive.nytimes.com/www.nytimes.com/interactive/2013/03/11/us/politics/democracy-tested.html#/#smallstate

Locke J (1996 [1690]) In: MacPherson EB (ed) Second treatise of government. Hackett Publishing, Indianapolis

Madison J (n.d.) The Federalist Number 10, [22 November] 1787. Founders Online. National Archives. https://founders.archives.gov/documents/Madison/01-10-02-0178

Marbury v. Madison. 1803. 5 U.S. 137

Morgan B (2020) Citing Anthony Fowler. University of Chicago News, 6 July 2020. https://news.uchicago.edu/story/does-voting-mail-increase-risk-voter-fraud

Naylor B (2022) The Senate is set to debate voting rights. Here's what the bills would do. National Public Radio. https://www.npr.org/2022/01/18/1073021462/senate-voting-rights-freedom-to-vote-john-lewis-voting-rights-advancement-act

Plato. ca. 375 BCE. Republic

Plessy v. Ferguson. 1896. 163 U.S. 537

Powell A (2022) Where are we going, America? Harvard Gazette. https://news.harvard.edu/gazette/story/2022/11/where-are-we-going-america/. Accessed 24 Dec 2022

Roe v. Wade. 1973. 410 U.S. 113

Rousseau J-J (2019 [1762]) On the social contract, 2nd edn (Trans. Donald A. Cress). Hackett Publishing, Indianapolis

Scolari F (2021) Why are there still hereditary peers in the House of Lords? Electoral Reform Society, 5 March 2021. https://www.electoral-reform.org.uk/why-are-there-still-hereditary-peers-in-the-house-of-lords/

Shapiro S, Brown C (2018) A look at civics education in the United States. American Federation of Teachers. https://www.aft.org/ae/summer2018/shapiro_brown

Laurence D. Houlgate is an American philosopher, Emeritus Professor of Philosophy, and former department chair at California Polytechnic State University, San Luis Obispo. He specializes in interpretations of the classics of Western philosophy, social ethics, philosophy of law, and political philosophy.

Truth Matters: Factual Accuracy, Theoretic Rationality, and the Legitimacy of Political Decision-Making

Joshua J. Kassner

The people is never corrupted, but it is often misled; and only then does it seem to will what is bad.—Rousseau (2004), p. 30.

Abstract This chapter probes the extent to which political legitimacy rests not merely on proceduralist accounts, but fundamentally on truth understood as factual accuracy and rational assessments of the available data, that is, on information we can share.

1 Introduction

In modern pluralist societies we are often faced with value laden policy choices defined by disagreements that can't be resolved by appealing to independent standards of evaluation or objective criteria. Despite such intractable disagreements, we must choose. Further, if we are to justify the demand that those affected by the decision respect it, our choices must be politically legitimate.[1] Since consensus on the correctness of any particular decision is unlikely, many have looked to decision-making procedures as the basis for political legitimacy.

To my mind, however, post-truth politics has revealed the limits of such proceduralist accounts of political legitimacy. In understanding the threat that post-truth politics poses to political legitimacy, one realizes that political legitimacy requires more than legitimate procedures alone. In an effort to supplement such accounts, I contend that in addition to employing legitimate decision-making procedures,

[1] Peter (2009).

J. J. Kassner (✉)
University of Baltimore, Baltimore, MD, USA
e-mail: jkassner@ubalt.edu

G. A. Babst et al. (eds.), *Liberal Constitutionalism and its Contemporary Challenges*, AMINTAPHIL: The Philosophical Foundations of Law and Justice 12, https://doi.org/10.1007/978-3-031-53602-1_3

political legitimacy requires that a community's political decision-making must respect factual accuracy and theoretic rationality. Post-truth politics poses a threat to political legitimacy because it undermines our collective ability to respect factual accuracy and theoretic rationality in our political decision-making. In a more structured form, the argument runs as follows:

- ***Premise 1:*** Political legitimacy requires respect for factual accuracy and theoretic rationality.
- ***Premise 2:*** Post-truth politics undermines respect for factual accuracy and theoretic rationality.
- ***Conclusion:*** Therefore, post-truth politics undermines political legitimacy.

If correct, we should be skeptical of the legitimacy of decisions made amidst post-truth politics, ***and*** of the demand that we respect those decisions, and we should pursue reforms to make our political decision-making (more) legitimate.

2 Post-Truth Politics

This simple statement of the argument belies its complexity. Beginning with "post-truth politics", it is important to separate two distinct, but related, questions: What is post-truth politics? And, what makes post-truth politics possible? As to the former, post-truth politics is a social phenomenon of a political culture defined by certain attitudes towards the nature and purpose of politics, including a win-at-all-costs approach to politics and an utter disregard for truth and reason. Post-truth politics has resulted in large portions of the electorate believing things that are demonstrably false; for example, that the 2020 United States Presidential election was stolen, or that the National Health Service of the United Kingdom would recover hundreds of millions of pounds a week should the nation choose to leave the European Union.

As to the second question, post-truth politics is enabled by the fact that our understanding of the world is fraught with cognitive dissonance and confirmation bias. These weaknesses are not insurmountable, but the technology available to us and the rise of social media platforms and the echo-chambers they encourage, allow us to shield ourselves from the intellectual discomfort that comes with being confronted by ideas that challenge our understanding of the world. It is just such discomfort that impels us towards greater knowledge and understanding.[2]

One might contend that post-truth politics is nothing new, that politics has always involved some degree of sophistry and misrepresentation. I would argue, however, that during much of the twentieth century, the space of public political deliberations included more effective, though perhaps not complete, checks against such

[2] For a thoughtful discussion of the dangers of social media and the echo-chambers they enable, see Sunstein (2017).

deception and fallacious reasoning, including engaged and informed public discourse that crossed ideological lines, and an independent press that was more committed to journalistic integrity and ***more likely*** to be held accountable for its reporting. It was simply harder for individuals to find safe harbor for their cognitive weaknesses. Today, public political deliberation plays out in ideological echo-chambers, not in anything resembling a Millian free market of ideas.

Admittedly, there have been occasions when such checks failed to protect against misrepresentations and failures of reason. One need only think of the lead up to the Spanish-American War as a possible counterexample, and the way in which newspapers in the United States wove a false narrative to provide the necessary public support for war. I believe that such failures were largely the exception, and not the rule. If I am incorrect and post-truth politics is not unique to the digital age, that doesn't mean we shouldn't be concerned. Rather, we should be skeptical of the legitimacy of past decisions as well, and this realization should serve as a clarion call to seek out a more legitimate path.

3 Political Legitimacy

As this argument is intended to shed light on our understanding the conditions necessary for political legitimacy, a brief explanation of what I mean by political legitimacy is in order. This explanatory task is only made more difficult by the fact that political legitimacy is taken to mean different things in different contexts and within different inquiries.[3] As such, let me begin by explaining what I do ***not*** mean by political legitimacy. First, it is not about why people ***believe*** in the legitimacy of a political institution or decision-making procedure.[4] Second, I am not concerned with the relationship between political legitimacy and the right to rule.[5] Finally, I am ***not*** seeking to understand the role political legitimacy plays in justifying a government's use of coercive force.[6] Though related to these other understandings, the notion of political legitimacy with which I am concerned is found in Fabienne Peter's work on democratic legitimacy.[7] For Peter, understanding political legitimacy is about understanding the conditions under which the decisions made by our political institutions deserve our respect.[8]

Thus, the ability to justify this demand for respect that is attendant to a politically legitimate decision is a *desideratum* that any viable account of political legitimacy

[3] For a thorough survey of the notion of political legitimacy and the many different roles the concept plays, see Peter (2017).

[4] For example, see Weber (1991). And see Weber (1964).

[5] For example, see Locke (1990). And see Rawls (2007). See also Raz (2006).

[6] For example, see Rawls (1993). And see Ripstein (2004).

[7] Peter (2009).

[8] *Ibid.*

must accommodate. In other words, any account of political legitimacy must be able to explain why those subject to a decision—especially those who disagree with it—ought to show it respect. Consequently, to understand this notion of political legitimacy, one must understand what is meant by "respect". On this point, it is important to distinguish respect from other attitudes. Respect requires more than mere acceptance; rather, respect is to be understood as a form of moral approval. This does not mean approval of the substantive correctness of the decisions reached, but approval of the way in which the decision was made.[9] If the decision was made in the right way, then the decision deserves our respect.

3.1 Proceduralist Understanding of Political Legitimacy

Though clarifying the relevant notion of political legitimacy, it begs the question regarding the conditions necessary for political legitimacy. I am assuming that the correct account of legitimacy is, neither a consequentialist nor an instrumental one,[10] but must be one grounded in the processes and procedures used to make a decision. Though there are a variety of such proceduralist accounts,[11] they share a commitment to the proposition that a procedure that adequately instantiates the right values produces legitimate decisions regardless of the substantive correctness of the decisions reached. In my considered judgment, the most convincing value commitment upon which such proceduralist accounts rely is the demand that political decision-making respect the equal moral worth of all affected by a decision.[12]

Before proceeding there is a point of possible confusion that needs to be discussed; namely, there are two conceptions of "respect" now being relied upon in this discussion. On the one hand, there is the notion of respect found in the account of political legitimacy being relied upon—respect as the proper moral attitude towards the outcomes of legitimate political decision-making. On the other hand, there is the notion of respect found in our understanding of what it is that makes a political decision-making procedure legitimate—that it must respect the equal moral worth of all affected by a decision. The latter is related to the former, but they are not the same. To be specific, respecting the moral equality of all affected by a decision is necessary for the claim that we ought to respect the outcome of a community's political decision-making. One is a property of our political decision-making processes, and the other is the reactive attitude that is appropriate to decisions made by

[9] See May (1952), pp. 680–684. And see Dahl (1956). See also Manin (1987). And see Rawls (1993). And see Bohman (1996). And see Waldron (1999). See also Gaus (1997). And see Christiano (2008). Further, see Kolodny (2014a). And see Kolodny (2014b).

[10] For examples of such accounts, see Mill (1998). And see Brink (1992). See also Ten (1998).

[11] For example, see Rawls (1993). And see, Christiano (2008). See also Kolodny (2014a, b).

[12] For example, see Waldron (1999).

legitimate political decision-making processes. In the discussion that follows, the context should make clear which notion is being used.[13]

3.2 *Proceduralist Understanding Revised*

This understanding of political legitimacy fits with the socio-political phenomena with which I am concerned and that follow nearly every election or referendum. Namely, a vote is held, a decision is made, and in the aftermath, we are admonished to respect the outcome because it was decided by a legitimate procedure. It is my contention that legitimate procedures alone, however, are not enough to justify the claim to political legitimacy or the attendant demand for respect. To understand why, we must consider the implications of the requirement that a community's political decision-making respect the equal moral worth of all affected by a decision. In addition, for reasons that I will discuss momentarily, the questions submitted to a political decision-making procedure must be the sort of questions that are appropriate for political decision-making. Consequently, we must also assess the implications this condition has for our understanding of political legitimacy.

3.2.1 When Is It Appropriate to Subject a Question to Political Decision-Making

The claim that only certain questions are appropriately subjected to political decision-making is not about how decisions are made, rather it is a constraint on when it is appropriate to use political decision-making procedures at all. It is thus a prior condition before political decision-making of any sort can be legitimate. There are at least two properties of a choice-situation that determine whether it is appropriate to subject the underlying question to political decision-making. First, there must be sincere disagreement, which requires that those involved in the disagreement hold their views in good faith.[14] This means that those engaged in the dispute believe that there is a right answer to the question at issue, they are committed to engaging in deliberation and collective decision-making to try to find that answer, and they are open to reasoned persuasion. The notion of "right answer" does not require a truth functionally correct answer. For example, a particular dispute may involve little more than the competition of interests or value judgments, but in advancing one set of interests or values over another, a party is implicitly supporting the prioritization of one set of interests or values as the right answer.

Second, to be appropriately addressed by political decision-making, the question at issue must not admit of epistemically accessible determinate answers. It is

[13] I want to thank Steven Scalet for pointing out this possible confusion to me.

[14] Waldron (1999), pp. 97–99.

important to understand that by "accessible" I intend to include those matters in which there is a determinate answer that can be discovered through empirical evaluation and exploration by experts using independent criteria, not that an answer is known at the moment. If such answers exist, no decision-making procedure can change the (il)legitimacy of those answers. For example, whether climate change is anthropogenic admits of an epistemically accessible determinate answer. Consequently, it would be illegitimate to address the question of whether climate change is anthropogenic through political decision-making because there is an epistemically accessible determinate answer. How we ***ought*** to respond to climate change does not, however, admit of an epistemically accessible determinate answer; consequently, it is appropriate for political decision-making.

3.2.2 Respect for the Equal Moral Worth of All Affected

As noted, to be politically legitimate a community's political decision-making must instantiate respect for the equal moral worth of all affected by a decision.[15] But, what constitutes such respect? Jeremy Waldron argues that to respect the moral equality of all affected, a community's political decision-making must be impartial between different possible outcomes.[16] In addition, it has also been argued that all who are affected by a decision must have an equal and meaningful—not merely formal—opportunity to participate in the community's political decision-making.[17] For the purposes of this argument, it makes little difference whether the choice being presented to the community is a matter of substantive policy or an individual seeking to represent the relevant community in a representative democracy like ours.

To clarify, impartiality is required because, in those matters appropriately subjected to political decision-making, there are no non-arbitrary reasons that justify treating some alternatives as more worthy than others prior to subjecting the underlying question to political decision-making.[18] Further, in value-laden policy matters, since they are permeated with issues in which there are no epistemically accessible determinate answers regarding what counts as the right or the good, respecting the equal moral worth of all affected by a decision requires that a community's political decision-making not predetermine the outcome.[19] To fail to remain impartial would be to treat some outcomes and those who hold them as superior to others.

As to the requirement that all affected by a decision have an equal opportunity to ***meaningfully*** participate, respecting the equal moral worth of all affected by a decision requires that those affected by a decision must, as a matter of practical effect, be treated equally within a community's political decision-making. This requires

[15] See Waldron (1999). And see Kassner (2006).

[16] Waldron (1999).

[17] Kassner (2006).

[18] Waldron (1999).

[19] *Ibid*, pp. 110, 114.

that each person be guaranteed the ability to participate in political decision-making on equal terms with others, failing to do so is to treat some as less capable than others at governing, again to treat some as inferior and others as superior.

3.2.3 Legitimate Decision-Making Procedures Are Not Enough

I have yet to defend the proposition that political decision-making procedures—even if legitimate in a narrow sense—are necessary but not sufficient for political legitimacy in a broad sense. To clarify, by a narrow sense of legitimacy I mean that the procedure instantiates certain procedural values, such as fairness and impartiality, and though necessary for political legitimacy in the broader sense, the fact that the procedure instantiates such values is not sufficient for political legitimacy in the broad sense, not enough to justify the demand that one respect the outcomes of the community's political decision-making.

If, however, it is possible to have (narrowly) legitimate procedures alongside failures to respect the two additional considerations just explored, then such (narrowly) legitimate procedures are not sufficient for political legitimacy. As a conceptual matter, this possibility should be clear. We can imagine a state of affairs in which a (narrowly) legitimate political decision-making procedure is employed in circumstances in which it is either the case that the question being addressed is one that ought not be subjected to political decision-making or the (narrowly) legitimate political decision-making procedure is employed in circumstances that by their very nature are incapable of demonstrating respect for the equal moral worth of all affected.

For example, imagine a political community that has responded to the climate crisis by subjecting the question of whether climate change is anthropogenic to a (narrowly) legitimate political decision-making procedure. Due to the fact that this question admits of an epistemically accessible determinate answer, whether climate change is anthropogenic is not appropriately addressed through political-decision making. Employing a (narrowly) legitimate political decision-making procedure cannot alter that fact.

Further, if the use of a (narrowly) legitimate political decision-making procedure were sufficient for political legitimacy, then we would not need to know anything else about the choice situation other than whether the political decision-making procedure was (narrowly) legitimate. Imagine, however, that as a political community, we are faced with the question of what we ought to do about climate change, and the broader context within which this decision is being made, is not merely conflict-ridden, but includes state controlled media that consistently presents only one side of the debate, the state institutes laws that have a chilling effect on views other than those advanced by the state and a prohibition on gatherings to discuss and protest the current administration and/or its policies, but the decision about what ought to be done in response to climate change is left to a narrowly legitimate decision-making procedure.

This scenario presents us with a sort of Orwellian dystopia in which a (narrowly) legitimate political decision-making procedure is used to make political decisions. The existence of such a (narrowly) legitimate political decision-making procedure amidst such circumstances fails to satisfy the demand that our political decision-making respect the equal moral worth of all affected by a decision under such circumstances. Thus, rendering the decisions reached illegitimate and not deserving of our respect.

Rejecting the idea that a (narrowly) legitimate decision-making procedure is sufficient for political legitimacy raises the question of what, if anything, is sufficient. My response relies on a distinction between political decision-making procedures and political decision-making processes. To my knowledge, the two notions are often used interchangeably. There is, however, an important distinction to be drawn between them that leads to significant implications both for our understanding of political legitimacy and the opportunities for reform.

As to what differentiates a decision-making process from a decision-making procedure, the latter is a formally institutionalized practice used to make final decisions embedded within a community's political decision-making processes. A political decision-making process includes both the broader informal space of public political deliberation and the formal procedures used by a political community. It is the nature of the overarching political decision-making process, not the final decision-making procedure alone, that determines whether a decision is legitimate, and thus deserving of our respect.

An example may help to clarify the distinction and their relationship. Imagine that the United States is engaging in a nation-wide policy debate over immigration reform. This issue is the topic of discussion on news programs, social media, around dinner tables and in the halls of legislative bodies. Many of these conversations are informal, meaning that they are not governed by formal rules and procedures, and are instead organized around social norms that provide structure to our civil discourse. Others, like specific floor debates, formal campaigns, referenda and legislative votes, are governed by formally institutionalized rules. The relevant political decision-making process includes the around-the-dinner-table conversations and the formally rule-governed deliberations and votes; the former providing a source of meaning, context and understanding for the latter.

As noted, this should not be taken as a rejection of the value of pure proceduralist theories, but as a recognition of their incompleteness. The introduction of the difference between political decision-making procedures and political decision-making processes is intended to fill the gap between narrow procedural legitimacy, which is explained by such proceduralist accounts, and the requirements of a broader political legitimacy capable of justifying the demand that the outcomes of a community's political decision-making be respected. In short, this is not an argument in opposition to procedural accounts, but a supplementation.

4 Political Legitimacy, Factual Accuracy and Theoretic Rationality

With this understanding of post-truth politics, political legitimacy and the distinction between political decision-making procedures and processes in hand, we can now shift our focus to assessing ***Premise 1***, that respect for factual accuracy and theoretic rationality are necessary for political legitimacy. To begin, however, assessing ***Premise 1*** requires that we have a working understanding of factual accuracy and theoretic rationality.

4.1 Factual Accuracy

Factual accuracy is an epistemic notion distinguishable from more robust notions like truth or knowledge. To be factually accurate, a claim must be justifiable to others based on the information available, but it needn't be "true" in a deeper metaphysical sense. Factually accurate claims are also provisional in nature. They are open to adjustment should new information dictate a change in one's understanding.

There are at least three questions raised by this understanding. First, what is it about factual accuracy that makes it an appropriate epistemic standard for political choices? Second, what kind of information can be assessed as factually (in)accurate? Third, and finally, how are factually accurate understandings provisional and why? Regarding the first question, our political choices often revolve around matters that admit of epistemically accessible determinate answers. Despite the relevance of such empirical matters to our policy choices, more robust epistemic standards like truth require a degree of certainty that is not appropriate for matters of politics. There is, nonetheless, value in recognizing the importance of epistemic justification when it comes to such matters. Factual accuracy leans towards truth while remaining practically effective in a world where collective decisions must be made amidst disagreement.

As to the second question, factual accuracy attaches to those aspects of a disputed policy question that admit of an epistemically available determinate answer. By determinate I mean that the matter admits of empirical assessment, confirmation or explanation that relies on an epistemically accessible independent standard of evaluation. Examples include historical, scientific, mathematical, statistical and similar claims. They are testable against the relevant epistemically available independent criteria. What can constitute good faith disagreement when discussing matters that admit of such determinate answers is extremely limited.

Finally, regarding its provisional nature, in one sense it is obviously true that factual accuracy must be provisional. As scholars, clinicians, scientists and others continue to experiment, investigate, test and contemplate our existence and our world, our understanding evolves. What we understand at present is always, and should be, subject to revision. For both conceptual, practical and historical reasons, it would be unreasonable to expect otherwise. It is also important to point out that in recognizing the provisional nature of factually accurate information we recognize the fact that even our best understandings are likely incomplete, and that we should not remain complacent with the status quo but should continue to seek improved understandings of ourselves and our world.

4.2 Theoretic Rationality

Theoretic rationality is about ***how*** we reason from the foundational reasons that serve as the bases for our beliefs to the beliefs themselves and from those theoretically rational beliefs to the various practical and theoretical inferences we draw from them. A belief is theoretically rational if it satisfies two conditions. Our reasons for the belief must be good reasons, and our beliefs must bear an appropriate relationship to such foundational reasons and each other.

But what constitutes a "good" reason? On this point, I am sympathetic to Thomas Scanlon's account of reasons.[20] For Scanlon, a reason is inexorably linked with our social and moral practices of explanation and justification.[21] Such practices are about offering reasons to others to explain or justify our actions or beliefs to one another. What needs to be justified (or explained) and to whom will depend on the nature of the explanation or justification needed. Therefore, what constitutes a good reason is context dependent.

For example, whether an individual's experience of religious revelation constitutes a good reason depends on what it is intended to explain or justify, and whether or to whom it is offered or owed. As an explanation of an individual's faith, it is a good reason since it provides others with an understanding of her faith. That explanation, without more, however, cannot justify coercion; consequently, her explanation would not—in-and-of-itself—justify coercing others to adopt her religion.

Understanding what constitutes a good reason is not, however, enough to understand theoretic rationality. It must also be the case that one's beliefs and actions are related to those reasons in the right way. A complete catalogue of the various relationships constitutive of this aspect of theoretic rationality isn't possible here, but there are several general rules worth recognizing. First, claims that suffer from basic logical fallacies are not theoretically rational. Second, brute subjective preferences, values, judgments, … etc. don't serve as justifications. Finally, theoretic rationality requires that principles of coherence and consistency be observed. These are minimal forms of rational inference and reasoning.

[20] Scanlon (2000).

[21] *Ibid.*

4.3 *Respect for Factual Accuracy and Theoretic Rationality as a Condition of Political Legitimacy*

I can now return to defending the claim that political legitimacy requires respect for factual accuracy and theoretic rationality. I take it to be largely uncontroversial that political legitimacy requires respect for the equal moral worth of all affected by a decision and respect for the fact that only certain questions are appropriate for political decision-making. Consequently, if failures to respect factual accuracy and/or theoretic rationality make it more likely that a political community either fails to limit its political decision-making to those questions appropriately addressed through political decision-making processes or fails to instantiate respect for the equal moral worth of all affected by a decision, then failures to respect factual accuracy and theoretic rationality undermine political legitimacy.

4.3.1 Impact of Failures to Respect Factual Accuracy and Theoretic Rationality on the Appropriate Use of Political Decision-Making

Looking first to the proposition that only those questions that admit of sincere disagreement ***and*** that do not admit of epistemically accessible determinate answers ought to be subjected to political decision-making, if failures to respect factual accuracy or theoretic rationality undermine either of these conditions, then whatever is decided cannot be legitimate since the question should not have be subjected to political decision-making in the first place. As to the former condition, sincere disagreement requires that parties to the disagreement are committed to the possibility and pursuit of a correct answer while also being open to persuasion by reasoned argument. A failure to respect factual accuracy, if not corrected once discovered, undermines both the possibility of pursuing a correct answer and the commitment to that pursuit, because such failures, by definition, disregard the existence of an identifiable best answer to the matter under consideration. It is to disregard both the answer and to fail to adopt the proper attitude regarding the pursuit of the answer.

As to the relationship between a failure to respect theoretic rationality and the possibility of sincere disagreement, sincere disagreement requires that the parties to the disagreement are open to reasoned persuasion. This requires an openness to some form of public deliberation, which can only function as a forum for sincere disagreement if the reasoning within the relevant deliberative space can be understood by all those participating in the relevant deliberations. The principles of theoretic rationality are the minimum needed to ensure that such reasoning can be so understood. Failures to respect theoretic rationality simply are—by definition—failures in minimally rational reasoning; thus, if uncorrected, failures to respect theoretic rationality prevent the pursuit of correct answers through public deliberation, undermining the possibility of sincere disagreement.

As to the requirement that questions that admit of epistemically accessible determinate answers not be subjected to political decision-making, failing to respect factual accuracy and theoretic rationality involves the willful disregard for the significance of epistemically accessible independent criteria capable of settling a disputed matter. Consequently, such failures are antithetical to the demand that we recognize and employ such epistemically accessible criteria, increasing the likelihood that a community will unjustifiably subject a question to political decision-making when—at least elements of—the question should be decided by such independent criteria and not subjected to political decision-making. One need only consider the recent case of Fox News (Fox), and their willful and intentional deception, knowing that the various conspiracy stories being offered in support of the false narrative that the 2020 Presidential election had been "stolen" were themselves untrue, Fox consciously and intentionally chose to spread lies to ensure the continued engagement of their audience rather than tell them the truth and bear the financial costs of doing so. Their lies have had a determinate impact on the health and legitimacy of our political decision-making, including the defeat of moderate Republicans and the rise of election-denying extremists in the Republican party.

4.3.2 Impact of Failures to Respect Factual Accuracy and Theoretic Rationality on the Ability of the Decision-Making Process to Respect the Moral Equality of All Affected by a Decision

As argued, respecting the equal moral worth of all affected requires that decision-making processes are both impartial between possible outcomes, and that all affected by a decision have an equal and meaningful opportunity to participate in the decision-making process. As to the requirement of impartiality, if a decision-making process fails to respect factual accuracy, then the process will have arbitrarily placed some outcomes at a (dis)advantage compared to others. Those outcomes supported by factually inaccurate claims, if uncorrected, have a distinct and unjustifiable advantage over those that are grounded in respect for factual accuracy, as the latter are being held to a different, and more demanding, standard.

To clarify, returning to our example of climate change, imagine that we are answering what ought to be done about climate change. This is a policy question appropriately addressed by political decision-making. Let us also assume that there are only two viable options, one prioritizes individual liberty over social welfare and the other prioritizes social welfare over individual liberty. Barring any changes to the political decision-making situation, the liberty-prioritizing option will win.

However, just weeks before the vote, new information arises that favors the welfare-prioritizing alternative and is deeply problematic for the liberty-prioritizing alternative. In fact, if this information is presented within an environment that respects factual accuracy, the welfare-prioritizing alternative will win. Those advocating for the liberty-prioritizing alternative effectively preclude this information from public deliberations through a combination of deceptive advertising and social media campaigning that unjustifiably calls the relevant empirical data into doubt.

These failures to respect factual accuracy are uncorrected by the process. A (narrowly) legitimate decision-making procedure is then employed to reach a decision. Under these circumstances, the political decision-making process is no longer impartial. The failure to respect factual accuracy privileged one alternative over another, and the outcome's claim to legitimacy has been undermined.

Though less clear, failures to respect theoretic rationality also undermine a political decision-making process's ability to remain impartial. Impartiality requires that the relevant political deliberations enable those affected to offer one another criticisms and justifications within a deliberative framework that is itself impartial. If, however, one fails to respect theoretic rationality and offers arguments and criticisms based in illicit reasoning that goes uncorrected, then those conceptions of the good and the alternatives supported by such illicit reasoning are provided with an unjustified advantage, again undermining the legitimacy of the outcome.

Returning to our example, imagine that those supporting the liberty-prioritizing alternative acknowledge the existence of the information that supports the social welfare-prioritizing alternative but actively employ illicit forms of reasoning that happen to be highly rhetorically persuasive. The outcome is that a majority of the population reaches the conclusion that is rationally inconsistent with the factually accurate information in question. If uncorrected, the liberty-prioritizing alternative has again been given an arbitrary advantage. In which case, the legitimacy of the outcome is again undermined.

Uncorrected failures to respect factual accuracy or theoretic rationality also have an impact on the ability of a political community's decision-making processes to ensure that all affected by a decision have an equal and meaningful opportunity to participate in the decision-making process. Those whose views benefit from such uncorrected failures have an unfair advantage over those whose views do not, resulting in the illicit privileging of some alternatives over others.

Returning to our example, in the scenarios discussed the welfare-prioritizing advocates are facing a tilted, rather than level, playing field. Those advocating for the liberty-prioritizing alternative, in failing to respect factual accuracy and theoretic rationality, are not playing by the same rules as those advocating for the welfare-prioritizing alternative, undermining the ability of the community's political decision-making processes to respect the right of those advocating for the welfare-prioritizing alternative to equal and meaningful participation in the decision-making process.

4.3.3 The Significance of 'Uncorrected' and 'Undermined'

The threat to political legitimacy posed by the failures discussed depends on those failures being ***uncorrected***. Such uncorrected failures ***undermine*** political legitimacy. Both notions require further clarification. Regarding the claim that the threat to political legitimacy depends on the failures being uncorrected, it is the ability of the overall process to respect factual accuracy and theoretic rationality that matters, not whether individual failures can be prevented in the moment of their occurrence. In other words, it is not that failures occur, but that the process doesn't correct them.

As to the significance of the proposition that uncorrected failures undermine political legitimacy, it is related to the fact that politically legitimate decisions are deserving of our respect. Respect is an attitude that admits of degrees. Implicit in this understanding of political legitimacy as respect is that political legitimacy is ***not*** an all-or-nothing proposition.[22] In arguing that failures to respect factual accuracy and theoretic rationality undermine political legitimacy, I am implicitly accepting that some decisions are ***more*** legitimate than others, thus deserving more respect than others.

5 Post-Truth Politics Undermines Factual Accuracy and Theoretic Rationality

To complete this argument, it is necessary to explain how post-truth politics threatens factual accuracy and theoretic rationality. First, and most directly, post-truth politics—by definition—includes an utter disregard for factual accuracy and theoretic rationality, resulting in an unavoidable tension between factual accuracy and theoretic rationality on the one hand, and post-truth politics on the other.

Second, in actual practice post-truth politics has undermined factual accuracy. Whether it is in the acceptance of the false rhetoric of emerging populist movements around the globe, the use of social media to advance partisan agendas by creating echo-chambers, or in campaigns that trade in disinformation, distortion and ignorance-based fear-mongering; post-truth politics has undermined factual accuracy. As a specific example one need only consider the claim by the Leave campaign in 2016 that if voters in the UK would choose to leave the European Union, then hundreds of millions of pounds a week would be repatriated to the United Kingdom (UK) for its beloved National Health Service. Under such false pretenses, that is exactly what the population of Great Britain chose to do.

Third, and finally, looking specifically at the conflict between post-truth politics and theoretic rationality, post-truth politics includes forms of reasoning not constrained by any rules or principles of rationality or reasonableness. Theoretic rationality, on the other hand, is committed to impartiality and reasoning that is constrained by minimal considerations of logic, consistency and coherence. Post-truth politics, in its single-minded commitment to victory at any cost, is defined by an attitude of utter disregard for theoretic rationality.

In response, one might argue that no process can effectively prevent ***every*** instance in which post-truth politics undermines factual accuracy or theoretic rationality, at least not without sacrificing other values that make political decision-making processes legitimate, such as freedom of expression and association. This

[22] For an example of a more binary understanding of legitimacy, see Applebaum (2019).

potential objection relies on a misunderstanding of what respect for factual accuracy and theoretic rationality requires. As noted, the claim is not that failures must be ***prevented*** for factual accuracy and theoretic rationality to be respected; rather, if such failures are not corrected ***at some point*** by the process, then the claim that the outcomes are legitimate and deserving of our respect is undermined to the degree to which the outcome is impacted by the failures in question.

6 Objection from the Requirement that Political Decision-Making Respect the Equal Moral Worth of All Affected by a Decision

There is one more point that begs for clarification. To be specific, someone like Jeremy Waldron might object that if we assume that respect for the equal moral worth of all affected by a decision requires impartiality between possible outcomes, then the claim that political legitimacy requires respect for factual accuracy and theoretic rationality may prove problematic because it places a prior constraint on the outcomes of our political decision-making processes. In which case, respecting factual accuracy and theoretic rationality would violate the commitment to impartiality.

The success of this objection depends on the commitment to factual accuracy and theoretic rationality predetermining the outcome or results, arbitrarily privileging some alternatives over others. Respecting factual accuracy and theoretic rationality constrains the process, not the content of the outcomes. In fact, if we accept our inability to determine which conception of the right or good is correct, then nearly all outcomes are compatible with factual accuracy and theoretic rationality. Thus, there is no unjustified or arbitrary bias in favor of some outcomes or conceptions of the good over others.

Undoubtedly some will find this response unsatisfying. A stronger version of the objection would begin by claiming that certain outcomes will *de facto* be excluded by any process that respects factual accuracy and theoretic rationality. To clarify, since it is possible that there are some outcomes that can only be supported by factually inaccurate information or theoretically irrational reasoning, then those outcomes will be excluded. If correct, then—the argument concludes—we must choose between respecting factual accuracy and theoretic rationality or respecting the requirement that the decision-making process remain impartial.

Even assuming this is true, this limitation doesn't warrant objection. A commitment to factual accuracy and theoretic rationality implies that only outcomes grounded in minimally rational beliefs and that don't disregard epistemically accessible determinate answers are worthy of our respect. This is not the same as limiting the substantive content of the possible outcomes, but merely ensuring that all outcomes are arrived at through a decision-making process that respects these minimal conditions. Further, the objection depends on there being a dilemma between our ability to respect the equal moral worth of all affected by a decision and our ability to respect factual accuracy and theoretic rationality. There is, however, no dilemma because, as argued, failures to respect factual accuracy and theoretic rationality unjustifiably privilege some outcomes over others. Consequently, to respect factual accuracy and theoretic rationality is to maintain, not undermine, respect for the equal moral worth of all affected by a decision.

Additionally, respecting factual accuracy and theoretic rationality requires that the same independently justified standards of epistemic and rational evaluation be used to distinguish between alternative outcomes. Impartiality doesn't require that we don't judge at all, only that our judgment is not biased in a way that unjustifiably privileges—for arbitrary reasons—some outcomes or conceptions of the good over others. Outcomes that are neither factually accurate nor theoretically rational don't deserve our respect because they fail to be consistent with our best empirical understanding of the world and/or fail to be supported by minimal rationality; neither are arbitrary reasons for making such judgments about possible outcomes.

Finally, the requirement that the decision-making process remains impartial is not valuable in-and-of-itself, rather the commitment to impartiality is justified as a means to fulfilling the requirement that we respect the equal moral worth of all affected by a decision. Thus, such impartiality is only valuable to the extent that it serves this core commitment. In the case of post-truth politics, for reasons already discussed, if we must choose, our commitment to the equal moral worth of all affected by a decision is better served by a commitment to factual accuracy and theoretic rationality, rather than a blind adherence to an unsophisticated understanding of impartiality that conflates it with simple neutrality.

7 Conclusion

So, in this age of post-truth politics what is needed if our political decision-making processes are to deserve our respect? To begin, we ought to adopt a holistic perspective on what constitutes the relevant deliberative and decision-making space, to focus on processes and political culture over procedures alone. Our assessment of whether the political decision-making processes we rely on respect factual accuracy and theoretic rationality should include every aspect of what we reasonably consider political fora in which public political deliberation takes place.

Failing to view our political decision-making in this more holistic fashion unnecessarily limits what's relevant to our understanding of a community's political decision-making, needlessly limiting our options for reform. For example, one might perceive a tension between free speech and commitments to respect factual accuracy and theoretic rationality, the latter arguably placing unjustifiable limits on the former. This concern is unwarranted, because by broadening the deliberative space and incentivizing the public competition of ideas rather than simply precluding ideas that we believe are problematic, we can both protect free speech and promote respect for factual accuracy and theoretic rationality. To paraphrase Justice

Brandeis, the answer to bad speech is not to ban it, but to provide venues for more and better speech.[23]

However, for more and better speech to "remedy" bad speech, it must be the case that there is a confrontation of ideas, that bad speech is challenged by good speech in fora in which the two are set against one another on equal terms. The threat post-truth politics poses to political legitimacy is exacerbated by the extent to which we avoid the sort of confrontation necessary for this free market of ideas to prove effective. Steven Scalet's notion of "confrontation respect" presents a compelling account of the sort of interactions necessary for public deliberations to both respect others and contribute to the necessary competition of ideas.[24]

When Michael Ignatieff states, "[r]espect actually means listening to something you'd rather not hear, and listening must include the possibility of recognizing that there may be right on the other side",[25] we are reminded of the fact that one of the most reliable ways to collectively pursue truth and reason is through rigorous argument and rational dialogue conducted in a good faith effort to seek out the better argument. If done well, we not only increase the likelihood that our political decision-making will respect factual accuracy and theoretic rationality, we increase the likelihood that we will move closer to more accurate, rational, and empathetic understandings of our world and each other.

In the end, if properly constructed, such fora and the deliberative political culture surrounding them would serve as a better means to respecting factual accuracy and theoretic rationality than would one that excludes problematic speech from the public square. Post-truth politics presents a significant challenge to our ability to create such fora, thus forcing us to consider novel schemes to create and foster such spaces of public reason and deliberation—to protect and incentivize a competitive free market of ideas.

One might wonder how realistic such proposals are. Such skepticism, though understandable, is not necessarily justified. Citizen assemblies present a practically possible approach to the challenge of creating such fora.[26] In such assemblies, large groups of randomly selected citizens are brought together for thoughtful, but open, conversations on various controversial policy issues.

Ultimately, what is essential is that our politics revolves around a commitment to seeking answers to wicked problems amidst reasonable disagreement, while also showing respect for the equal moral worth of all affected by our decisions, thus justifying the demand that we respect the outcomes of our collective political decision-making. Respect for factual accuracy and theoretic rationality must be recognized as an essential part of this task.

---

[23] For Justice Brandeis's version of this argument regarding the First Amendment of the US Constitution, see *Whitney v. California* 274 U.S. 357(1927). For a more philosophical defense, see *On Liberty* from Mill 1998.

[24] Scalet (2010).

[25] Ignatieff (2000), p. 23.

[26] See "Amateurs to the rescue", *The Economist* (September 25, 2020), pp. 15–16.

References

(2020) Amateurs to the rescue. The Economist. September 25, pp 15–16
Applebaum A (2019) Legitimacy: the right to rule in a Wanton world. Harvard University Press, Cambridge
Bohman J (1996) Public deliberation. MIT Press, Cambridge
Brink D (1992) Mill's deliberative utilitarianism. Philos Public Aff 21:67–103
Christiano T (2008) The constitution of equality. OUP, Oxford
Dahl R (1956) A preface to democratic theory. Chicago University Press, Chicago
Gaus G (1997) Reason, justification, and consensus: why democracy can't have it all. In: Bohman J, Rehg W (eds) Deliberative democracy. MIT Press, Cambridge, pp 205–242
Ignatieff M (2000) The rights revolution. House of Anansi Press, Toronto
Kassner J (2006) Is everything really up for grabs? The relationship between democratic values and a democratic process. J Polit Philos 14:482–494
Kolodny N (2014a) Rule over none I: what justifies democracy. Philos Public Aff 42:195–229
Kolodny N (2014b) Rule over none II: social equality and the justification of democracy. Philos Public Aff 42:287–336
Locke J (1990) Second treatise on civil government. Hackett, Indianapolis
Manin B (1987) On legitimacy and political deliberation. Polit Theory 15:338–368
May K (1952) A set of independent, necessary, and sufficient conditions for simple majority decision. Econometrica 20:680–684
Mill J (1998) On liberty and other essays. OUP, Oxford
Peter F (2009) Democratic legitimacy. Routledge, New York
Peter F (2017) Political legitimacy. In: Zalta E (ed) The Stanford encyclopedia of philosophy. https://plato.stanford.edu/archives/sum2017/entries/legitimacy/
Rawls J (1993) Political liberalism. Columbia University Press, New York
Rawls J (2007) Lectures on the history of political philosophy. Harvard University Press, Cambridge
Raz J (2006) The problem of authority: revisiting the service conception. Minn Law Rev 90:1003–1044
Ripstein A (2004) Authority and coercion. Philos Public Aff 32:2–35
Rousseau J (2004) The social contract. Penguin Books, London
Scalet S (2010) Legitimacy, confrontation respect and the binding of freestanding liberalism. J Soc Philos 41:92–111
Scanlon T (2000) What we owe to each other. Belknap Press, Cambridge
Sunstein C (2017) #Republic. Princeton University Press, Princeton
Ten C (1998) Democracy, socialism, and the working class. In: Skorupski J (ed) The Cambridge companion to Mill. CUP, Cambridge, pp 372–395
Waldron J (1999) Law and disagreement. Clarendon Press, Oxford
Weber M (1964) The theory of social and economic organization. Free Press, New York
Weber M (1991) Politics as a vocation. In: Gerth H, Mills CW (eds) From Max Weber: essays in sociology. Routledge, London, pp 77–128
Whitney v. California 274 U.S. 357(1927)

Joshua J. Kassner is a Professor of Philosophy at the University of Baltimore. His research and teaching are focused on normative and applied ethics, political philosophy, global justice, and the philosophy of law.

Learning How to Read: Legal Hermeneutics

Wade L. Robison

Abstract Among all the problems bedeviling our Constitutional democracy, one that may well prevent their solution is reading the Constitution as though it were limited in its meaning to what those who framed it and those who adopted it understood it to mean—as though words have definitive meanings, tethered to the time and place they were uttered or written, to be uncovered through an examination of the text in which they occur and what ordinary individuals could have thought they meant.

That view of language betrays a serious misunderstanding of how language works and fails to capture what Chief Justice Marshall put so well when he remarked that the provisions of the Constitution are "intended to endure for ages to come." The version of originalism we shall assess ties us to a time long past.

1 Introduction

When Americans won the Revolutionary War, they ceased being subjects of the King. When they adopted the Constitution, they completed the revolution, becoming citizens who were to govern themselves. The Constitution embeds that ideal, but certainly did not meet it then.

The Constitution's mode of adoption illustrates just how far we were from realizing it. Only white males, and only some of those, were thought to be citizens, capable, that is, of ruling themselves and so capable of deciding whether the Constitution should be adopted.

We have come farther in realizing that ideal. Women have the right to vote, for instance. There are impediments to achieving more, however. Some are structural. Having two Senators for each state, regardless of size, was necessary to obtain the agreement of the small colonies, but that arrangement gives the citizens in those

W. L. Robison (✉)
Rochester Institute of Technology, Rochester, NY, USA

G. A. Babst et al. (eds.), *Liberal Constitutionalism and its Contemporary Challenges*, AMINTAPHIL: The Philosophical Foundations of Law and Justice 12, https://doi.org/10.1007/978-3-031-53602-1_4

states far more leverage in fashioning legislation and in Presidential elections than their numbers would justify were every citizen's vote to count equally. And then we have political parties doing what they can to diminish the voting power of the other party's supporters.

These problems are not minor since they may prevent us from solving social, economic and political issues we face, but there is another problem that lurks beneath them. That is the problem of determining the meaning of the Constitution's provisions.

The Constitution is the bedrock of our legal system and thus of our society, and yet some of its most momentous provisions are subject to dispute. Most troubling for progress in achieving the Constitution's ideal, as well as maintaining the stability of our country, is the appeal to a form of originalism to understand its provisions. Originalism requires that we read the Constitution's provisions as they would have been read and understood at the time of their adoption. The provisions mean what they meant.

Whatever that may mean, and originalists differ on that, what is not at issue is that we are to look back to what the provisions meant at the time they were adopted. We are then supposedly understanding them as they were understood by the future citizens of the United States. Their approval gave the Constitution legitimacy, and since they approved what they thought it meant, originalism argues that we are obligated to find that meaning and use it in any judicial decision involving the Constitution.

Put that way, originalism may sound plausible, but the version I will examine appeals to a theory of meaning that makes it anything but plausible. I first lay out two conditions any version of originalism must satisfy to be viable and then the condition that has recently become a dominant feature. We will then examine a historic case where that version was used before going on to examine the nature of language and its relevance to originalism.

2 Originalism

Ideas can mutate when they enter a new mind, and so there are a variety of versions of originalism. However much variants may differ, and they can differ significantly, any viable variant must satisfy the first two conditions we will examine. The most problematic variant for realizing the Constitution's ideal adds a third.

1. First, a viable variant must appeal to something accessible to anyone who wants to understand and assess an interpretation. However obvious this condition may seem, it does exclude one form of originalism, an appeal to the framers' intentions, what they intended a provision to mean. We have no guarantee that those framing the Constitution's provisions, or those approving it, had the same intentions, and even if they did, we cannot know what they were. Appealing to the framers' intentions is thus not a viable form of originalism (Rakove 1997,

pp. 15–37). A viable form must appeal to something public, something accessible to anyone concerned to understand and assess an interpretation.
2. The Constitutional text satisfies that criterion, but since it is what is open to competing interpretations, we need to ensure that we are reading it the right way. We do that by determining what the words meant "in the ordinary language of the day" (60 U.S. 410) and by making use of external sources "that might reveal the public meaning of the text at the time it became law" (O'Neill 2005, p. 2).

   "Legislative powers," "Commerce," and "domestic Tranquility," for instance, all would seem to mean today what they meant in 1788. So an originalism that satisfies these two conditions might seem like a plausible theory of interpretation. But whether plausible or not, some originalists add to these conditions a third.
3. Part of what the words mean is what those using those words *could* have had in mind in using them. So the Constitution refers to "citizens," and when Chief Justice Taney argued that Dred Scott could not be a citizen, even if free, he pointed out that when the Constitution was adopted, no one could have had in mind that "a negro, whose ancestors were imported into this country, and sold as slaves," could be a citizen (60 U.S. 403ff.). No citizen would count a slave a citizen.

We are not to look at what a word meant, at its intension, but to its extension, to what those who used the word would have recognized as falling under that word. If the meaning of "search and seizure" is constituted by what those who read the words could have had in mind in 1788, we get a far thinner protection than we might assume. It never would have occurred to those living in 1788 that someone could search your luggage without opening it up or seize details of your life by hacking into your phone.

It is originalism as defined by all three conditions that we will examine because it is originalism with this third condition that is becoming dominant in judicial decisions. We have a good example of the damage it can cause in *United States v. Zackey Rahimi*. Rahimi was subject to "an agreed civil protective order" after allegedly assaulting his ex-girlfriend (*Rahimi*, No. 21-11001, 2). It is no secret that the fear of those who ask for a protective order is that the person who assaulted them will do so again or do worse, killing them, and Texas passed a law prohibiting those under such an order from possessing firearms.

Rahimi argued that the law was unconstitutional, that he had a right under the Second Amendment to the pistol and rifle he had. He was certainly not a law-abiding citizen, having been involved in at least five shootings prior to his arrest. But the US Court of Appeals for the Fifth Circuit held that the Texas law was unconstitutional because the government could not point to "historical precedent from before, during, and even after the founding [that] evinces a comparable tradition of regulation" (*Rahimi*, 10). It held that the ban on the possession of firearms in such a situation is an "outlier that our ancestors would never have accepted" (*Rahimi*, 22).

A similar case involved a New York law banning carrying concealed weapons on such public modes of transportation as subways. A federal judge declared it unconstitutional because "historical analogues exist containing specific exceptions permitting…carrying firearms while travelling" (*Antonyuk et al v. Kathleen Hochul et al*, 1:22-CV-0986, 37). New York cannot *now* prohibit carrying concealed weapons on public transportation because it was legal *then*, when the second amendment was adopted, to carry firearms while traveling. To determine what the second amendment means, we are to look to how far the right to bear arms extended when it was written and adopted.

Just as our ancestors would have counted carrying firearms while traveling as protected by the second amendment, so they would not have counted being under a protective order as precluding possessing firearms. Put another way, the claim is that it would never have occurred to our ancestors that the second amendment's right to bear arms would be overridden by a concern for someone who had been assaulted or by a concern for the safety of other travelers.

Our concern is that originalism with this third condition will so constrain the Constitution's provisions as to make us unable to reach the Constitution's ideal of all citizens governing themselves or cover new circumstances not anticipated when the Constitution was adopted.[1]

3 Initial Problems

Two problems need to be addressed before we can examine the assumptions that power the version of originalism we are examining:

1. Nothing in the Constitution tells us how to read it. So originalism cannot find its source in any provision in the Constitution.
2. Nothing in the Constitution empowers courts to assess the Constitutionality of any legislation.

We have with originalism a theory of interpretation that on its own terms has no Constitutional support and is to be used by the judicial branch to do what, on originalist grounds, it has no power to do.

There is nothing in the Constitution, or from the Constitutional Convention, giving the judiciary authority to determine if legislation is constitutional. The idea had support, primarily by the Federalists, "but not by most Republicans and probably not by the bulk of the American people" (Wood 2009, p. 452). But no matter how many may have shared the view, originalists hold that we must appeal to what the Constitution says. To found their theory of interpretation on even widespread agreement about judicial review puts it on a much weaker footing than it would have were it stated in the Constitution.

[1] Doerfler and Moyn (2022) They argue that "constitutions — especially the broken one we have now — inevitably orient us to the past and misdirect the present into a dispute over what people agreed on once upon a time, not on what the present and future demand for and from those who live now."

The first case involving that power illustrates even the judiciary's hesitation about having that power. The case is not *Marbury v. Madison*, but *Hayburn's Case*, decided in 1792 by a federal district court in Pennsylvania composed of two Supreme Court justices and the district judge. Congress had passed a law requiring the justices to decide pension claims made by veterans injured in the Revolutionary War, their decisions to be reviewed and perhaps reversed by the Secretary of War and Congress. The court declared the law "unconstitutional on the grounds that engaging in non-judicial activities that were subject to revision by other branches of government violated judicial independence." What is intriguing is that the justices "apologized for their decision" (Wood 2009, p. 453).

They were clearly reluctant to exercise the power of review, but unless they did, there would be no real separation of powers. *Hayburn's Case* was the first in a series of judicial decisions that carved out a judicial role distinct from any administrative or legislative role.

Since we must go beyond anything in the Constitution or from the Constitutional Convention to justify the judiciary having the power of review, originalists are in the position of exercising a power of review originalism would deny they had the power to exercise. That is arguably an incoherent position (Chemerinsky 2022, pp. 73–114).

Originalists do not seem at all bothered by this. They know, as we know, that judicial review is not going to disappear. The reasons for having it have nothing to do with originalism, but with the arguments for and against having an institution within a constitutional democracy that is counter-majoritarian, empowered to overturn what the majority in Congress has decided is lawful. So originalists are going to continue to exercise judicial review using originalism, regardless.

Were originalism mandated by the Constitution, or by the Constitutional Convention, we would not question it as the method for interpreting the Constitution's provisions. But since nothing in the Constitution tells us how to interpret it, and the Convention did not issue a set of instructions, originalism must be justified on other grounds. We cannot use originalism to justify itself.

Originalists justify it on three grounds. First, they claim that judges can determine exactly what Constitutional provisions mean through originalism. Their judicial rulings will thus be objective. Using originalism to interpret those provisions means they will not bias their rulings with their own political views. Second, we get stability in the legal system because of that objectivity. Different justices, at different times, will make the same judicial rulings. And, third, their rulings will be justified by appealing to what those who adopted the Constitution understood its provisions to mean. Justices are reading the Constitution as those who approved it read it. That legitimizes their rulings.

Or so it is claimed. We should note, however, that just as the judges in *Hayburn's Case* appealed to the consequences of their ruling to justify it, originalists appeal to the consequences of using originalism to justify it. That tells us that originalists think it perfectly reasonable to appeal to something other than what originalism requires to justify claims about how to interpret the Constitution.

On its own terms, originalism cannot be the only contender for interpreting the Constitution. Other modes of interpretation with other consequences can be contenders as well.

Originalism has another problem. Using it does not necessarily lead to clarity about the meaning of Constitutional provisions. We will examine why by looking at a case where the Court did what originalism requires, providing a detailed textual analysis and backing that analysis with an examination of the historical record that explained why the provision was adopted and why it had to mean what the Court claimed it meant.

4 An Example: *Dred Scott*

Originalism is supposed to provide us with an objective reading of what the Constitution meant "when it came from the hands of its framers, and was voted on and adopted by the people of the United States" (60 U.S. 426). Words can change meaning over time, and appealing to what was originally meant "in the ordinary language of the day" insures that we are not importing new meaning into the Constitution's provisions (60 U.S. 410).

The passages quoted are from Chief Justice Taney's opinion in *Dred Scott v. Sandford*, and it provides us with a test case for originalism. He is insistent that the Constitution "must be construed now as it was understood at the time of its adoption. It is not only the same in words, but the same in meaning" (60 U.S. 410). The Court's duty, he argues, is "to administer it as we find it, according to its true intent and meaning when it was adopted" (60 U.S. 405).

Representatives were elected or chosen in each state to meet and vote on whether to adopt the Constitution. What they voted on and approved was what the Constitution's words meant to them at the time—not on what the words might come to mean, not on what someone might think they could or should mean, but on what they did mean. It is only by appealing to that meaning, the Chief Justice is arguing, that a court's opinion can have legitimacy.

The ultimate issue in *Dred Scott* was whether Scott had become a citizen by living for a time in the free state of Illinois or in that part of the Louisiana Territory that Congress had designated as free in the Missouri Compromise. Taney argues, as we saw, that at the time of the Constitution's adoption, no one thought that Negroes, even free Negroes, were citizens of the United States, saying that

> …they are not included, and were not intended to be included, under the word "citizens" in the Constitution, and can therefore claim none of the rights and privileges which that instrument provides for and secures to citizens of the United States (60 U.S. 404).

He supports this claim with detailed analyses of the wording of the Declaration of Independence, of the legislation of various states before and after the adoption of the Constitution, and of how, in their ordinary lives, white citizens, and even Negroes, enslaved or free, thought that Negroes were not citizens.

So even if Scott became free by living in Illinois or what would become Minnesota, he would not have become a citizen and so could not have standing to bring a suit to the Court. But Taney does not stop there. He argues that Scott did not become free by living in what became Minnesota because the only provision that could empower Congress to pass the Missouri Compromise has a far more limited scope.

That provision is Article IV, Section 3:

> The Congress shall have Power to dispose of and make all needful Rules and Regulations respecting the Territory or other Property belonging to the United States; and nothing in this Constitution shall be so construed as to Prejudice any Claims of the United States, or of any particular State.

Taney's argument that Section 3 is limited in scope relies on originalism in two different ways.

First, he appeals to the meaning of "Rules and Regulations," arguing that "they are not the words usually employed…in giving supreme power of legislation" (60 U.S. 437). They are not used in that way "in any other part of the instrument," noting passages where the terms are "employed…in speaking of some particular specified power"—as in granting the power "to establish an uniform *rule* of naturalization" and "to coin money and *regulate* the value thereof." Those terms are not used "when granting general powers of legislation" (60 U.S. 440).

Second, if we look to external sources "that might reveal the public meaning of the text at the time it became law," we find that Section 3 empowered Congress to establish rules and regulations for the territory that had been and would be ceded to the United States by the states.

> It does not speak of *any* territory, nor of *Territories*, but uses language which, according to its legitimate meaning, points to a particular thing, *the* territory of the United States — that is, to a territory then in existence, and then known or claimed as the territory of the United States (60 U.S. 436).

Taney claims this reading is backed by the second sentence in Section 3, that "nothing in this Constitution shall be so construed as to Prejudice any Claims of the United States, or of any particular State." That clause is "to exclude the conclusion that either party, by adopting the Constitution, would surrender what they deemed their rights" (60 U.S. 437). That sentence "relates…obviously to the unappropriated lands not yet ceded by the States" while the "first clause makes provision for those then actually ceded." The conclusion Taney draws is that "it is impossible, by any just rule of construction, to make the first provision general, and extend to all territories, which the Federal Government might in any way afterwards acquire, when the latter is plainly and unequivocally confined to a particular territory,…" (60 U.S. 437–8).

So Taney appeals first to the meaning of the terms in Section 3 and then to what the framers could have had in mind. Both appeals are central to the version of originalism we are assessing. We are to determine what a provision means by what it meant, but determining what it meant requires not just an appeal to what the words meant in the ordinary language of the day, but what those who understood them could have had in mind.

Taney finds nothing in the Constitution that authorizes the Federal Government to pass rules and regulations for any additional territory it might later acquire. “There is certainly no power given by the Constitution to the Federal Government to establish or maintain colonies…nor to enlarge its territorial limits in any way, except by the admission of new States” (60 U.S. 446). Congress has a duty to help a territory become a new state (60 U.S. 448), but it must exercise that duty Constitutionally, and in particular, cannot deprive any person “of life, liberty, and property, without due process of law” (60 U.S. 450).

The Missouri Compromise prohibited anyone from carrying their slaves, their property, that is, into the Louisiana Territory above parallel 36°30′ north, and so, Taney concludes, it “is not warranted by the Constitution, and is therefore void.” So “neither Dred Scott himself, nor any of his family, were made free by being carried into this territory” (60 U.S. 452). That is according to Taney’s originalist reading of the Constitution.

5 An Alternative Reading

My brief summary has no doubt failed to do justice to Taney’s examination of Section 3, but even a detailed account will not parry two implications which should make us chary of his reading.

His reading means that once the United States provided for the territory and property belonging to it as of June 21, 1788, when the Constitution came into effect, Article IV, Section 3 became moot. The government could make rules and regulations for what it owned as of that date in 1788, but not for anything newly acquired. Donations, gifts from foreign countries, ships seized at sea, imports for which duties had not been paid—the list is long and varied, but Taney’s reading prevents the government from doing anything with such property.

The second problem is that it is more than a little odd that the framers would clutter the document that lays out the structure and powers of the new government with a provision that would quickly become irrelevant. It would remain in the Constitution, with no further purpose, dead to later generations.

But there is a more compelling reason for questioning Taney’s reading. It was primarily Gouverneur Morris who pulled together the various matters that the Convention had agreed to and, in 4 days, converted it into the Constitution. In a letter to Henry W. Livingston in 1803, he wrote,

> I always thought that, when we should acquire Canada and Louisiana it would be proper to govern them as provinces, and allow them no voice in our councils. In wording the third section of the fourth article, I went as far as circumstances would permit to establish the exclusion. Candor obliges me to add my belief, that, had it been more pointedly expressed, a strong opposition would have been made (Sparks 1832, 3.192).

The readings Taney gives Section 3 and that Morris says he gave to it are at odds, but we do not have to choose between them to make my point. It is far more difficult than it may first appear to determine the original meaning of a provision in the Constitution. Morris was a native speaker, and in pulling together into a single coherent document what the Convention had agreed to, he surely understood what his words meant to his fellow framers and to the future citizens of the United States.

We should note his caution. He "went as far as circumstances would permit to establish this conclusion." His words were chosen with care, that is, and whatever their ambiguities, he surely was not saying what Taney's reading would have him say. Far from referring "to the particular territory" the United States would come to possess upon its creation, Morris meant it to apply "to territory which the new Government might afterwards obtain from a foreign nation," including Louisiana and Canada (60 U.S. 441–2).

Whatever we might think of his singular view that we should not admit either of those as states, it suggests that he carefully avoided language that might imply the more sweeping power given Congress in general, but chose "Rules and Regulations" to imply that Congress would be administering any new territory "as provinces."

In any event, what matters is what he said he meant in fashioning Article IV, Section 3, and what he said he meant is directly counter to what Taney claimed it meant. That is all we need to know to make us chary of drawing any firm conclusion from even a careful textual and historical analysis of what a word or phrase meant "in the ordinary language of the day." If anyone knew what was meant by "Rules and Regulations" as it was used elsewhere in the Constitution, it would surely be Morris.

6 How to Read

Chief Justice Taney assumes that Article IV, Section 3 has a meaning that we can determine by reading it carefully, taking care to examine almost every word if necessary, and by understanding what its contemporaries could have meant by it. It may seem paradoxical to use an appeal to a framer's intent to undermine an originalist's reading of a constitutional provision, but that appeal makes the point that we cannot determine a provision's meaning in the way originalism requires. Because the framer's intent contradicts the originalist meaning Taney provides, originalism fails to pass a test it must pass to be a viable form of interpretation.

Originalism cannot provide us the meaning of Art. IV, Section 3, putting in doubt its capacity to determine the meaning of any Constitutional provision. There are reasons for that.

First, we must always interpret. As Francis Lieber wrote in 1838, we "are continually obliged to resort to interpretation" (Lieber 1994, p. 28). He provides an example of a housekeeper who gives some money to a servant to "fetch some soup-meat" and thereby makes a great many assumptions. She assumes the servant understands that the money is not a gift, but is given to buy the meat, that the servant is to get the meat at the butcher's and not wander around asking everyone he meets if they have soupmeat he can purchase, that the servant is to bring the meat back to the housekeeper and not keep it himself, and so on. Making all these assumptions explicit so as "to exclude all *possibility* of misunderstanding" would not help at all, Lieber says, because each specification of an assumption would presuppose further assumptions, and on and on. Whatever we say depends upon assumptions we do not state, and stating them would entail "new ones. Where would be the end?…We are constrained then," he concludes, "always, to leave a considerable part of our meaning to be found out by interpretation, which, in many cases must necessarily cause greater or lesser obscurity with regard to the exact meaning, which our words were intended to convey" (Lieber 1994, p. 30).

This feature of language should be no surprise. Individuals may make different assumptions so that the same statement may be read one way by one individual and in quite another way by another individual. We thus have no assurance that others will find a text to mean what we find it to mean.

Originalists will say that they are doing exactly what Lieber says must be done: they are providing interpretations. But that misses the skepticism in Lieber's view. We can never be sure we have got the assumptions right and so can never be sure we understand a provision's meaning. We can be sure, however, that originalists have failed to get the meaning of the Constitution's provisions.

For the second problem they have is that their interpretations limit the meaning of terms to what the public could have had in mind upon reading or hearing it. What would they have recognized as an example? They limit the meaning to a term's extension at the time it was used. But this betrays a serious misunderstanding of how language works and, in particular, how the general terms in the Constitution work.

What makes a term general, and not just a name, is that we project the term onto objects we have not seen before (Cavell 1979, pp. 169ff.). Children have no trouble learning that "puppy" does not mean a particular puppy. They quickly learn that such general terms are not names of particular dogs, like "Ollie" or "Joey," but are to be projected onto new instances, like new breeds of dogs, that satisfy the relevant criteria we use in recognizing an animal as a dog. The possibility of projection is what makes them general terms rather than names. Were general terms constrained as originalists of the sort we are examining require, children would never learn to speak and understand a language. They would live in a world of names (Wittgenstein 2009, §2ff.).

The general terms of the Constitution are just like any other general terms. Consider the term "Commerce" in Art. I, §8 where Congress is given the power "to regulate Commerce with foreign Nations, and among the several States, and with the Indian Tribes." Clearly all that the framers and those who adopted the Constitution could have had in mind was someone carrying commercial goods from one state to another, going by foot or horse or boat. The meaning of "interstate commerce" did not change when steamboats began to ply American rivers. New York state claimed it did, but as Chief Justice Marshall pointed out, to exclude navigation from Congressional control would "restrict a general term, applicable to many objects, to one of its significations" (*Gibbons v. Ogden*, 22 U.S (9 Wheat)1, 189 (1824)). Nor did the meaning of "commerce" change when railroads began to run from one state to another, carrying cargo, or when motor vehicles or airplanes began to do the same.

Terms are general just because their meanings are *not* constrained by what anyone has in mind. When I utter a word, its meaning does not depend upon what I have in mind or on what everyone who hears it could have in mind, but, to put it paradoxically, on what it means. Consider how Robert Frost ends *The Road Not Taken*:

> Two roads diverged in a wood, and I—
>
> I took the one less traveled by,
>
> And that has made all the difference (Frost 2015, p. 128).

Frost did not have in mind a particular intersection where he happened to take one road rather than another. He is making a point about how decisions in our lives have consequences and especially about choosing something other than the ordinary. We understand what he has written only because we take his meaning in a general sense, something we learned to do as children when we learned to talk.

Originalists do not want to apply to the Constitution's provisions the lesson even they picked up quickly as children and what they use today in communicating to us through their opinions, for instance. They write using general terms, but by their own originalist criteria, what they write can only mean what we take it to mean today, what we could have in mind when we read their words. That position undercuts the precedential value of their opinions and so discourages the stability they claim to value in a legal system.

7 Principles

The most problematic words and phrases in the Constitution share two characteristics:

1. They are essentially contested.
2. They embody principles.

"Essentially contested" is W. B. Gallie's phrase. There are many examples in our ordinary language. Who is the best baseball player? Those who think hitting is the most important feature of the game will pick one kind of player. Those who think pitching most important will pick another, and those who think an all-round hitter and fielder will pick another. The "best baseball player" is an essentially contested concept because disagreements about its meaning are "not resolvable by argument of any kind," but "are nevertheless sustained by perfectly reasonable arguments and evidence" (Gallie 1968, p. 158).

Just so, "freedom of speech," "equal protection," and "due process" are open to competing interpretations of their meaning that can be "sustained by perfectly reasonable arguments and evidence," and yet cannot be resolved.

Consider what is meant by equal protection. Does it mean what it meant when the 14th amendment was adopted? If those who framed and adopted it had disabled Civil War soldiers in mind, they did not have in mind special ramps or doors for wheelchairs. Does equal protection require that students are to gain leverage to enter higher education because of some background condition, like their ancestors having been slaves? Or is that itself a denial of equal protection? The history of the court cases on affirmative action is a telling example of an essentially contested concept being interpreted first one way and then another. [2]

Perhaps more telling about what we might call the range of the concept of equal protection is *Brown v. Board of Education of Topeka* (347 U.S. 483 (1954)). The framers of the 14th amendment certainly did not have in mind "Negroes" and whites going to school together, and yet the decision in Brown turned on the claim that "equal, but separate" was in no way equal.

The point of such examples is to illustrate that the concepts in question— equal protection, due process, and so on—are short-hand for principles that are, as principles, to be applied to new cases. When we say that no state shall "deny to any person within its jurisdiction the equal protection of the laws," we are articulating a principle that far from being limited to what its framers or the citizens may have considered unequal protection, is by its nature open to situations that no one had considered—provided that a reasonable argument can be made that the situation denies equal protection.

8 Seeing Connections

We should add one further way in which Constitutional provisions resist being limited in the way the version of originalism we are assessing maintains. It is a relatively common phenomenon for us to discover that a variety of things we thought distinct from each other turn out to share a common feature that we have come to find only by looking at those things in a different way.

That common feature was always there, but we were not in a position to discern it, not having yet come to grips with the ideas that would allow us to discern it. The right to privacy is a prime example. When we examine the cases that Warren and Brandeis laid out in their 1893 seminal article on the right, we can see both how the cases might have been thought to be quite distinct and how we can now see that they share a common feature (Warren and Brandeis 1890, pp. 193–220).

The two that come to mind are the case of photographers and newsmen invading the wedding of Warren's daughter and the case of the stranger in a Michigan case who came with a physician into the house of a woman about to have a baby. She thought he was helping the physician. The physician thought it was the woman's

[2] Compare the *Regents of the University of California v. Bakke* (438 U.S. 265 (1978)) and *Grutter v. Bollinger et al* (438 U.S. 265 (1978)).

husband. He had the man touch the woman's abdomen to feel the movement of the fetus, and when it was discovered that he was a stranger, he was accused of a battery, of touching the woman without her consent. But as Warren and Brandeis make clear, the man really invaded the woman's privacy—although that concept was not available in the law at the time of the incident. Only afterwards, when the two introduced the right to privacy, did we have the intellectual instruments to see it for what it was.

It shared that feature with the invasion of the wedding of Warren's daughter. Here were uninvited individuals coming to a gathering of guests and intruding on the proceedings. It was impossible to ignore them since they were busy taking photographs and presumably talking to guests to get their stories, but, in any event, they were as invasive as the man in Michigan.

It is not amiss to look at the Constitution with an understanding we did not come to have until long after its adoption. What we would find is what Justice Douglas found. We might find a better way of describing the common features he found among disparate rights articulated in the Constitution than his "penumbra," but he was correct that several Constitutional rights exemplify the right to privacy. [3] What is the right against search and seizure other than the right of citizens not to have their privacy invaded? What is the right against self-incrimination other than the right not to have one's private thoughts used against oneself? What is the right not to have troops quartered in one's home other than the right not to have one's private residence invaded? What is the right against a state's prohibiting a couple using contraceptives other than a right against the state's invading the bedroom of one's home?

It is no surprise that the founding fathers did not articulate a right to privacy since we did not come to the concept until Warren and Brandeis wrote about it, but now that we have the concept, we can certainly use it to understand how what might appear to be unrelated provisions in the Constitution are instances of the same right, articulated in different contexts. Given that the right is there, it is certainly not amiss to argue that it covers other contexts than those referred to in the Constitution.

9 Concluding Remarks

As the competing analyses of Art. IV, Section 3 show, originalism cannot provide us with the determinate meaning of a Constitutional provision. That one failure is enough to reveal its basic problem: it fails to understand how language works. That failure is particularly egregious when it is the Constitution that is to be interpreted. No one has put the point better than Chief Justice Marshall in justifying the federal government's establishing a national bank:

[3] Justice Douglas wrote in *Griswold v. Connecticut* 381 U.S. 484 (1965) that "specific guarantees in the bill of rights have penumbras, formed by emanations from those guarantees that help give them life and substance."

> This provision is made in a Constitution intended to endure for ages to come, and consequently to be adapted to the various *crises* of human affairs. To have prescribed the means by which Government should, in all future time, execute its powers…would have been an unwise attempt to provide by immutable rules for exigencies which, if foreseen at all, must have been seen dimly, and which can be best provided for as they occur. To have declared that the best means shall not be used,…would have been to deprive the legislature of the capacity to avail itself of experience, to exercise its reason, and to accommodate its legislation to circumstances (*McCulloch v. Maryland*, 17 U.S. (4 Wheat.) (1819), 415).

As he puts it earlier in the opinion, "we must never forget that it is *a Constitution* we are expounding" (407).

So when we are unclear what a provision means, we do not turn to the version of originalism we are assessing, but, as Chief Justice Marshall says, to the "well settled rule, that the objects for which it was given, especially when those objects are expressed in the instrument itself, should have great influence in the construction" (*Gibbons v. Ogden*, 22 U.S (9 Wheat)1, 224 (1824).

References

Cavell S (1979) The claim of reason. Oxford University Press, New York

Chemerinsky E (2022) Worse than nothing: the dangerous fallacy of originalism. Yale University Press, New Haven

Doerfler RD, Moyn S (2022) The constitution is broken and should not be reclaimed. The New York Times, 19 August 2022

Frost R (2015) The road not taken and other poems. Penguin, New York

Gallie WB (1968) Philosophy and the historical understanding, 2nd edn. Schocken Books, New York

Lieber F (1994) Legal and political hermeneutics. Gryphon Editions, New York

O'Neill J (2005) Originalism in American law and politics: a constitutional history. The Johns Hopkins University Press, Baltimore

Rakove J (1997) Original meanings. Vintage Books, New York

Sparks J (ed) (1832) The life of Gouverneur Morris, with selections from his correspondence and miscellaneous papers, 3 vols. Boston

Warren SD, Brandeis LD (1890) The right to privacy. Harv Law Rev 4(5)

Wittgenstein L (2009) Philosophical investigations, 4th edn. Wiley-Blackwell, Oxford

Wood GS (2009) Empire of liberty: a history of the early republic, 1789-1815. Oxford University Press, New York

Wade L. Robison is the Ezra A. Hale Professor of Applied Ethics at the Rochester Institute of Technology. He has published extensively in philosophy of law, David Hume, and practical and professional ethics. His book *Decisions in Doubt: The Environment and Public Policy* (University Press of New England, 1994) won the Nelson A. Rockefeller Prize in Social Science and Public Policy. His latest book is *Practical and Professional Ethics* (Bloomsbury Press).

Deference Without Virtue: A Concern for Common Good Constitutionalism

Renée Nicole Souris

Abstract Adrian Vermeule's book *Common Good Constitutionalism* presents a profound challenge to the reigning schools of American legal thought in an effort to return to our classical roots. Vermeule describes his theory as methodologically Dworkinian in that he intends it to fit and justify American law, but unlike Dworkin's judge-centered theory of law as integrity, common good constitutionalism argues for judicial deference to political authorities—legislative and executive officials—who have 'primary competence for promoting the common good.' Indeed, common good constitutionalism urges political authorities to show a 'candid willingness to legislate morality.' The deference expected of judges toward legislators is part of common good constitutionalism's 'role morality' within our constitutional system, though the theory is presented as 'agnostic at the level of institutions' such that it does not require any particular institutional scheme. I challenge common good constitutionalism's argument for judicial deference to legislators from within the classical tradition itself by showing that within this tradition, deference depends upon a presumption of virtue among legislators which is untenable in our institutional environment. From here, I argue that common good constitutionalism either needs a new basis beyond virtue for judicial deference to legislators, or that Vermeule needs to revise the theory's institutional commitments so that it rules out those institutions that fail to cultivate political virtue among our legislators.

R. N. Souris (✉)
Florida Institute of Technology, Melbourne, FL, USA
e-mail: nsouris@fit.edu

G. A. Babst et al. (eds.), *Liberal Constitutionalism and its Contemporary Challenges*, AMINTAPHIL: The Philosophical Foundations of Law and Justice 12, https://doi.org/10.1007/978-3-031-53602-1_5

1 Introduction

Adrian Vermeule's book *Common Good Constitutionalism* presents a profound challenge to the reigning schools of American legal thought in an effort to return to our classical roots.[1] Common good constitutionalism seeks to revive the classical tradition of natural law and rejects legal positivism for failing to capture the fundamentally moral character of our law. With respect to constitutional interpretation, it aims to dispel originalism as an illusory approach that cannot make good on its promises to avoid questions of political morality—and, for Vermeule, originalism fails in this regard because we cannot divorce American law from political morality.[2] Common good constitutionalism also argues that while progressive constitutionalism appeals to political morality, it does so superficially and to a misguided account of our political morality.[3]

Vermeule describes his theory as methodologically Dworkinian, but unlike Dworkin's judge-centered theory of law as integrity, common good constitutionalism argues for judicial deference to political authorities—legislative and executive officials—who have 'primary competence for promoting the common good.'[4] While this deference depends upon a 'rebuttable presumption of authority,'[5] common good constitutionalism urges political authorities to show a 'candid willingness to legislate morality' and also asks judges to show deference to the moral judgments of political authorities so long as they act non-arbitrarily and with 'good faith.'[6] This is part of common good constitutionalism's 'role morality'[7] within our constitutional system, though the theory is presented as 'agnostic at the level of institutions' such that it does not require any particular institutional scheme.[8] Vermeule further argues in a distinctly Dworkinian fashion that common good constitutionalism both fits and justifies American law,[9] which gives us reason to take his theory as both descriptive and normative, and by no means simply a work in ideal theory.

My aim is to challenge common good constitutionalism's insistence on deference to non-judicial decisionmakers (specifically legislators) from within the classical tradition itself. Within this tradition, deference to decisionmakers makes sense because they are expected to have virtue, which disposes them toward the common good. For this model to work here and now, we need confidence that those to whom we are deferring moral judgment are similarly disposed toward the common good in the exercise of their lawmaking power. But Vermeule does not provide an

[1] Vermeule (2022).

[2] Vermeule (2022), Chapter 3, 'Originalism as Illusion,' 91–116.

[3] Vermeule., Chapter 4, 'Progressive and Developing Constitutionalism,' 117–153.

[4] Vermeule (2022), p. 5, 69.

[5] Vermeule (2022), p. 46.

[6] Vermeule (2022), p. 71.

[7] Vermeule (2022), p. 38, 43.

[8] Vermeule (2022), p. 10.

[9] Vermeule (2022), p. 69.

argument for this. He recognizes that lawmakers can make mistakes about the common good, but he presents these mistakes as a sort of anomaly rather than the ordinary state of affairs. While it would be desirable for our representatives to have virtue (and indeed consistent with the views of the framers who hoped they would), I argue that current institutional realities make it unreasonable to simply assume our lawmakers cultivate and practice virtues in the course of their official capacities—and further, that there are countervailing reasons to think our institutions actually dispose our lawmakers toward various kinds of personal and political vices. Hence, for common good constitutionalism to fit and justify our practice, as Vermeule intends it to do, we either need a new basis beyond virtue for judicial deference to legislators, or we need to rethink the institutional commitments of the theory so that it rules out institutions and practices that fail to cultivate virtue among lawmakers.

In Sect. 2, I present textual evidence to show that common good constitutionalism, like Dworkin's theory of law as integrity, is intended to capture actual practice of American law and is not an exercise in ideal theory. In Sect. 3, I then connect common good constitutionalism's presumption of deference to the moral judgments of non-judicial decisionmakers to the tradition of natural law and show that, within that tradition, deference also depended on a presumption of virtue among lawmakers within a context that made the presumption reasonable. In Sect. 4, I argue that institutional pressures facing our lawmakers fail to cultivate virtue and may actually dispose them toward vice. Insofar as the aretaic assumptions of common good constitutionalism are not tenable in our system, then the theory either needs a new basis beyond virtue for judicial deference to non-judicial authorities, or different institutional commitments that offer a more promising path for promotion of the common good. Section 5 provides a summary of my argument.

2 Common Good Constitutionalism as Methodologically Dworkinian

Vermeule describes common good constitutionalism as 'methodologically Dworkinian' in that it is intended to fit and justify the practice of American law.[10] For this reason, we are right to regard it (as we do Dworkin's) as a partly descriptive, partly normative project. This section lays out relevant parts of Dworkin's theory of law as integrity, and then shows how common good constitutionalism draws on Dworkin's theory as well as departs from it. The aim is (a) to establish that common good constitutionalism is not a work in ideal theory, so can and should be evaluated in terms of how well its assumptions hold true in our world, and (b) to show how common good constitutionalism sees itself within contemporary legal and political theory.

[10] Vermeule (2020), Vermeule (2022).

In an early essay, Dworkin presents an account of law that he describes as a kind of 'naturalism' because it asks judges to decide hard cases by 'interpreting the political structure of their community' in a special way, that is, by 'trying to find the best *justification* they can find, in principles of political morality, for the structure as a whole, from the most profound constitutional rules and arrangements to the details of, for example, the private law of tort or contract.'[11] Hard cases, for Dworkin, are those that implicate the political morality *in the law itself* and cannot be reduced to factual or semantic disagreement.[12] In *Law's Empire*, Dworkin explains that because the law makes some conduct mandatory and uses coercion in seeking compliance, there is always 'a standing risk of a distinct form of public injustice,' which makes there 'inevitably a moral dimension to an action at law.'[13] He further argues that because of law's coercive force, any theory of law must be able to explain how past political decisions justify present coercion. Dworkin's own answer is found in the political virtue of integrity, which could be interpreted to capture the theory's conception of the common good.

Two principles guide law as integrity: 'a legislative principle, which asks lawmakers to try to make the total set of laws morally coherent, and an adjudicative principle, which instructs that the law be seen as coherent in that way, so far as possible.'[14] While law as integrity asks legislators to craft morally coherent laws, it is not a work in ideal theory; it recognizes that legislators often appeal to policy considerations rather than moral principle. In a utopian society, integrity would not be a political virtue because the laws would already be just and fair in a morally coherent way, but in our imperfect society, law as integrity entrusts judges to bring principled moral coherence—or integrity—to law made on policy grounds.[15] In other words, the theory seems to accept that legislators may not be oriented toward the common good, understood here as oriented to craft laws in a morally principled and coherent way. Judges promote integrity, according to Dworkin, by engaging in an interpretive method that examines hard cases along two dimensions: fit and justification.

Fit asks judges to make the law as a whole coherent, fitting the answer to the present case with as much of the past legal history as possible, to present the law as if it was made by a single author: 'the community personified.'[16] In a 'community of principle,' where integrity is the guiding ideal, the law is not seen as the result of compromises for power among competing policy positions, but as a reflection of the values of the community and a principled resolution of conflicts between those values. As such, the dimension of justification asks judges to exercise moral judgment

---

[11] Dworkin (1982), p. 165.

[12] By contrast, Vermeule maintains that hard cases are those 'in which the rule the lawmaker prescribed for ordinary cases is ambiguous, or is vague, or otherwise misfires — fails to track the common good – due to unusual circumstances.' Vermeule (2022), p. 111.

[13] Dworkin (1986), p. 1.

[14] Dworkin (1986), p. 176.

[15] See Dworkin (1986), Chapters 6–7.

[16] Dworkin (1986), p. 225.

when deciding hard cases. In engaging with the political morality in the law, judges consult justice, fairness, and procedural due process in an effort to put the law in its best light. In doing so, judges aim to *justify* what politicians did and said, through a sort of legal and political story worth telling within a larger practice worth preserving.[17]

With that background of law as integrity in view, let us now turn to Vermeule's common good constitutionalism. In an *Atlantic* article that attracted much scholarly attention, Vermeule described his theory as 'methodologically Dworkinian,' and he continues to do so in his book, *Common Good Constitutionalism*.[18] The theory laid out therein, which like the title, is called common good constitutionalism draws inspiration from the classical tradition of natural law and from the parts of Dworkin's theory that are consistent with it.[19] There are two aspects to common good constitutionalism: an administrative part (which supports the current practice of judicial deference to agency officials, who are part of the executive branch) and a constitutional part (which calls for judicial deference to legislators). I am mainly concerned with the latter here.

Vermeule explains that, in relation to Dworkin's theory of law as integrity, common good constitutionalism,

> [S]hares the view that the positive provisions of the *ius civile,* including at the constitutional level, can only be interpreted in light of principles of political morality that are themselves part of the law. And it urges that the classical law is the best of our tradition, with the emphasis on both 'best' (justification) and 'tradition' (fit). But it advocates a different set of substantive moral commitments and priorities and a different account of rights from Dworkin's, which were all of a conventionally left-liberal and individualist bent… I reject his liberal theory of rights, as trumps over collective interests, in favor of a classical theory of rights as *ius,* founded in the injunction of justice to give every person what is due to them in a political order devoted to the common good.[20]

In a footnote directly after that passage, Vermeule adds that he rejects Dworkin's distinction between principles and policies because it assumes 'a typical liberal opposition between 'individual rights' and 'collective interests,' imagining the latter as aggregated social utility that may or may not 'override' individual rights.'[21] Common good constitutionalism also rejects the central interpretive role that law as integrity affords to judges. For Dworkin, law as integrity 'requires a judge to test his interpretation of any part of the great network of political structures and decision of his community by asking whether it could form part of a coherent theory justifying the network as a whole,' which he acknowledges is a Herculean task, but one that actual judges can approximate.[22] For Vermeule, common good constitutionalism, by

[17] Dworkin (1986), p. 227.

[18] Vermeule (2020, 2022).

[19] Vermeule (2022), p. 5.

[20] Vermeule (2022), p. 6.

[21] Vermeule (2022), 190fn17.

[22] Dworkin (1986), p. 245.

contrast, expects far less of judges, requiring them to subordinate their judgment to non-judicial decisionmakers. He writes,

> [O]ne might see the common good framework as Dworkinian-plus-deference, just with a better account of justification than the one Dworkin offers. In line with Dworkin's law-as-integrity, combining 'fit' and 'justification,' the common good framework attempts to 'fit' the developing law while also providing justifications for that law in light of a political morality of the common good, understanding political morality to itself include a morality of *institutional roles that commits primary competence for promoting the common good to political authorities*. On this view, the coherence and integrity of law include arguments from political morality for *deference to nonjudicial decision-makers*, within reasonable boundaries.[23]

It is important to note that Vermeule qualifies this deference as a 'rebuttable presumption of deference' that can be overridden where political authorities do not act in 'good faith' in their efforts to promote the common good. To evaluate whether political authorities act in good faith, common good constitutionalism asks judges to examine their determinations of the common good using a rational basis test and an 'arbitrariness review.'[24] By arguing that courts ought to embrace a rational basis test for all cases, Vermeule, in effect, argues that those laws that infringe on our fundamental rights would no longer be subject to the kind strict scrutiny that the Supreme Court has used for decades. While one might think Vermeule is only concerned with deference *outside* of the fundamental rights that are contained in the Bill of Rights, he rejects the autonomy-driven focus on individual rights that he associates with progressive constitutionalism. He suggests, moreover, that we ought to determine the scope and application of the rights contained in the Bill of Rights through the lens of the common good itself, where it is the common good that determines the sphere of conduct that those rights protect. I will return to this concern in the next section, but for now, let us outline common good constitutionalism's argument for deference into the following propositions:[25]

First, the purpose of law is to promote the common good,
Secondly, the promotion of the common good requires political virtue ('regnative prudence')
Thirdly, the group of officials who are more institutionally equipped to have political virtue have primary competence to promote the common good and less institutionally equipped officials should be bound by a presumption of deference to their judgments,
Fourthly, non-judicial decisionmakers are more institutionally equipped than judges to have political virtue,

[23] Vermeule (2022), p. 69 (italics added).

[24] Vermeule (2022), p. 63. The next section further explains this point, though it is worth noting here that the strict scrutiny test developed by the Supreme Court to examine the constitutionality of government acts that infringe upon fundamental rights is the kind of approach that common good constitutionalism would reject in favor of deference.

[25] This is my outline and not one provided by Vermeule.

Conclusion: judges should be bound by a presumption of deference to the judgments of non-judicial decisionmakers in their promotion of the common good

Because my aim is ultimately to critically examine common good constitutionalism from *within* the classical tradition, I do not dispute the first or second of the above propositions. These are assumptions within his theory that we can accept for the sake of argument. The third proposition can be constructed by several of Vermeule's assertions. For instance, he maintains that there is no specific institutional distribution of authority required by common good constitutionalism, but that the distribution should promote the common good. The problematic part of the argument is the fourth proposition. Vermeule asserts early on that non-judicial decisionmakers have 'primary competence for promoting the common good,'[26] which we must interpret as the conclusion to an ancillary argument that is not fully provided.

Vermeule cannot, of course, argue that lawmakers have this competence because we the people have given it to them. That is, he cannot appeal the idea of *consent* to ground the putative competence of non-judicial lawmakers for promoting the common good because that would anchor his theory in a central concept of the liberal philosophical tradition, which he aims not to do. We must, then, assume that this competence is substantive and not simply the result of a transfer of lawmaking authority from individuals to lawmakers via some sort of social contract. Moreover, he does adequately explain why judges shouldn't also promote the common good when a case or controversy before them concerns the meaning of the law and where there are multiple reasonable views of the common good and given that whatever Congress passes is the result of compromise. Here, too, Vermeule seems naïve: as if the common good were a cloud floating above Congress and all they need do is look up with their binoculars (and virtue) and they will the same thing.[27]

As the fourth proposition captures a crucial assumption in common good constitutionalism, we need to examine whether it can be sustained in application to the system he intends for his theory to fit and justify—the American system. In Sect. 4, I take on this task, but before doing so, the next section engages more deeply with the classical tradition. There, I trace common good constitutionalism's argument for deference to the classical tradition and show that this deference also depended upon a reasonable presumption of virtue among lawmakers, which justified the central role they had to promote the common good.

3 The Dependence of Deference Upon Virtue

Common good constitutionalism revives and adapts the classical tradition of natural law associated with Aristotle, Cicero, and Aquinas to argue for a purposive account of American law oriented toward the common good. It relies on Aquinas' definition

[26] Vermeule (2022), p. 5.

[27] I thank Gordon Babst for articulating the point this way.

of law as an ordinance of reason for the common good promulgated by political authorities to argue that the primary function of political authority is to promote the common good through law.[28] While the natural law does not require any particular form of government or institutional scheme,[29] Vermeule argues that, within the American system, judges should largely defer to the determinations of the common good of legislative and executive officials, rather than try to work out the common good on their own through the exercise of their adjudicative capacity.

This deference is different from the deference expected by originalism and positivism. It is not deference to the original public meaning of a written text or to the rules or commands of some person or group with recognized lawmaking power. Rather, the basis for judicial deference to non-judicial decisionmakers within common good constitutionalism is the assumption that the latter are more likely than the former to competently determine and enact the common good. That is, it is deference to non-judicial lawmakers because of their presumed competence, which is deference on substantive rather than procedural grounds. Indeed, such political authorities are expected to have what Vermeule calls (following Aquinas) 'regnative prudence,' which furnishes them with good judgment concerning the common good.[30] In this section, I trace this aspect of common good constitutionalism to the classical tradition, under which the promotion of the common good was believed to be dependent on rulers having virtue.

Under the natural law tradition, the most complete good is the happiness of the community as a whole, an idea that the tradition takes from Aristotle. Because communal flourishing within the *polis* is the most complete good, it is also good for individuals, according to Vermeule.[31] Communal flourishing depends on promoting the common good, which humans are uniquely able to do through reason. According to the part of the tradition associated with Aquinas, who Vermeule mentions as inspiration throughout his book,[32] there are two modes of rational participation with the natural law: deduction and determination.[33] According to common good constitutionalism, moreover, 'deference flows from determination,'[34] which is 'the process of giving content to a general principle drawn from a higher source of law, making it concrete in application to particular local circumstances of problems.'[35] This process of determination is carried out 'by means of the faculty of prudential judgment—more specifically, the virtue that is called 'regnative prudence.' This is the prudential judgment, oriented toward justice, of a public authority who is charged with the care of the *res publica*, whether by election, delegation, or some

[28] Aquinas (2002); Vermeule (2022), p. 9.

[29] Vermeule (2022), pp. 9–15.

[30] Aquinas (2002); Vermeule (2022), p. 9.

[31] Aristotle (2017); Vermeule (2022), p. 14.

[32] Vermeule (2022), pp. 3, 44–46, 48, 74–76, 120–121.

[33] George (2001), p. 2279.

[34] Vermeule (2022), p. 152.

[35] Vermeule (2022), p. 9.

other mode of selection.'[36] It could, of course, be argued that judges should join our non-judicial decisionmakers in caring for the *res publica* by consulting the common good and that doing so would reflect the design of our government as three coequal branches sharing power. Instead, though, Vermeule argues that judges can contribute to the care of *res publica* in a different way—by supporting our non-judicial decisionmakers in *their* determinations of the common good, unless, that is, their determinations lack a rational basis.

The dependence of deference on determination and determination on virtue within common good constitutionalism is consistent with the natural law tradition, under which the common good depended upon political authorities having virtue, which inclines them toward the common good. In a revealing passage that identifies the assumptions of his own theory, Vermeule quotes Aquinas, who in turn, quotes Aristotle (or 'the Philosopher'):

> As the Philosopher says (Rhet. I, 1), 'it is better that all things be regulated by law, than left to be decided by judges': and this for three reasons. First, because it is easier to find a few wise men competent to frame right laws, than to find the man who would be necessary to judge aright of each single case. Secondly, because those who make laws consider long beforehand what laws to make, whereas judgment on each single case has to be pronounced as soon as it arises: and it is easier for man to see what is right, by taking many instances into consideration, than by considering one solitary fact. Thirdly, because lawgivers judge in the abstract and of future events; whereas those who sit in judgment of things present, towards which they are affected by love, hatred, or some kind of cupidity; wherefore their judgment is perverted. Since then the animated justice of the judge is not found in every man, and since it can be deflected, therefore it was necessary, whenever possible, for the law to determine how to judge, and for very few matters to be left for the decision of men.'[37]

Here, Aquinas may be taken to interpret Aristotle to mean that a sort of deference to lawmakers is reasonable where it is reasonable to expect them to (a) be wise, (b) make general rather than particular judgments, and (c) exercise reasoned foresight of future events rather than impassioned judgments of present controversies.[38] Now, it is reasonable to think that those who are wise and institutionally equipped to act with reasoned generality and foresight are capable of promoting the common good, but whether we can expect this as characteristic of non-judicial lawmakers in America's contemporary institutional scheme is a separate issue that I take up later in Sect. 4.

Arguably, it could be expected in the ancient Athens of Aristotle's time where there were no official judges, but rather ordinary (legally untrained) citizens pronounced legal judgments *en masse,* as depicted of Socrates' trial in Plato's *Apology.*[39] Any citizen (free-born Athenian male) over the age of 30 was able to participate in the *dikastai,* which was the body that pronounced such judgments, but the group

---

[36] Vermeule (2022), p. 9.

[37] Aquinas (2002); Vermeule (2022), pp. 74–75.

[38] I will come back to this in the next section but notice that (a) - (c) make personal and institutional assumptions.

[39] I thank Jeffrey Turner for raising this point with me in conversation.

was often comprised of men over 60 who were too old to work.[40] Under such institutional circumstances, it is reasonable to think that the common good would be better promoted if not left in the hands of these 'judges.' Doing so would offer no institutional protections against mob rule, as latter generations recognized.

Beyond these sorts of appeals to ancient thinkers and the natural law tradition, common good constitutionalism needs a better way to convince us that non-judicial lawmakers in a system like ours actually have political virtue to determine the common good as well as an institutional environment that encourages them to promote it through law. For classical thinkers, it is not an absolute that lawmakers have the requisite virtue but a precondition for the common good that they do. Aquinas, for instance, recognizes that sometimes lawmakers make mistakes about the common good, but he further argues that unjust laws are not always simply mistakes or failures of reasoning. They can also be what results when lawmakers legislate with moral vices. Within the classical tradition, ruling for the common good is always contrasted with a perverse form of rule that aims for private advantage. In discussing Aquinas' view, Vermeule rightly points out that when private advantage rather than the common good is the end of a law, it is not 'as though it had never been created; rather, it results in a perverted caricature of law.'[41] Given the dependence of deference on determination and determination on virtue within this tradition, we need more assurance from common good constitutionalism that judicial deference to non-judicial decisionmakers for the sake of the common good won't create a caricature of the law.

Granted, Vermeule tells us that, under common good constitutionalism, judges are bound by a 'rebuttable presumption of authority' to the determinations of the common good by non-judicial lawmakers, which we are to suppose is expressed in the legislation they craft. He writes,

> Deference is essentially that favorite tool of the classical lawyer: the rebuttable presumption of authority. It can be overcome, of course, when the public authority acts in such a way as to forfeit its claim to be implementing law at all, either because (1) a particular body acts outside its sphere of legal competence, or (2) it pursues aims that have no imaginable public purpose, or (3) it acts in an unreasoned manner, arbitrarily and capriciously. Because law is an ordinance of reason for the common good by one charged with care of the community, fulfillment of any of these conditions puts the act of the public authority outside of law and thus forfeits its claim to be engaged in determination of the natural law. But the presumption is important nonetheless.[42]

In this quotation, Vermeule presents a strikingly low standard of review to which common good constitutionalism is committed. The first condition does not exclude much as outside the sphere of legal competence of the public authority, given the natural law underpinnings of the theory. This is because common good constitutionalism considers the aims of law to be 'the classical triptych of peace, justice, and abundance, and their modern equivalents and corollaries' which 'include health,

[40] The Kosmos Society (2018).

[41] Vermeule (2022), pp. 120–121.

[42] Vermeule (2022), pp. 47–48.

safety, and a right relationship to the natural environment.'[43] All of these aims must be taken as within the sphere of legal competence of non-judicial lawmakers under the theory, and because of its natural law underpinnings, legal competence concerning these aims is a moral competence. In other words, the theory calls for deference to the *moral judgments* of lawmakers about peace, justice, abundance, health, safety, and the natural environment. And, to recall, this deference depends upon their competence to make reasonable determinations about these aims *insofar as such lawmakers are also reasonably presumed to have virtue.*

The second and third conditions contained in the above quotation provide the limits of deference, or when it may be overridden, we gather, by judges—that is, only when lawmakers act without any imaginable public purpose, arbitrarily, or capriciously are judges then empowered to have a more important role in the process of determining the common good. This is what Vermeule calls a 'good faith' standard of review. This means that the Supreme Court's current and long-standing practice of using heightened and strict scrutiny to adjudicate cases involving gender or suspect classifications, and those where governmental acts infringe on the fundamental rights, would be replaced by something akin to current rational basis test. An important and concerning practical consequence of this on American constitutional practice would be fewer protections for individual rights—especially the rights of those with less influence over legislatures. Not only does Vermeule's proposal put individual rights at risk, but it provides hardly any protections to minority groups from being trampled by any given majority in Congress. To protect against the cost to the common good that would result from such trampling of rights, we could rely on the solution that Vermeule rejects: affording courts and judges authority to discern the common good and enact it, where necessary, *against* that majority in Congress.

Indeed, Vermeule concedes that common good constitutionalism would uproot the current constitutional practice of 'balancing' individual rights against governmental interests. Yet, he finds this to be a merit rather than demerit of the theory. Common good constitutionalism aims to replace the current constitutional practice of protecting individual rights with one derived from the classical tradition. For Vermeule, the current approach depends upon a problematic autonomy-driven, quasi-utilitarian conception of rights, whereas under the classical tradition, the common good has primacy and determines the proper scope of individual rights.[44]

Granted, where common good constitutionalism requires judges to embrace a 'good faith' approach to adjudication where they defer to the judgments of non-judicial decisionmakers concerning the common good, it nonetheless recognizes that there are circumstances where our institutions do not function properly. Vermeule calls these 'unusual circumstances' and a 'state of exception' when 'the malfunctioning of subsidiary institutions means that the common good requires extraordinary intervention by the highest levels of public authority in the juridical

[43] Vermeule (2022), p. 36.

[44] Vermeule (2022), pp. 166–167.

order, for the purpose of helping those subsidiary institutions function correctly in an overall scheme that conduces to the common good.'[45] For this reason, the highest authority in our juridical order—our Supreme Court—also needs regnative prudence and the power to exercise it.[46] Yet, this power should not be exercised except, when necessary, in the face of 'unanticipated and exception breakdowns' in the functioning of government.[47] Now, where Vermeule thinks that the ordinary course of affairs within the American institutional scheme is one where non-judicial lawmakers can ordinarily be entrusted with promoting the common good, I challenge the aretaic assumptions of common good constitutionalism in the next section. Of course, he explains that 'The classical tradition rests, in the end, on the overarching principle of *bona fides*, good faith. Where such good faith is systematically absent, the law may misfire, but in such a scenario the misfiring of law would be the least of the polity's problems.'[48] As we can see, a lot then rests on the presumption of virtue among our lawmakers.

4 Do Our Political Institutions Cultivate Virtue Among Legislators?

So, how well do the aretaic assumptions of common good constitutionalism apply to the American polity? This section argues not well enough for us to embrace the theory of common good constitutionalism as currently formulated by Vermeule. I argue that not only does our system fail to clearly meet the aretaic assumptions of common good constitutionalism, but there is also concern that it fosters personal and political vices among lawmakers. As we saw above, the purpose of political authority under the classical tradition is to promote the common good and the happiness of the community as a whole. Virtuous lawmakers are needed to promote communal flourishing, which is carried out primarily though not exclusively through the production of legislation. Lawmakers with virtue would also help their citizens develop the right sort of habits so that they, too, could develop virtue and live flourishing lives.

Our system, however, does not cultivate virtue among our lawmakers. Various institutional pressures make it such that they are constantly trying to keep power once they have it. The point of various different voting schemes tries to correct this, but with limited success. It takes a tremendous amount of money even to mount a legislative campaign at the federal level and it is not much different at the state level, especially in high profile elections. While there are no term limits for these positions, there are recurring elections every few years. Because of this, legislators face

[45] Vermeule (2022), pp. 154–155.

[46] Vermeule (2022), p. 161.

[47] Vermeule (2022), p. 161.

[48] Vermeule (2022), p. 70.

constant institutional pressures to campaign, a phenomenon that political scientists call the 'permanent campaign.'[49] The concept refers to the blurring of boundaries between governing and campaigning where legislators (and executive officials) 'exploit the resources and opportunities of their offices, with increasing energy and sophistication, to advance their reelection prospects.'[50] The pressures associated with the permanent campaign undermine the cultivation of virtue among lawmakers as they spend more effort trying to keep their power than using their power to promote the common good.

Granted, legislators cannot *only* campaign, but must have some success at translating their ideas into law, or else they risk being unseated for an opposing candidate who will. This, though, creates further institutional pressure that disposes them away from virtue, and toward vice. As Cohen explains, 'a pervasive belief among modern political consultants is that elections have become 'base dominant,''[51] which means legislators increasingly appeal to a small but vocal segment of their constituency. Our legislators also respond especially to lobbyist who represent powerful and wealthy interest groups in order to get the big donations they need to get re-elected. Sometimes these loud voices are not even their constituents but reflect the wishes of an industry that may actually be counter to their constituents' interests. If elected again, legislators then face pressures to serve the groups' private interests as a debt and in anticipation of the next election cycle. Amy Gutmann offers the insightful point that in a pluralist democracy like our own, promoting the common good requires some degree of compromise, but that 'candidates inspire supporters less effectively when they talk more about prudent compromises than about steadfast commitments.'[52] This attenuates legislative attention to parochial interests, rather than fosters a virtuous disposition toward the common good. Even Vermeule recognizes the principle that where public power serves private interests, the result is government by faction, which is hostile to the common good.[53]

Gutman further argues that campaigning requires mistrust of other candidates because politics is a zero-sum game.[54] This can breed too much trust in one's own views, and a sort of epistemic arrogance that undermine conditions for deliberation among those who disagree. Moreover, this puts further pressure on legislators to pander to the beliefs and values of their base, even, perhaps, when they are wrong, as we have seen recently with conspiracy theories and fake news becoming talking points for politicians. Where one's constituents are uncompromising and uninformed, virtuous legislators would not pander to their bases, but would try to educate them. However, in the midst of the permanent campaign that exists within our system, legislators may be more disposed toward epistemic vices than Aquinas'

[49] Blumenthal (1980).

[50] Ornstein and Mann (2000), p. vii.

[51] Cohen (2021).

[52] Gutmann and Thompson (2013).

[53] Vermeule (2022), p. 27.

[54] Gutmann and Thompson (2013).

regnative prudence in their efforts to keep power. Epistemic vices are character traits—such as indifference to knowledge—that 'interfere with acquiring, maintaining, and transmitting knowledge.'[55]

Mark Button's account of political vices is also helpful to elucidate concerns over common good constitutionalism's assumption of virtue among our non-judicial decisionmakers.[56] He explains that,

> Political vices are qualities and dispositions that, while taking form within specific sociopolitical settings, undermine the virtue of politics and its promise of relating parts to whole through language and the practice of cooperative virtues… Political vice, as a general category, is the habitual disposition to act in ways that would install a part over the whole without justification, or, contrawise, it describes the attitude and settled disposition that motivates the "whole" (or those who claim to speak on its behalf) to ignore and/or dominate over a part without sound reason.[57]

Political vices are not merely institutional vices—that is, built into certain institutional designs—but also socio-epistemic vices because they affect how we perceive, think about, and judge ideas and events in the political realm. Because of its socio-epistemic orientation, this view of political vice fits within much of the recent literature on institutional vice, which regards institutional vices to have a dual nature as both ethical and epistemic vices.[58] Vermeule's vision of how to promote the common good in America seems woefully naïve insofar as it obscures or neglects the realities of our system that it is reasonable to expect incline our nonjudicial decisionmakers to such vices.

In our constitutional regime, promoting the common good crucially depends on cooperation and compromise among a plurality of governmental actors, and political vices are those entrenched habits that work against the deliberative pluralism upon which our constitutional scheme rests. Button specifically describes how the political vices of hubris, moral blindness, and recalcitrance 'represent a standing challenge to the principles and values of the mixed political regime we call liberal democracy,'[59] but there are arguably other vices to worry about, too. In a system like ours where legislators are permanently campaigning to ever polarizing bases, the office of the non-judicial decisionmaker makes demands on the moral characters of legislators, and politics too often becomes a contest to keep power that is more likely to incline lawmakers toward vice than toward virtue. This makes it unreasonable to expect them as a group to (a) be wise, (b) make general rather than particular judgments about what is good for the country, and (c) exercise reasoned foresight of future events rather than impassioned judgments of present controversies—the precise qualities associated with regnative prudence that would make a rebuttable presumption of deference to them defensible out of concern for the common good.

---

[55] Meyer et al. (2021).

[56] Button (2016).

[57] Button (2016), p. 15.

[58] Fricker (2021).

[59] Button (2016), p. 3.

What is more, Cohen (2021) explains that a 'new permanent campaign' is evolving due to technology, which he hypothesizes will only exacerbate these problems over time. This augments the concerns with common good constitutionalism. Unless we have reason to believe legislators cultivate and sustain virtues in the affairs of their offices, common good constitutionalism neither fits nor justifies the American legal practice. Ultimately, to adequately cultivate and safeguard the virtue of our legislators—especially their ability and desire to engage in the kind of prudential judgment that constitutes regnative prudence—we need to first extricate those practices within our system that tend to incline legislators toward the opposite.

5 Conclusion

In this paper, I showed that a crucial assumption of common good constitutionalism's argument for judicial deference to non-judicial decisionmakers is that the latter could reasonably be assumed to have the virtue needed to determine the common good and enact it through law. Yet, Vermeule does not provide a persuasive account of why we should think this to be true in our system, which undermines the aims he has for the theory to fit and justify our practice. From here, I then argued that political realities within our system, such as the permanent campaign and other institutional pressures facing legislators, makes it such that they are more likely to cultivate vices than virtues while seeking and preserving their power. More work is needed to examine how our complex institutional scheme affects (and is affected by) the moral characters of agents working within it and to identify those practices that frustrate the cultivation of regnative prudence among our lawmakers. In the end, as currently formulated, common good constitutionalism either needs a new basis beyond virtue for its argument for judicial deference to legislators, or we need to revise the institutional requirements of the theory to rule out those that fail to cultivate political virtue.

References

Aquinas (2002) Summa Theologica. In: Dyson RW (ed) *Thomas aquinas political writings*. Cambridge University Press, Cambridge and New York

Aristotle (2017) Politics (trans: CDC Reeve). Hackett, Indianapolis

Blumenthal S (1980) The permanent campaign: inside the world of elite political operatives. Beacon Press, Michigan

Button M (2016) Political vices. Oxford University Press, New York

Cohen M (2021) Modern political campaigns: how professionalism, technology, and speed have revolutionized elections. Rowman and Littlefield, Lanham

Dworkin R (1982) 'Natural' law revisited. Fla Law Rev 34:165–118

Dworkin R (1986) Law's empire. Belknap Press of Harvard University Press, Cambridge

Fricker M (2021) Institutional vices: the case of inferential inertia. In: Kidd IJ, Battaly H, Cassam Q (eds) Vice epistemology. Routledge, New York

George RP (2001) Natural law, the constitution, and the theory and practice of judicial review. Fordham Law Rev 69:2269–2283

Gutmann A, Thompson DF (2013) Valuing compromise for the common good. Daedalus 142:285–198

Law and Courts in Ancient Athens: A Brief Overview (2018) The Kosmos Society of Harvard University. https://kosmossociety.chs.harvard.edu/law-and-courts-in-ancient-athens-a-brief-overview/. Accessed 21 June 2022

Meyer M, Alfano M, de Bruin B (2021) The development and validation of the epistemic vice scale. Rev Philosophy Psychol. https://doi.org/10.1007/s13164-021-00562-5

Ornstein N, Mann T (2000) The permanent campaign and its future. AEI and Brookings Press, Washington DC

Vermeule A (2020) Beyond originalism. The Atlantic. https://www.theatlantic.com/ideas/archive/2020/03/common-good-constitutionalism/609037/ . Accessed 23 Apr 2023

Vermeule A (2022) Common good constitutionalism. Polity Press, Cambridge

Renée Nicole Souris is an Assistant Professor of Law & Society at the Florida Institute of Technology where she researches issues that lie at the intersections of law, morality, and politics. Much of her work examines the relation between moral development and criminal responsibility, especially as applied to child soldiers. Her research also adopts an interdisciplinary virtue ethics methodology to examine issues of domestic and global concern.

Dworkinian Protestantism, Civil Disobedience, and Democratic Citizenship

Win-chiat Lee

Abstract In this chapter, I develop the idea of obeying the law with what Dworkin calls the protestant attitude. Given the protestant attitude, I argue, obeying the law might require citizens paradoxically to disobey it, i.e., the prevailing authoritative account of it, and subject their own interpretation to the test by the courts. I discuss the implication of this approach for democracy. As the protestant attitude has the potential of seeing settled law as unsettled, the paper ends with a brief discussion of the protestant attitude in relation to *Dobbs* and the development of the right to abortion and its future in American law.

1 Introduction

In *Law's Empire* (1986), Ronald Dworkin puts forward a jurisprudential view he calls "protestantism," or "the protestant attitude." Dworkin does not say very much about this protestantism about law in Dworkin (1986) (or any of the later work), but it is quite clear that it is a doctrine central to his overall theory of law as integrity. Law as integrity, briefly, is the theory that the law is not any individual political decision of the community, such as a piece of legislation or a court decision, but, rather, the principles that can be identified, presumably by interpretation, as the

I dedicate this chapter to the memory of Kenneth Henley, a long-time member of AMINTAPHIL who passed away in January, 2022. Henley (1990) has influenced my thinking about the subject. I am also grateful to the participants in the Wake Forest Philosophy Department Work-in-Progress Workshop and 2022 AMINTAPHIL Conference for their comments on earlier drafts of this chapter. I am particularly indebted to Imer Flores for his written commentary, which is incorporated in Flores (2024).

W.-c. Lee (✉)
Wake Forest University, Winston-Salem, NC, USA
e-mail: leew@wfu.edu

G. A. Babst et al. (eds.), *Liberal Constitutionalism and its Contemporary Challenges*, AMINTAPHIL: The Philosophical Foundations of Law and Justice 12, https://doi.org/10.1007/978-3-031-53602-1_6

community's commitments to justice and fairness that render the political decisions of the community, *as a whole,* morally consistent, i.e., containing the virtue of integrity.

The central importance of the protestant attitude to Dworkin's theory of law as integrity and the citizens' role in interpreting the law it implies is made evident by his reference to it in the very last paragraph of *Law's Empire*:

> It is a protestant attitude that makes each citizen responsible for imagining what his society's public commitments to principles are, and what these commitments require in new circumstances. The protestant character of law is confirmed, and the creative role of private decisions acknowledged, by the backward-looking judgmental decisions, and also by the regulative assumption that though judges must have the last word, their word is not for that reason the best word. Dworkin (1986), p. 413.

Earlier in the book, Dworkin also writes,

> Political obligation is …not just a matter of obeying the discrete political decisions of the community one by one, as political philosophers usually represent it. It becomes a more protestant idea: fidelity to a scheme of principle each citizen has a responsibility to identify, ultimately for himself, as his community's scheme. Dworkin (1986), p. 190.

Dworkin's use of the term "protestantism" is to emphasize the direct role individuals have in identifying the law for themselves, be they judges or individuals, instead of simply deferring to an account of it dictated by an authority, as a legal parallel to the doctrine of "the priesthood of all believers" in the sixteenth century protestant reformation in Christianity.[1]

In Lee (2015), I have given an account of Dworkin's protestantism about law.[2] On my account, Dworkin's protestantism is part and parcel of his theory of law as integrity. This is because integrity is the property of a system of law as a whole. The interpretive approach proposed by Dworkin in law as integrity is therefore holistic. The law is determined by what is the best interpretation of the system as a whole and not, as Dworkin puts it, "the discrete political decisions of the community one by one." (Dworkin (1986), p. 90, quoted above) Even when an authoritative account of the law is given by the court or the legislature, we only have one more discrete political decision to take in as the data for the interpretation of the law. It does not take away the need for interpretation by either a judge or an ordinary citizen in each new situation. In this way, the protestant attitude can lead to seeing settled law as unsettled or an authoritative act to settle the law as leaving the law still unsettled.

In this chapter, I would like to explore further the implication of the protestant attitude towards law for a citizen's political obligation, i.e., her duty to obey the law. Paradoxically, as I will argue, a certain kind of civil disobedience by citizens is in fact a proper way of obeying the law on Dworkin's protestant view about law. Indeed, one might even argue that the protestant attitude *requires* citizens commit

[1] The title of Lee (2015), "The Judgeship of All Citizens: Dworkin's Protestantism about Law," is to make this parallel explicit.

[2] Lee (2015) contains a more complete and detailed account of Dworkin's protestantism that I can give in this chapter.

that kind of civil disobedience if that is the proper way of discharging one's duty to obey the law. But, as I also argue, that might also be too demanding of citizens.

I will also address what seems to be a suggestion in Dworkin's remarks in the two quoted passages about democratic citizenship that has less to do with the citizens' relation to the making of the law (the legislative) and more to do with the identification of it (the judiciary). We are generally more familiar with the former than with the latter. The latter may, however, be an interesting and novel take on the idea of democracy. Since this novel aspect of democratic citizenship involves engagements with the judiciary, I will also discuss this interpretation of Dworkin's view in the context of criticisms of judicial review as constraints on democracy, such as those made by Jeremy Waldron.

Finally, I will conclude with some brief remarks about the fate of abortion rights in American law as the consequence of the protestant attitude at work especially in unsettling settled law.

2 Dworkin's Protestantism and Authority in Law

Dworkin's protestantism about law has two elements. One is a thesis about political obligation. According to Dworkin, every citizen has to interpret the law for herself in discharging her duty to obey the law. (That includes judges too in discharging their duty to apply the law in deciding cases.) The other main element of Dworkin's protestantism is the view that what the law is (or one might say what the law *really* is) in relation to a particular case is, in principle, always up to interpretation even if an authoritative account (by a court decision or a legislative act) has already been given. As mentioned before, even if a recent court decision or piece of legislation has been rendered, it is simply yet another item, albeit with the proper weight assigned,[3] to be thrown in with all the other data to be interpreted *as a whole* to determine what account of the law will give the law *as a whole* the greatest integrity.

These two theses are clearly related. If what the law *really* is, is always up to interpretation, then clearly one cannot blindly follow authority, so to speak, in order to discharge one's obligation to obey the law. However, this does not mean that in most cases one would actually need to engage in interpretation oneself. This is because in most cases it probably would not make a difference if one does so oneself. In these cases, reasonable interpretations of the law would not differ much from one another or from the authoritative account of the law.

Drawing a parallel with the use of the term Protestantism in Christianity, one could perhaps argue that Dworkin's protestantism about law should simply deny

[3] There may not be a general account of how to assign weight to a new political decision in interpreting the law in accordance with the theory of law as integrity. The fact that the decision, either in the form of a court decision or a piece of legislation, is recent and new may carry a greater weight for an interpretation if it conflicts with an earlier decision. Even that, however, is not absolute and would require judgement and the use of other considerations.

that there is authority in law or that there is an authoritative account of the law. This is, however, not a promising line of thinking. Authority is essential to the rule of law while, arguably, it need not be in the case of religion. Especially for an existing case involving conflicting accounts of the law, it is essential that there be an authoritative determination of what the law is. That job usually falls on the judiciary and ultimately on the land's highest court, but it need not. In addition, law performs many of its functions, such as coordinating the actions of citizens, by providing preemptive or exclusionary reasons for action, i.e., by being authoritative.

Authority is so essential to law that any protestant view of law cannot do away with the idea of authority in law, but rather it will have to show how it can have an account of the authority in law compatible with the view that the law is always up to interpretation—either by individual citizens or by the courts—and indeed compatible with the idea that it is their duty to interpret the law *for themselves*.

The key to resolving this apparent conflict between authority and individual interpretation in law, both of which are essential to law as integrity, is the distinction between the finality of a court's decision (or any other body's determination) and its infallibility—a distinction first invoked by H.L.A. Hart in Hart (1961).[4] I take this to mean that a court's account of the law may be authoritative in the practical sense (i.e., in commanding actions), but not necessarily in the theoretical sense (i.e., in getting the law right). Following Hart, Dworkin makes the point that the land's highest court may have the last word on what the law is, but it need not have the best word on it. Using the language of Dworkin's interpretive approach, which may not have use for the idea of getting the law right, but only a better or worse interpretation of it, one can say that the interpretation of the law given by the court may carry authority without being the best interpretation of it.

The distinction between finality and infallibility, in my view, is what allows for a protestant attitude towards law even as one recognizes that authority is essential to the rule of law. It makes room for interpretation or further interpretation by individual citizens (as well as future courts) that might yield a better account of the law even when the court has rendered its *final* interpretation. Even though such opening for further interpretation would open up interesting intellectual exercises, the protestant attitude of citizens (and future courts) would ultimately be futile as a practical matter unless the "final" interpretation of the court is not so final after all or only final for the time being. That is, a protestant attitude towards law would make practical sense only if the rule of law allows for the possibility that even the "final" interpretation of the law can be revised by the reversal of earlier court decisions within the system of law itself.

This protestant attitude towards law will therefore require precedents set by court decisions to have a dual and seemingly contradictory characteristic. To accommodate the idea of authority, which the protestant attitude must if it is an attitude about *law*, precedents set by court decisions must carry special weight and cannot be easily overturned, especially if they have been repeatedly reaffirmed in later court

[4] Pp. 138–144.

decisions.[5] However, if the idea that the law is always up to interpretation is not futile, it must be the case that precedents can be overturned, albeit not easily so because of the special weight they carry that is difficult to overcome, especially when the precedents have been reaffirmed. To put it in the language of law as integrity, which is the basis of Dworkin's protestantism, integrity requires precedents be both respected and open to repeal.[6]

In Dworkin's legal protestantism, not only are judges supposed to take the interpretive approach towards the law in discharging their duty to apply the law, but ordinary citizens are also required to do the same in discharging their duty to obey the law. Just as there is no distinction between priests and ordinary believers in Christian Protestantism in their relation and approach to God, there is no distinction between judges and ordinary citizens in Dworkin's legal protestantism in their relation and approach to the law. There is, however, an important disanalogy between religious and legal protestantism. In the legal case, a main difference between judges and ordinary citizens is that the latter's interpretation of the law is not authoritative and carries no practical weight as a determination of the law without being litigated and accepted by the courts. In view of this, one can perhaps argue that in Dworkin's protestantism, it is indeed the duty of a citizen, in discharging her duty to obey the law, to put forward her interpretation of the law to be tested and contested before the courts, especially in important matters, if it differs from the existing authoritative account of the relevant law. This, in my view, would justify or even require a citizen to commit a defiant act of civil disobedience in order to put forward her interpretation of the law to be tested. Doing so would also be a way of acknowledging legal authority from a protestant attitude.

3 Two Kinds of Civil Disobedience

Just now I have referred to the defiant act of challenging the existing account of the law as an act of civil *disobedience*. Such an act, in truth, might turn out to be not an act of disobedience after all if, upon adjudication, the law turns out to be contrary to what it is generally understood to be. (Also, we might not know if the case is not adjudicated.) Such an act could turn out to a more profound kind of fidelity to the law of the community—a fidelity to what the law of that community really is and not to what it has hitherto been identified to be.

In 1961, for example, the Executive Director of the Planned Parenthood League of Connecticut, Estelle Griswold, and medical volunteer Dr. C. Lee Buxton, open a

[5]These cases are sometimes referred to as "super-precedents". *Roe v. Wade,* to be discussed later, is an example.

[6]There are the two dimensions of legal interpretation in law as integrity, namely, fit and appeal. It should also be noted that this view about precedents is consistent with *stare decisis*, which gives precedents authority and makes them difficult to overturn, as long as it does not preclude the possibility that they can be overturned with very weighty considerations.

birth control clinic in New Haven, Connecticut, in defiance of the Connecticut law prohibiting the use and distribution of contraceptives, with the intention of challenging that law by getting themselves arrested, tried and found guilty by state courts so that they could appeal the case all the way to the US Supreme Court. This resulted in the famous US Supreme Court decision in *Griswold v. Connecticut* which not only struck down the Connecticut anti-contraceptives law, but did so based on finding a constitutional right to privacy not explicitly stated in the US Constitution. There are numerous examples of such challenges to the existing understanding of the law by "disobeying" it, some more successful than others, in both federal and state courts in the United States.

Many of these challengers to the law have no interest in violating the law in secret or evading law enforcement. To the contrary, the point of their defiant acts is to be public so that they can be arrested, charged, and have their cases adjudicated. There are also others who launch challenges to the law more or less as an afterthought. That is, they may have initially violated the law as is understood without the intention of challenging it. After they are caught, arrested and subject to adjudication, however, they pose challenge to the law as it is applied to them. (I have in mind for example the famous US flag-burning case of *Texas v. Johnson*). Others may be recruited by civil rights organizations such as ACLU as plaintiffs to challenge the existing understanding of the law. (Examples are *Roe v. Wade* and *Loving v. Virginia*.) For present purposes, I will treat these cases similarly and regard them all as cases of civil disobedience and consider them to be cases of obeying the law with a protestant attitude in Dworkin's sense.

An interesting point to observe is that these acts of civil obedience with the intention to challenge and change the current understanding of the law would not succeed if the prosecutors do not prosecute and the courts do not adjudicate these cases. In some of these cases, the prosecutors and the courts are quite willing to drop the case or take a plea for a lesser crime. For the dissenters or, more accurately, those who intend to obey the law with a protestant attitude, they would have to refuse the plea bargain and otherwise step up the pressure in order to have their day in court. This seems to be rather consistent with the stronger interpretation of political obligation under Dworkin's protestantism.

The important point is that these acts of civil disobedience, i.e., these challenges to existing understanding of the law, shape to a great extent the law in the United States as we know it today. Even when it does not involve a more dramatic act of the violation of the law, launching any legal challenge to the existing understanding of the law through the courts would require a protestant attitude toward law.

The kind of civil disobedience—let's call it "protestant obedience"—I have described so far would appear to be quite different from the classic kind of civil disobedience in which an act of disobeying the law is committed for the sake for the higher or moral law. The conflict is between law and morality in classic civil disobedience and not between competing interpretations of the law. One can say that classic civil disobedience is fidelity to a higher law (instead of the community's law) as opposed to a deeper fidelity to the community's law that motivates protestant obedience. Martin Luther King's famous act of civil disobedience in 1963 is an example of classic civil disobedience.[7]

However, the difference should not be exaggerated. As Dworkin has observed in his earlier—pre-law as integrity—discussion of civil disobedience, in American law moral arguments about a law are not totally unrelated to arguments about its constitutionality, because of the presence of clauses, such as due process, equal protection and cruel and unusual punishment, in the US Constitution that are inherently moral considerations.[8] I do not intend to assess the merit of this argument. Here I would like to pursue a different relation between the two kinds of civil disobedience under Dworkin's theory of law as integrity.

Law as integrity does not require the law to be moral, but morally consistent. That is, on law as integrity, it is important that the law, upon interpretation, can be seen to contain a scheme of principles of justice and fairness that are consistently embodied in all laws. These principles of justice and fairness do not have to be correct objectively, but they are the community's principles because they are interpreted to be what are consistently embodied in that community's system of law. This gives Dr. King another route to justify his act of civil disobedience. Instead of justifying his defiance of segregation laws morally by arguing they are unjust, he could have justified legally his defiance by arguing that the segregation laws are in violation of the principle of equality that is embodied in the US Constitution and would render American law morally inconsistent. The legal argument, from the point of view of law as integrity, is also a moral argument, but a moral argument that is based on the political morality interpreted to be contained in American law.

There is a further problem. If taking the protestant attitude is a matter of political obligation, then that attitude may *require* a citizen to commit what I have called protestant obedience. But that may be asking the citizen to bear too heavy a burden in some cases. Especially if she likely faces an unfriendly court and the law she is required to disobey and pose interpretive challenge is a criminal law, she may be asked to bear unreasonable risk of years of imprisonment or other heavy punishments. Therefore, if the protestant attitude is a matter of political obligation, whether that protestant attitude should result in an actual requirement for action, i.e., to "disobey" the law, should be limited by the amount of risk involved. However, from the protestant perspective, it would also seem to be the case that the more egregious a law is a violation of what one interprets to be the integrity of the law, the greater the action requirement will be for one to "disobey" that law to pose a legal challenge. But these are likely also cases where the risk involved in the "disobedience" is high.[9] In my view, it is correct to think that our obligation to "disobey" a law will

[7] Martin Luther King states very clearly in *Letter from Birmingham Jail* that his justification for parading without a permit is that the permit ordinance was *unjust* because it is "used to preserve segregation and to deny citizens the First Amendment Privilege of peaceful assembly and peaceful protest…" King continues, "Of course, there is nothing new about this kind of civil disobedience."

[8] Dworkin (1977), Ch. 8.

[9] I am grateful to Nikki Souris for pointing out this difficult problem to me.

become more stringent as the law becomes more egregiously incompatible with the integrity of law, but only up to a point. There are risks beyond which it would be unreasonable to expect someone to bear as a matter of political obligation.[10] An alternative would be for the court to adopt a more lenient approach to credible cases of protestant obedience.[11] But that might require judges also to have the protestant attitude.

4 Protestantism and Democracy

According to this account of protestantism, a community ruled by law is a community of interpreters, be they judges or ordinary citizens, who participate in an ongoing collective project of interpreting and determining what the law is. As Dworkin writes (in Dworkin (1986), p. 413 and quoted above), "It is a protestant attitude that makes each citizen responsible for imagining what his society's public commitment to principles are, and what these commitments require in new circumstances." One might find this way of thinking of the rule of law rather attractive, especially from the point of view of democracy. If nothing else, the participatory and self-government aspects of this conception of the rule of law certainly evokes democratic ideals. We tend to focus on the legislative aspect of government, i.e., the making of law, in talking about democracy. But Dworkinian protestantism allows us a way of thinking about the application of law (which for Dworkin is not always distinguishable from the making of it) itself as democratic, as a way in which citizens participate in governing themselves, even as judges are not typically elected in an otherwise democratic society. In fact, this kind of democracy in the application of law would be independent of democracy in legislation. Even if the law is made in a way that is not democratic, the protestant attitude in the interpretation of the law will still introduce a significant democratic element in the law. It is important to note that the significance of this democratic element in a community of law will greatly depend on the judiciary also taking the protestant attitude towards law as a partner in the ongoing project of interpreting the law. If the judges in that community do not interpret the law for themselves or are unreceptive to citizens' interpretation of the law for themselves, citizens' taking the protestant attitude in obeying the law will be in vain.

[10] For example, a doctor contending with a state law that treats performing abortion at any stage of pregnancy as murder might think such a law egregiously incompatible with what she interprets to be the political morality in the law. Should she feel obligated to violate that law to bring a challenge to it? There would be too much at risk in such a challenge, in my view, for it to be a matter of political obligation, but more a matter of political supererogation, so to speak.

[11] Dworkin writes in Dworkin (1977), "…the government has a special responsibility to those who act on a reasonable judgment that a law is invalid. It should make accommodation for them as far as possible, when this is consistent with other policies." (p. 217)

They will not only have no influence on the shape of the law in that community, but, worse, expose themselves to potential punishments unnecessarily.[12]

There is, however, a different angle from which one can look at this democratic element of protestantism and find it undemocratic and worrisome. From that angle, not only is it the case that, as Dworkin says, the courts cannot be presumed to have the best word on what the law is even if they have the last word, it is also the case that the legislature does not have the best word on the law either even as they engage in the *making* of it. So even after the legislature has legislated on a certain issue, it is still a matter of interpretation for the courts, as well as ordinary citizens, as to what the law is on that issue. Even more controversial in relation to the protestant attitude when taken up by the judges is the idea of what Jeremy Waldron calls, "strong judicial review," by which the courts may strike down a legislation or severely limit its application on the grounds that it is unconstitutional, improperly made, or for a number of other kinds of reasons.[13] In a system in which the legislature is democratically elected and the judiciary is not, the protestant attitude of the judges and their power to overturn or limit the application of legislation can be considered to be decidedly undemocratic or even anti-democratic.

One might think that the anti-democratic nature of Dworkinian protestantism may be mitigated by the fact the protestant attitude towards law is to be taken up not only by judges, but also by ordinary citizens as well. In Dworkin's protestantism, citizens, like judges and especially appellate judges, are supposed to interpret the law for themselves even if the law is made by a democratically elected legislature. So legislation may be overturned or severely limited in its application from the point of view of an ordinary citizen taking up the protestant attitude. But such thinking or interpretation on the part of ordinary citizens carries no legal authority. It becomes authoritative only by being adopted by the courts in the judges' own exercise of the protestant attitude. So, ultimately, one can argue that the anti-democratic nature of strong judicial review is not canceled out by the participation of ordinary citizens in the review. In fact, one can perhaps even say that as a consequence of their protestant attitude towards law, ordinary citizens "colluded" with judges in subverting the law-*making* by the legislature and thus, paradoxically, in an important sense, subvert *their own* law-*making* if the legislature is democratically constituted. On the other hand, it is also important to note that in a system where the legislature is not democratic, the protestant attitude towards law does add a democratic dimension to the system.

Waldron's objection to strong judicial review is, however, not entirely or even fundamentally about its undemocratic nature. More important, Waldron's objection is based on the claim that the judiciary is less competent than a democratically elected legislature as the protector of individual rights, assuming that the democratically elected legislature is serious about rights and about the fact that there are

[12] I am grateful to Gordon Babst for a comment that has promoted me to clarify this point about the democratic significance of the protestant attitude.

[13] Waldron (2006), pp. 1354–1355.

profound disagreements about some of them. Similarly, despite the democratic flavor of Dworkin's protestantism (for example, everyone is responsible for the shape of the community or something like that), ultimately it is also not motivated by democratic interests.[14] Ultimately it is the concern for the legitimacy of a society's rule of law that motivates the protestantism in Dworkin's jurisprudence.

For Dworkin, it is the integrity of law that legitimizes the exercise of coercion in the rule of law and give us reason to obey the law as law. By "integrity," Dworkin means moral consistency. For the law to have integrity, in Dworkin's view, it must contain within it a coherent scheme of principles of justice and fairness. So on this view, for any law in a community to have legitimacy and give us reason to obey, it must flow from the community's scheme of principles of justice and fairness embodied in its law as a whole. For Dworkin, however, all claims about the integrity of the law are matters of interpretation, including claims about its scheme of principles of justice and fairness, based on, ideally, "data" from the whole body of law. The legislature, democratically constituted or not, may or may not have the integrity of law in mind when it legislates. The judiciary, held democratically accountable or not, may or may not have the integrity of law in mind when it decides cases. Regardless, legislation and court decisions simply add more to the pool of "data" for individual citizens and future courts to interpret to get at the integrity of the law. Judges and ordinary citizens alike are under an *obligation* to interpret the pool of "data" in order to see what they have (preemptory or exclusionary) reason to follow. It is this normative demand and the logic of law as integrity, I contend, that requires the protestant attitude.[15]

Democracy is not a fundamental value or the grounds of legitimacy in law as integrity. It is equality, i.e., the equal concern and respect for all, that motivates the moral consistency required in law as integrity. However, it would be hard to imagine that a community with a coherent scheme of principles of justice and fairness does not have respect for some individual rights and does not have democratic institutions to determine such rights. It might also be hard to imagine in such a society, *contra* Waldron, not to have judicial review to provide some safeguard against democratic legislative processes to protect some of those rights. Regardless, whether and to what extent there should or should not be strong judicial review in a democratic society is a matter of law of that society and, in Dworkin's view, will be subject to interpretation relating to that society's principles of justice and fairness.

[14] One can perhaps say that it is also motivated by the concern for individual rights. But that would require making the connection between the Rights Thesis in Dworkin's earlier work and law as integrity in Dworkin (1986), a connection that I cannot make here.

[15] One can transform Waldron's question about whether the courts are more competent or better at identifying and protecting rights than a democratic legislature into a question, for the purposes of the protestant attitude, whether the courts are better at and more appropriate than a democratic legislature for identifying the scheme of principle of the community. Dworkin seems to think the courts are the place for it. He refers to courts as "forums of principle." I would only add that for courts to be forums of principles, it would be helpful that some of the cases they have to decide involve matters of principle. That might depend on citizens taking the protestant attitude in deciding how they comply with the law, as in what I call protestant obedience.

A protestant attitude towards law is what allows us to reflect on these issues as matters of law.

5 Leaving Settled Law Unsettled: The Protestant Attitude from *Roe* to *Dobbs*

Recently, the US Supreme Court, taking what arguably is the protestant attitude, handed down the decision of *Dobbs v. Jackson Women's Health Organization,* reversing the long-standing and repeatedly reaffirmed precedent of *Roe v Wade*. The consequence of that decision for women's right to abortion is dire in many states. Essentially, that right as a constitutional right is taken away. Under *Dobbs*, access to abortion is entirely a matter of state law and there is virtually no limit to what states may do to restrict access to or criminalize abortion.

The Dworkinian protestant response to this decision seems to be quite straightforward. The Court might have the last word *for now* on the subject, but not necessarily the best word. What that means, on the theory of law as integrity, is that when the law is taken as a whole, even with the recent decision of *Dobbs* added, one might still find the best interpretation of the law and its moral consistency requires one to see *Dobbs* and the overturning of *Roe* as a mistake.

For those who think so, this might not be the best time to commit the kind of protestant obedience I have described to try to subject *Dobbs* to further interpretive test through the courts. This, however, may be more a matter of strategy than of principle. Perhaps more time needs to have passed for any meaningful direct challenge to *Dobbs* to be launched. More important, perhaps more of the other issues related to abortion that might erode *Dobbs* should be litigated before any direct challenge to *Dobbs* be launched. This might accumulate the number of cases that would make a stronger case for interpreting *Dobbs* as a mistake.

Regardless, what is important to observe is that this protestant attitude toward law was precisely what many pro-life activists and politicians can be said to have taken toward *Roe* and the subsequent cases affirming *Roe,* such as *Casey*, that were, in their view, wrongly decided.[16] While they may have recognized these decisions as authoritative, they did not think these political decisions one by one (as Dworkin would put it) determine what the law really is. They may even have adopted the most important aspect of the protestant attitude, i.e., to treat obeying the law as "fidelity to a scheme of principle each citizen has a responsibility to identify, ultimately for himself, as his community's scheme." (Dworkin 1986, p. 190, quoted above.) Even the principal activities abortion opponents had engaged in over a long period of time since *Roe* to subject *Roe* and the prevailing understanding of abortion

[16] One might take issue with the anti-abortion activists' interpretation of the law that regards *Roe* or *Casey* as a mistake from the point of view of law as integrity. That, however, does not detract from the claim that they were taking a protestant attitude toward the law.

law constantly to further interpretive tests can be said to be what I have called protestant obedience. While the state legislative processes that produced state anti-abortion legislation are legitimate in most cases, the laws that were produced were so clearly in violation of the *Roe* framework that they were acts of defiance that can easily be construed as disobedience. The point of these legislative acts was to get *Roe* re-litigated through the courts again.

The greatest irony is that *Roe* itself was also the result of the protestant attitude towards law and an act of protestant obedience. With *Dobbs* overturning *Roe,* however, we are not going back to square one, i.e., the state of the law pre-*Roe*. From the Dworkinian perspective, we now have a recent US Supreme Court decision overturning *Roe* to contend with in our interpretation of law as a morally consistent whole. This does not mean that *Roe* simply disappears from the "data" for future interpretation of the law. If nothing else, the fact that *Roe* was overturned by *Dobbs* and the reasons for overturning it given by *Dobbs* would have to figure prominently in any future interpretation of the law. None of this, however, precludes the possibility of seeing *Dobbs* as a mistake on further interpretation on law as integrity, but there is more to overcome in that interpretation.

This goes to show that the protestant attitude towards law advocated by Dworkin is a double-edged sword. Its potential of not leaving any law settled is quite troubling. On any contentious issue that divides the citizenry, whichever side the law settles on, it opens the possibility for those citizens on the other side not to see the law as settled and pose interpretive challenge to the law when opportunities arise. Taking the protestant attitude, furthermore, is not a guarantee that one would come up with a good interpretation of the law that is difficult to challenge. Nor is it likely that the courts, taking the protestant attitude, would produce an interpretation that is the "best word" on the law and not leave room for other parties taking the protestant attitude to reinterpret the law and challenge their decisions.[17]

The pendulum that is the law would therefore swing back and forth until the citizenry reaches what amounts to some kind of consensus about the issue involved—a consensus that would make any reasonable interpretative account of the law by a reasonable person taking the protestant attitude to contain some version of the consensus as part of that community's scheme of principles. When that point is reached, then there will be few, if any, occasions for citizens with the protestant attitude to disagree about the law (or the relevant part of it) and feel the need to commit an act of protestant obedience to challenge the existing authoritative understanding of the law. We have perhaps reached that stage with some issues. The has not been any serious challenge to *Brown v. Board of Education,* for example.

[17] This is what I take to be a central point of Flores (2024).

References

Literature

Dworkin R (1977) Taking rights seriously. Harvard University Press, Cambridge
Dworkin R (1986) Law's empire. Harvard University Press, Cambridge
Flores I (2024) Authority, Fidelity, and Integrity in Law. In: Babst G, Souris RN, McGregor J (eds) Liberal constitutionalism and its contemporary challenges, Springer
Hart HLA (1961) The concept of law. Oxford University Press, Oxford
Henley K (1990) Protestant hermeneutics and the rule of law: Gadamer and Dworkin. Ratio Juris 3(1):14–28
King Jr. ML (1963) Letter from Birmingham Jail. https://billofrightsinstitute.org/primary-sources/letter-from-birmingham-jail. Accessed 22 May 2023
Lee W-C (2015) The judgeship of all citizens: Dworkin's protestantism about law. Law Philosophy 34:25–53
Waldron J (2006) The core of the case against judicial review. Yale Law J 115(6):1346–1406

Court Cases

Brown v. Board of Education of Topeka, 491 U.S. 397 (1989)
Casey v. Planned Parenthood of Southeastern Pennsylvania, 505 U. S. 833 (1992)
Dobbs v. Jackson Women's Health Organization, 97 U. S. ____ (2022)
Griswold v. Connecticut, 381 U.S. 479 (1965)
Loving v. Virginia, 381 U.S. 479 (1967)
Roe v. Wade, 410 U.S. 113 (1973)
Texas v. Johnson, 491 U.S. 397 (1989)

Win-chiat Lee is Professor of Philosophy and Tatum Family Faculty Fellow at Wake Forest University. His main research interest is in the philosophy of law, especially the philosophy of international criminal law, and global justice. He is currently completing a paper on the human right to a nationality, and also working on a book on universal jurisdiction. He also serves as the Executive Director of AMINTAPHIL.

Constructive Interpretation, Democracy, and the Protestant Attitude

Imer B. Flores

Abstract This paper concerns Ronald Dworkin's notion of a 'protestant attitude' in interpreting constitutional provisions and offers an additional interpretation of Dworkin's work, finding it useful for a constructive interpretation of the constitution and a partnership conception of democracy.

1 Introduction

Adopting a protestant attitude to law and seeing what appears to be settled as unsettled are not necessarily problematic. It is quite the opposite: it is a proper way not only of discharging one's duty to obey the law by critically following its authority, displaying fidelity, and exhibiting integrity, but also by identifying and correcting previous mistakes (or even making new ones with the further possibility of revising and correcting them). After this introductory section, I will commence, in Sect. 2, by reviewing another reading of Dworkinian Protestantism and will focus on one aspect that some find problematic, mainly the implication of this approach for democracy. As Win Chiat Lee, for example, suggests: "the protestant attitude… is a double-edged sword. Its potential of not leaving any law settled is quite troubling".[1] I will continue, in Sect. 3, by revising three aspects of Ronald Dworkin's theory to clarify my own position and to respond to alternative readings, such as Lee's, by

[1] This is a revised and expanded version of "Authority, Fidelity, and Integrity in Law: Commentary on Lee's Dworkinian Protestantism, Civil Disobedience, and Democratic Citizenship", prepared for 2022 AMINTAPHIL Conference "Protecting Democracy, Liberty, the Common Good", Rollins College, Winter Park, Florida, October 6–8, 2022. See Lee (2024).

I. B. Flores (✉)
Legal Research Institute and Law School, UNAM (National Autonomous University of Mexico), Mexico City, Mexico
e-mail: imer@unam.mx

G. A. Babst et al. (eds.), *Liberal Constitutionalism and its Contemporary Challenges*, AMINTAPHIL: The Philosophical Foundations of Law and Justice 12, https://doi.org/10.1007/978-3-031-53602-1_7

suggesting that despite the fact that the protestant attitude appears to be a double-edge sword, which might yield good and bad results, it is not problematic especially for those of us, who—following Dworkin—advocate for both a constructive interpretation and a partnership conception of democracy. I will conclude, in Sect. 4, by briefly revisiting George Orwell's *Animal Farm* as a way of reinforcing why Jeremy Waldron's critique of stronger versions of judicial review is misled: in a democracy there are no final words and neither the legislator nor the judge nor any other legal official has—and much less should have—the last word. Albeit there are still right answers, and judges, despite not being the only ones, are most of the time better suited to reach them due to their independence from ordinary day-to-day politics.

The most outstanding features of liberal constitutionalism, as a limited government under a constitution, includes the determination of the liberties and rights of the people, and the division of power among the different branches of government. These features, if accompanied both with judges' independence and strong judicial review, enable the courts to be the guardian of the constitution. Since most of the challenges to our liberal constitutional democracies come from inside, the response must also come from inside and not surprisingly judges are better suited to resolve disputes and to respond to those threats, as well as to keep powers not only separated but also checked and balanced. In short, to safeguard the individual, minorities, and even governmental bodies threatened by the force of majoritarian politics and from elected officials, who would not only turn out to be autocrats, but also tend to exceed their powers.

As we will see, law is not exhausted by a catalogue of rules and its justifying principles, but requires an argumentative, constructive, interpretative, self-reflective, and even fraternal attitude, which Dworkin labeled as "protestant", to suggest that citizens, judges, and other legal officials as partners in self-government must be critical of what appears to be settled law, instead of blindly following its authority, they must interpret it by themselves to figure out what law really is and not inventing new law.

2 Another Reading of Dworkinian Protestantism

Lee correctly claims in both his current and previous accounts of Dworkinian Protestantism about law[2] that what Dworkin calls the protestant attitude has the potential of seeing settled law as unsettled[3] and so requiring that citizens and judges, as well as legislators and other legal officials, must adopt the protestant attitude not only to be critical of the prevailing account of law but also to be willing to interpret and reinterpret it by themselves. However, as already advanced, although the prot-

---

[2] See Lee (2024) and compare Lee (2015). See also Postema (1987), Henley (1990), Bustamante (2021).

[3] Lee (2024).

estant attitude toward law advocated by Dworkin may appear to be a double-edged sword, which can certainly yield *Roe* and even *Dobbs*, I reject Lee's view that its potential of not leaving any law settled is quite troubling.[4]

After the U.S. Supreme Court's overturning of *Roe* with *Dobbs*, the protestant attitude might be our last hope either to show that *Dobbs* was in fact a mistake and that it should be overturned, or to challenge the constitutionality either of a federal or state legislature abortion ban, which would criminalize women and neglect their right to decide to interrupt a pregnancy. Imagine that Congress or a given state legislature enacts an absolute abortion ban and consider whether a woman, an obstetrician, or someone else, will be able to challenge the statute or even practice civil disobedience.

I further agree not only that citizens and judges, but also legislators and legal officials, in the process of fulfilling their duty to obey the law, must figure out what the law is instead of merely following it. Therefore, I also accept the implication of the protestant attitude towards law for a citizen's political obligation, i.e., their duty to obey the law. Although certain kinds of actions are implied by the protestant attitude, including civil disobedience, which is paradoxically a proper way of obeying the law, I am not sure that—as Lee suggests—it is required: "*requires* citizens commit that kind of civil disobedience if that is the proper way of discharging one's duty to obey the law", because as he acknowledges "that might also be too demanding of citizens."[5] (I will return to this point below to suggest a friendly amendment: what is required is not to disobey, but to critically determine whether to obey or disobey what appears to be settled law.)

3 Ronald Dworkin's Protestantism

3.1 Protestant Attitude

Indeed, in *Law's Empire*,[6] Dworkin emphasizes a "protestant attitude" toward the law and mentions it only three times in this book, but with implications of utmost importance.[7] Though he does not say very much about it elsewhere, as Lee affirms: "it is quite clear that it is a doctrine central to his overall theory of law as integrity."[8] It is worth mentioning that Dworkin labeled and relabeled his theory many times, and not surprisingly the protestant attitude appears under different names, i.e., argumentative, constructive, interpretive, fraternal, and self-reflective attitudes, through-

[4] Lee (2024).

[5] Lee (2024).

[6] See Dworkin (1986).

[7] For this reason, I will recharacterize the "protestant attitude" as the "three times a lady thesis": (1) lady authority; (2) lady fidelity; and (3) lady integrity.

[8] Lee (2024).

out *Law's Empire* (the last four in its last paragraph),[9] but remained at the core of his account of law which was finally recharacterized: "law as interpretivism".[10]

After distinguishing between "two principles of political integrity: a legislative principle, which asks lawmakers to try to make the total set of laws morally coherent, and an adjudicative principle, which instructs that the law be seen as coherent in that way",[11] Dworkin suggests that "Integrity expands and deepens the role individual citizens can play in developing the public standards of their community because it requires them to treat relations among themselves as characteristically, not just spasmodically, governed by these standards."[12] Immediately, after, Dworkin alludes to the "protestant attitude"—as "protestant idea"—for the first time:[13]

> For the expressive value is confirmed when people in good faith try to treat one another in a way appropriate to the common membership in a community governed by political integrity and to see each other as making this attempt, even when they disagree about exactly what integrity requires in particular circumstances. Political obligation is then not just a matter of obeying the discrete political decisions of the community one by one, as political philosophers usually represent it. It becomes a more *protestant* idea: fidelity to a scheme of principle each citizen has a responsibility to identify, ultimately for himself, as his community's scheme.

As Lee acknowledges Dworkin's Protestantism about law has two elements, which seem to challenge the authority of law, i.e., its authoritative nature. One the one hand, "every citizen has to interpret the law for herself in discharging her duty to obey the law. (That includes judges too in discharging their duty to apply the law in deciding cases.)".[14] On the other hand, it is clear that "what the law is (or one might say what the law *really* is) in relation to a particular case is, in principle, always up to interpretation even if an authoritative account (by a court decision or a legislative act) has already been given."[15] Furthermore, "If what law *really* is, is always up to interpretation, then clearly one cannot blindly follow authority, so to speak, in order to discharge one's obligation to obey the law."[16] Thus, taking authority seriously means, not following it blindly, but figuring out critically what the law in fact is as a matter of interpretation and as such not merely as providing peremptory or

---

[9] See note 24. See also Flores (2015, 2018).

[10] See Dworkin (2004a, 2006, 2011). See also Flores (2022).

[11] Dworkin (1986), p. 176.

[12] Dworkin (1986), p. 189.

[13] Dworkin (1986), p. 190 (emphasis added). From my point of view, following Dworkin, it includes not only judges, but also legislators discharging their duty to make new law or reforming the preexisting one, as well as any other legal officials discharging their different duties within their distinctive and respective legal competences, by adopting something like H.L.A. Hart's "critical reflective attitude" or John Rawls's "reflective equilibrium". See Hart (1961), p. 56 [(1994), p. 57]; and, Rawls (1971), pp. 20–21, and 48–51 [(1999), pp. 18–19 and 42–45]. See also Flores (2002), pp. 155–156; Flores (2009b), p. 62.

[14] Lee (2024).

[15] Lee (2024).

[16] Lee (2024).

exclusionary reasons for action, but by adopting H.L.A. Hart's critical reflective attitude or John Rawls's reflective equilibrium.[17]

Although, I agree that citizens must put forward their dissenting interpretations of the law to be tested by the courts and civil disobedience is a great example, i.e., one appears to disobey a law, but in fact one is obeying the law, by adopting what Lee calls a "protestant obedience".[18] Nevertheless, I would like to introduce my friendly amendment: citizens must critically not only put forward their dissenting interpretation by disobeying a law or even objecting it as a matter of conscientious refusal, but also by challenging its content, including precedents, in a court and even by promoting an initiative to make a new law and an amendment or reform in the legislative arena. In sum, by challenging the prevailing account of law, citizens and legal officials reinforce its authority, not by following it literally or mechanically, but by figuring out what law's authority really allows or requires, confers or imposes, permits or prohibits. Certainly, they must provide additional reasons to debunk the prevailing account and replace it with a different interpretation, very much like the way precedents work. In other words, what is required is not to disobey the law itself, but to critically determine whether the best way to obey the law is by following what appears to be settled law or disobey it by appealing to a higher law or its purposive end, including rules and its justifying principles.

The second time that Dworkin mentions the "protestant attitude", he affirms that it is the attitude favored by his notion of integrity. But let me suggest that the passage also reinforces the importance of fidelity to law, because both citizens and judges, as well as legislators and other legal officials, not only must interpret the law, but also must do it within practical boundaries:[19]

> Dividing departments of law to match that sort of opinion promotes predictability and guards against sudden official reinterpretations that uproot large areas of law, and it does this in a way that promotes a deeper aim of law as integrity. If legal compartments make sense to people at large, they encourage the *protestant* attitude integrity favors, because they allow ordinary people as well as hard-pressed judges to interpret the law within practical boundaries that seem natural and intuitive.

Following Lon L. Fuller's distinction between "intelligent and unintelligent fidelity",[20] the fidelity that Dworkin advocates resembles the former and not the latter. The latter is associated with a more literal or textual approach to the law, deferent to whatever the authority has already enacted as law, whereas the former with a more interpretive or purposive approach to law, which requires as Dworkin suggests: "fidelity to a scheme of principles".[21] As Lee argues not only courts do not

---

[17] See note 13. See also Hart (1982, p. 262). Nevertheless, Hart cannot have it both ways. Either law provides peremptory reasons or law requires a critical reflective attitude. But not both. Following Dworkin and Lee, what law requires is a protestant attitude and obedience, consistent with Hart's critical reflective attitude or Rawls's reflective equilibrium.

[18] Lee (2024).

[19] Dworkin (1986), p. 252 (emphasis added).

[20] Fuller (1949), p. 616.

[21] See Flores (2016, 2017).

have the best word on what the law is even if they have the last word, but also legislatures does not have the best word on the law either even as they engage in the making of it. So even after the legislature has legislated on a certain issue, it is still a matter of interpretation for the courts, as well as ordinary citizens, as to determine what the law is on that issue.[22] Keep in mind Fuller's assertion: "The correction of obvious legislative errors or oversights is not to supplant the legislative will, but to make it effective."[23]

The third and last time that Dworkin refers to the protestant attitude—he does it twice under "protestant" and four more times with other words, such as "constructive", "fraternal", "interpretive", and "self-reflective"—in the last paragraph of the last section: "Epilogue: What is Law?" of the last chapter "Law Beyond Law" of *Law's Empire*:[24]

> What is law?... Law is not exhausted by any catalogue of rules or principles, each with its own dominion over some discrete theater of behavior. Nor by any roster of officials and their powers each over part of our lives. Law's empire is defined by attitude, not territory or power or process... It is an *interpretive*, *self-reflective* attitude addressed to politics in the broadest sense. It is a *protestant* attitude that makes each citizen responsible for imagining what his society's public commitments to principles are, and what these commitments require in new circumstances. The *protestant* character of law is confirmed, and the creative role of private decisions acknowledged, by the backward-looking judgmental decisions, and also by the regulative assumption that though judges must have the last word, their word is not for that reason the best word. Law's attitude is *constructive*: it aims, in the interpretive spirit, to lay principle over practice to show the best route to a better future, keeping the rights faith with the past. It is, finally, a *fraternal* attitude, an expression of how we are united in community though divided in project, interest, and conviction. That is, anyway, what law is for us: for the people we want to be and the community we aim to have.

This lengthy paragraph insists on the importance of citizens and judges—as well as other legal officials—adopting a protestant attitude by themselves as a way not only of contesting the authority of law, but also of displaying an intelligent fidelity to law, which is favored by Dworkin's conception of integrity to law as coherence, i.e., fit and justification. Additionally, it includes a caveat: though judges must have the last word, their word is not for that reason the best word. This suggests not only that sometimes citizens, judges, and other legal officials—even if they claim to adopt the protestant attitude—fail to reach the best or right answer and do commit mistakes, as in *Dobbs*, where the court was inventing new law rather than interpreting the existing one, but also that such mistakes must be corrected, as *Brown* did with *Plessy*.

---

[22] Lee (2024).

[23] Fuller (1949), p. 626.

[24] Dworkin (1986), p. 413 (emphasis added).

3.2 *Constructive Interpretation* aka *Interpretivism*[25]

Ever since the publication of his book review on Rawls' *A Theory of Justice,* Dworkin distanced himself from a "natural" model and endorsed a "constructive" one.[26] The "natural" model presupposes a philosophical position that describes an objective moral reality, which is not created by human beings, but rather discovered by them, as the laws of physics. On the contrary, the "constructive" model "treats intuitions of justice not as clues to the existence of independent principles, but rather as stipulated features of a general theory to be constructed, as if the sculptor set himself to carve the animal that best fits a pile of bones he happened to find together".[27] Later on, he reaffirmed: "moral judgments are constructed, not discovered: they issue from an intellectual device adopted to confront practical, not theoretical, problems".[28]

After his exchange with Stanley Fish[29] on legal *vis-à-vis* literary interpretation[30] and throughout his works, but especially in *Law's Empire*, Dworkin reinforced not only that the model is constructive and to some extent creative but also clarified that it is not inventive but interpretive of the practice.[31] In other words, since law is an "interpretive concept" the proper method requires a "constructive interpretation" of the practice. As he defined: "constructive interpretation is a matter of imposing purpose on an object or practice in order to make of it the best possible example of the form or genre to which it is taken to belong".[32] Furthermore "constructive interpretations… try to show legal practice as a whole in its best light, to achieve equilibrium between legal practice as they find it and the best justification of that practice".[33] In that sense, Dworkin's interpretive model is argumentative as well.[34]

It is well known Dworkin delineates three stages of constructive interpretation: (1) "Preinterpretive" in which the interpreter identifies the rules and standards taken to provide the tentative content of the practice; (2) "Interpretive" in which the interpreter settles on some general justification for the main elements of the practice identified at the preinterpretive stage; and (3) "Postinterpretive" in which the interpreter adjusts the sense of what the practice "really" requires so as better to serve the justification accepted at the interpretive stage.[35]

---

[25] See Flores (2013, 2015, 2022).

[26] See Dworkin (1973) and compare Dworkin (1982a). See also Rawls (1971).

[27] Dworkin (1977) [and (1978)], p. 160.

[28] Dworkin (2011), p. 63.

[29] See Fish (1982, 1983).

[30] See Dworkin (1982b, 1983).

[31] Dworkin (1985), p. 1; Dworkin (1986), pp. 66, 67, 366; Dworkin (2006a), p. 15.

[32] Dworkin (1986), p. 52.

[33] Dworkin (1986), p. 90.

[34] Dworkin (1986), p. 13.

[35] Dworkin (1986), pp. 65–68. See Flores (2012).

Although Dworkin seemed to deemphasize both the evaluative and the descriptive, it was in the process of emphasizing the interpretive.[36] At the end, he has been endorsing a moral reading of the practice, which requires references to value and even value judgments that are certainly done by subjects but not necessarily subjective but objective.[37] On the one hand, propositions of law are neither merely descriptive nor are they simply evaluative, but interpretive of legal history, which combines elements of both description and evaluation but is different from both.[38] On the other hand, clarified (with the "rules of courtesy" as example) that the "interpretive attitude" has two components, *i.e.* an assumption that it has an objective value (or point) and a further assumption that it is sensitive to it: "People now try to impose *meaning* on the institution—to see its best light—and then to restructure it in the light of that meaning".[39]

In *Law's Empire* Dworkin advanced his conception of "law as integrity", which includes both coherence and fit.[40] In his words "[Law as integrity] argues that rights and responsibilities flow from past decisions and so count as legal, not just when they are explicit in these decisions but also when they follow from the principles of personal and political morality the explicit decisions presuppose by way of justification".[41] What's more "Law as integrity… insists that legal claims are interpretive judgments and therefore combine backward- and forward-looking elements… So law as integrity rejects as unhelpful the ancient question whether judges find or invent law; we understand legal reasoning, it suggests, only by seeing the sense in which they do both and neither".[42] Hart replied in the "Postscript" to The Concept of Law:[43]

> It is true that when particular statutes or precedents prove indeterminate, or when the explicit law is silent, judges do not just push away their law books and start to legislate without further guidance from the law. Very often, in deciding such cases, they cite some general principle or some general aim or purpose… This indeed is the very nucleus of the 'constructive interpretation' which is so prominent a feature of Dworkin's theory of adjudication… But… though this procedure certainly defers, it does not eliminate the moment for judicial law-making.

Dworkin responded by developing an argument against a detached conception of values and for an integrated one.[44] In a few words, "political values are integrated rather than detached" and we "must try to understand them holistically and interpretively, each in the light of the others, organized not in a hierarchy but in a fashion of

[36] See Dworkin (1982b).

[37] See Dworkin (1983); Dworkin (1996), pp. 1–38.

[38] Dworkin (1985), p. 147.

[39] Dworkin (1986), p. 47.

[40] See Dworkin (1986), pp. 94–96.

[41] Dworkin (1986), p. 96.

[42] Dworkin (1986), p. 225. See Flores (2013), pp. 115–123.

[43] Hart (1994), pp. 274–275. See Flores (2011).

[44] See Dworkin (2004b).

a geodesic dome".[45] Similarly, Dworkin acknowledged that theories of law have been divided into roughly two groups: "positivist" theories of law, which insist that what the law of any jurisdiction requires or permits is only a matter of social fact, and "anti-positivist" theories, which claim that what the law requires sometimes depends not on social facts alone but also on controversial normative issues including moral issues. Regarding "hard cases" in which what lawyers regard as settled law does not decide the immediate issue according to a positivist theory, judges "must exercise discretion to make new law", whereas in an anti-positivist theory, judges "must aim at integrity in their decisions". However, "what integrity requires will often, perhaps usually, be controversial, so that a fresh judgement is needed".[46] And so, Dworkin restates Rawls' "reflective equilibrium"[47] as a method for legal philosophy: "We try to generate principles of some general scope and to match those general principles to the concrete judgements about what is just and unjust with which we begin, shifting our views about either principles or concrete judgments, or both, as becomes necessary to achieve an interpretive fit".[48]

3.3 *Partnership Conception of Democracy*[49]

Although "democracy means self-government" and "is valuable because in a democracy the people govern themselves" as Dworkin acknowledges,[50] the concept of democracy is an interpretive and a very contested one: people disagree about what democracy is.[51] In short, democracy means government by the people, but there are at least two competing and conflicting rival conceptions of democracy, i.e., the *majoritarian* and the *partnership*,[52] which attempt to answer in two radically different ways the question: Who are the people? On one side, for the "majoritarian" conception, it "means government by the largest number of the people. On this majoritarian view, the democratic ideal lies in a match between political decision and the will of the majority or plurality of opinion." On the other, for the "partnership" one, it "means government by *all* the people, acting together as full and equal partners in a collective enterprise of self-government".[53]

[45] Dworkin (2006a), pp. 159–160.

[46] Dworkin (2006a), p. 242.

[47] Rawls (1971), pp. 48–51. See Waluchow (2006) and Flores (2009b).

[48] Dworkin (2006a, p. 246).

[49] See Flores (2010, 2021).

[50] Dworkin (1998), p. 453.

[51] Dworkin (2011), pp. 379 and 382.

[52] It is worth to mention that Dworkin originally characterized it as the "constitutional conception of democracy" in the "Introduction" to *Freedom's Law* (1996), pp. 1–38, but later in a comment to Frank I. Michelman (1998), re-characterized it as the "partnership conception of democracy". See Dworkin (1998).

[53] Dworkin (2000), pp. 357–358.

As far as I know this distinction can be traced all the way back to John Stuart Mill, who in his *Considerations on Representative Government*, under the epigraph "Of True and False Democracy: Representation of All, and Representation of the Majority Only", acknowledged:[54]

> Two very different ideas are usually confounded under the name democracy. The pure idea of democracy, according to its definition, is the government of the whole people by the whole people, equally represented. Democracy as commonly conceived and hitherto practiced is the government of the whole people by a mere majority of the people, exclusively represented. The former is synonymous with the equality of all citizens; the latter, strangely confounded with it, is a government of privilege, in favor of the numerical majority, who alone possess practically any voice in the State.

In Dworkin's account, on one side, according to the *majoritarian* conception: democracy is government by majority will, i.e., in accordance with the will of the greatest number of people, expressed in elections with universal or near universal suffrage. There is no guarantee that a majority will decide fairly; its decisions may be unfair to minorities whose interests the majority systematically ignores. If so, then the democracy is unjust but no less democratic for that reason.[55] On the other, according to the *partnership* conception: democracy means that the people govern themselves each as a full partner in a collective political enterprise so that a majority's decisions are democratic only when certain further conditions are met that protect the status and interests of each citizen as a full partner in that enterprise. On the partnership view, a community that steadily ignores the interests of some minority or other group is for that reason not democratic even though it elects officials by impeccably majoritarian means.[56] What's more, Dworkin insisted—contra *inter alia* Robert C. Post—that democracy couldn't be reduced to a *procedural* ideal as the majoritarian conception purports but to a *substantive* one as the partnership conception proclaims:[57]

> The majoritarian conception purports to be purely procedural and therefore independent of other dimensions of political morality; it allows us to say, as I indicated, that a decision is democratic even if it is very unjust. But the partnership conception does not make democracy independent of the rest of political morality; on that conception we need a theory of equal partnership to decide what is or is not a democratic decision, and we need to consult ideas about justice, equality, and liberty in order to construct such a theory. So on the partnership conception, democracy is a substantive, not a merely procedural, ideal.

Hence, Dworkin emphasizes one fundamental and relevant difference between the *majoritarian* and *partnership* conceptions of democracy:[58]

> Citizens play two main roles in a mature democracy. They are, first, the judges of political contests whose verdicts, expressed in formal elections or in referenda or other forms of direct legislation, are normally decisive… Citizens are also, however, participants in the

[54] Mill (1958), pp. 102–103.

[55] Dworkin (2006b), p. 131.

[56] *Id.*

[57] Dworkin (2006b), p. 134. See Post (1995).

[58] Dworkin (2000), p. 358.

> political contests they judge: they are candidates and supporters whose actions help, in different ways, to shape public opinion and to fix how the rest of the citizens vote. The majoritarian conception of democracy pays exclusive attention to the first of these roles… The partnership conception recognizes both roles, because it supposes that in a true democracy citizens must play a part, as equal partners in a collective enterprise, in shaping as well as constituting the public's opinion.

First and foremost, Dworkin was adamant in his critique of a supposedly neutral account of democracy: democracy is government according to the will of the majority expressed in reasonably frequent elections with nearly full suffrage after political debate with free speech and a free press. Furthermore, he challenged: "Is democracy, understood as majority rule, something valuable in itself?" And even questioned: "Why should the fact that numerically more people favor one course of action over another signal that the more favored policy is either fairer or better?" To prove his point, i.e., majority rule is not intrinsically fair in all circumstances, he recognized "We might say: when people locked in a joint enterprise disagree about what should be done, the only fair solution is to count heads. But that must be rejected as a universal default principle of fair play: it is not automatically true." He reinforced his point not only by asking a rhetorical question: "But if democracy means majority rule… then why should we care so much to protect our democracy [from majority rule]?".[59] But also, by answering: "According to the alternative view of democracy… majority rule isn't even legitimate, let alone democratic, unless [certain] conditions are at least substantially met."[60] In fact, as Rickard Parker emphasized "the animating *mission* of modern constitutional law is conventionally described as the correction of failures allegedly endemic to majority rule".[61]

Clearly the mission is to safeguard the individual, minorities, and even governmental bodies supposedly threatened by the force of majoritarian politics. Since such task has been conferred upon courts via a strong judicial review, some—following Alexander M. Bickel—considered it as the "counter-majoritarian difficulty"[62] and are against it—most notably Jeremy Waldron.[63] Nevertheless, Dworkin and some authors, such as John Hart Ely and Wilfrid J. Waluchow,[64] have argued that allowing the country to be governed in part by judges is not necessarily antidemocratic, once it is accepted that the objective for democracy is to get the different decisions resolved in accord with the best or right conception of a democratic regime, which assures equal concern and respect to every citizen and their rights.[65] Certainly, allowing society to be governed by the judiciary alone can be a grave threat to democracy.[66] On the contrary, it is necessary to guarantee that neither many

[59] Dworkin (2011), pp. 347–348.

[60] Dworkin (2006a), p. 134.

[61] Parker (1994), p. 69.

[62] Bickel (1986), p. 16.

[63] See Waldron (2006).

[64] See Ely (1980). See also Waluchow (1994), p. 252.

[65] See especially Dworkin (1977) [and (1978)].

[66] See Berger (1977).

nor few, but all are part of the partnership, both majority and minority. Additionally, it is also necessary to transcend the debate about who is or should be the absolute or final authoritative interpreter: the legislator, the judge or someone else?[67] Both have a very important duty, either to legislate political rights (and constitutional norms that remain under-enforced) or adjudicate legal rights, according to the constitution and the law.[68] In a democracy, everyone has and must have a say and its share: it implies a division of labor.[69]

4 Conclusion

To conclude, as a way of reinforcing that adopting the protestant view and seeing settled law as unsettled are not necessarily problematic, a passage of George Orwell's *Animal Farm* is pertinent:[70]

> None of the other animals on the farm could get further than the letter A. It was also found that the stupider animals, such as the sheep, hens, and ducks, were unable to learn the Seven Commandments by heart. After much thought Snowball declared that the Seven Commandments could in effect be reduced to a single maxim, namely: "Four legs good, two legs bad." This, he said, contained the essential principle of Animalism. Whoever had thoroughly grasped it would be safe from human influences. The birds at first objected, since it seemed to them that they also had two legs, but Snowball proved to them that this was not so.

In a few words: (1) a general constitutive assembly, i.e., of animals, had enacted a Constitution, *i.e.*, the *Seven Commandments*; (2) an authority, i.e., Snowfall, exercising a secondary rule of legislation or change, proceeded to amend or reform it by declaring that the seven commandments can be reduce to one single maxim: "Four legs good, two legs bad"; (3) a class, fraction or group, i.e., the birds, acknowledging that they have two legs, and wondering whether they are bad for that reason, objected the content of the new rule; and (4) an authority, *i.e.*, Snowfall, exerting a secondary rule of adjudication, overruled their objection, proving them wrong, and upholding the one single maxim.

However, I am not convinced that the last adjudicative decision, regardless of being authoritative, is the right one, i.e., despite having two legs the birds were excluded from the application of the one single maxim. If we adopt the protestant attitude, we will have to critically keep interpreting it to determine if the birds were

---

[67] See Bishop Benjamin Hoadly (sermon before the English King in 1717) quoted by Grey (1986), p. 50: "Whoever hath an absolute authority to interpret any written or spoken laws, it is he who is truly the Law-giver to all intent and purposes, and not the person who first wrote or spoke them." See also Robert Jackson concurring opinion in *Brown v. Allen* (1953): "We are not final because we are infallible, but we are infallible only because we are final."

[68] See Dworkin (2011), pp. 405–407, 412–413. See also Sager (1978, 1993).

[69] See Flores (2005, 2007, 2009a, b).

[70] Orwell (1945), Book III.

rightfully excused or not. Let me suggest that the essential principle of animalism requires the recognition, sooner or later, of an additional qualification to exempt the birds: "Four legs good, two legs bad (with the exception of feathery animals)" or even "Four legs good, two legs bad (if accompanied by two hands with opposable thumbs)".

From my point of view, the morals of this part of the Orwellian fable are: What appears to be a final word is not infallible, but fallible, as all human endeavors—or animal ones. Furthermore, what seems to be a last word is not definitive, but tentative. In other words, what is settled for a time being remains unsettled over time and can be revised later by adopting the protestant attitude not only by citizens but also by legal officials, in their different capacities as legislators, judges, and so on, according to law and the duties imposed and powers conferred upon them. In sum, there are no final or last words in law, especially in a democracy, where everyone is entitled to have a say: framers, amenders, legislators, judges, other legal officials, and specially the citizens, if we are committed to pursue a true democratic citizenship of partners in self-government, who for that reason must adopt the protestant attitude: The people then, now, and forever more.

Cases

Brown v. Allen, 344 U.S. 443, 540 (1953)
Brown v. Board of Education of Topeka, 347 US 483 (1954)
Dobbs v. Jackson Women's Health Organization, 597 U. S. ____ (2022)
Plessy v. Ferguson, 167 US 537 (1896)
Roe v. Wade, 410 U.S. 113 (1973)

References

Berger R (1977) Government by the judiciary. The transformation of the fourteenth amendment. HUP, Cambridge

Bickel AM (1986) The least dangerous branch, 2nd edn. YUP, New Haven [original publication: Bobbs-Merrill, Indianapolis, 1962]

Bustamante T (2021) Is protestant interpretation an acceptable attitude toward normative social practices? An analysis of Dworkin and Postema. Am J Jurisprud 66:1–25

Dworkin R (1973) The original position. Univ Chic Law Rev 40:500–533

Dworkin R (1977) Taking rights seriously. HUP, Cambridge [There is a 2nd ed. "With Reply to Critics": 1978]

Dworkin R (1982a) 'Natural' law revisited. Univ Fla Law Rev 36(2):165–188

Dworkin R (1982b) Law as interpretation. Tex Law Rev 60:527–550

Dworkin R (1983) My reply to Stanley Fish (and Walter Benn Michaels): please don't talk about objectivity anymore. In: Mitchell WJT (ed) The politics of interpretation. Chicago University Press, Chicago

Dworkin R (1985) A matter of principle. HUP, Cambridge

Dworkin R (1986) Law's empire. HUP, Cambridge
Dworkin R (1996) Freedom's law. HUP, Cambridge
Dworkin R (1998) The partnership conception of democracy. Calif Law Rev 86:453–458
Dworkin R (2000) Sovereign virtue. HUP, Cambridge
Dworkin R (2004a) Rawls and the law. Fordham Law Rev 72:1385–1405
Dworkin R (2004b) Hart's postscript and the character of political philosophy. Oxford J Leg Stud 24:1–37
Dworkin R (2006a) Justice in robes. HUP, Cambridge
Dworkin R (2006b) Is democracy possible here? PUP, Princeton
Dworkin R (2011) Justice for hedgehogs. HUP, Cambridge
Ely JH (1980) Democracy and distrust. HUP, Cambridge
Fish S (1982) Working on the chain gang: interpretation in law and literature. Tex Law Rev 60:551–568
Fish S (1983) Wrong again. Tex Law Rev 62:299–316
Flores IB (2002) In the dark side of the conventionality thesis. In: Villanueva E (ed) Studies in social, political, and legal philosophy. Rodopi, Amsterdam, pp 143–156
Flores IB (2005) The quest for legisprudence: constitutionalism v. legalism. In: Wintgens LJ (ed) The theory and practice of legislation: essays on legisprudence. Ashgate, London, pp 26–52
Flores IB (2007) Legisprudence: the forms and limits of legislation. Problema. Anuario de filosofía y teoría del derecho 1:247–266
Flores IB (2009a) Legisprudence: the role and rationality of legislators —vis-à-vis judges— towards the realization of justice 1/2:91–110
Flores IB (2009b) The living tree constitutionalism: fixity and flexibility. Problema. Anuario de filosofía y teoría del derecho 3:37–74
Flores IB (2010) Ronald Dworkin's *Justice for hedgehogs* and *Partnership conception of democracy* (With a comment to Jeremy Waldron's "A majority in the lifeboat"). Problema. Anuario de filosofía y teoría del derecho 4:65–103
Flores IB (2011) H.L.A. Hart's moderate indeterminacy thesis reconsidered: in between Scylla and Charybdis? Problema. Anuario de filosofía y teoría del derecho 5:147–173
Flores IB (2012) Natalie Stoljar's wishful thinking and one step beyond: what should conceptual legal analysis become? Problema. Anuario de filosofía y teoría del derecho 6:81–105
Flores IB (2013) The problem about the nature of law *vis-à-vis* legal rationality revisited: towards an integrative jurisprudence. In: Waluchow WJ, Sciaraffa S (eds) The philosophical foundations of the nature of law. OUP, Oxford, pp 101–126
Flores IB (2015) The legacy of Ronald Dworkin (1931-2013): a legal theory and methodology for Hedgehogs, Hercules, and one right answers. Problema. Anuario de filosofía y teoría del derecho 9:157–192
Flores IB (2016) Intelligent or unintelligent fidelity? In: Book review symposium on fidelity to our imperfect constitution: six views and a response. Const Comment 31(3):407–423
Flores IB (2017) Constitutional interpretation, intelligent fidelity, and (im)perfection: on James E. Fleming's fidelity to our imperfect constitution. Problema. Anuario de filosofía y teoría del derecho 11:31–58
Flores IB (2018) Taking (human) dignity and rights seriously: the integrated legal, moral, and political philosophy of Ronald Dworkin. In: Khurshid S, Malik L, Rodriguez-Blanco V (eds) Dignity in the legal and political philosophy of Ronald Dworkin. OUP, New Delhi, pp 101–129
Flores IB (2021) Dworkin, Ronald: partnership conception of democracy. In: Sellers M, Kirste S (eds) Encyclopedia of the philosophy of law and social philosophy. Springer, Dordrecht
Flores IB (2022) Dworkin, Ronald: constructive interpretation *aka* interpretivism. In: Sellers M, Kirste S (eds) Encyclopedia of the philosophy of law and social philosophy. Springer, Dordrecht
Fuller LL (1949) The case of the speluncean explorers. Harv Law Rev 62:616–645
Grey JC (1986) A realistic conception of law. In: Feinberg J, Gross H (eds) Philosophy of law, 3rd edn. Wadsworth, Belmont

Hart HLA (1961) The concept of law. OUP, Oxford [there is a 2nd ed With a Postscript edited by Bulloch PA and Raz J (1994)]
Hart HLA (1982) Essays on Bentham. OUP, Oxford
Henley K (1990) Protestant hermeneutics and the rule of law: Gadamer and Dworkin. Ratio Juris 3(1):14–28
Lee W (2015) The judgeship of all citizens: Dworkin's protestantism about law. Law Philos 34:25–53
Lee W (2024) Dworkinian Protestantism, civil disobedience, and democratic citizenship. In: Babst GA, Souris RN, McGregor J (eds) Liberal constitutionalism and its challenges. Springer, Dordrecht
Michelman FI (1998) Brennan and democracy —the 1996-97 Brennan symposium lecture. Calif Law Rev 86:399–427
Mill JS (1958) Considerations on representative government. The Liberal Arts Press, Indianapolis [original publication: 1861]
Orwell G (1945) Animal Farm
Parker RD (1994) Here, the people rule. HUP, Cambridge
Postema GJ (1987) "Protestant" interpretation and social practices. Law Philos 6:283–319
Post RC (1995) Constitutional domains. Democracy, community management. HUP, Cambridge
Rawls J (1971) A theory of justice. HUP, Cambridge [there is revised ed (1999)]
Sager LG (1978) Fair measure: the legal status of underenforced constitutional norms. Harv Law Rev 91:1212–1264
Sager LG (1993) Justice in plainclothes: reflections on the thinness of constitutional law. Northwest Univ Law Rev 88:410
Waldron J (2006) The core of the case against judicial review. Yale Law Rev 115:1346–1406
Waluchow WJ (1994) Inclusive legal positivism. OUP, Oxford
Waluchow WJ (2006) A common law theory of judicial review. The living tree. CUP, Cambridge

Imer B. Flores is a Professor-Researcher at the Legal Research Institute and Law School, UNAM (Mexico). He is author of several articles, chapter and books on jurisprudence, legal, moral, and political philosophy, and constitutional law and theory; co-editor of *Law, Liberty, and the Rule of Law* (Springer, 2013); contributor to the *Encyclopedia of the Philosophy of Law and Social Philosophy*; and co-founder of *Problema. Anuario de Filosofía y Teoría del Derecho.* He has been Visiting Scholar in institutions in the USA, UK, and Latin America.

Part II

Structural Injustices in the Educational System, Inequality, and Its Effects on Democracy

Joan McGregor

Abstract This paper evaluates the woeful lack of Black, Latino/-a, and Native American students in higher education, a concern made all the more relevant in the light of the Court's recently announced decision in Students for Fair Admissions, Inc. v. President and Fellows of Harvard College (2023).

This paper was first presented at the AMINTAPHIL meeting at Rollins College in 2022. I would like to thanks the attendees for their helpful comments on this paper. I would also like to thank my CSRC fellow, Sydney Tran, who did research on this topic for me. Her work was invaluable for this project.

> I know no safe depository of the ultimate powers of the society but the people themselves; and if we think them not enlightened enough to exercise their control with a wholesome discretion, the remedy is not to take it from them, but to inform their discretion by education. This is the true corrective of abuses of constitutional power.[1]

> Those persons, whom nature hath endowed with genius and virtue, should be rendered by liberal education worthy to receive, and able to guard the sacred deposit of the rights of their fellow citizens, and …should be called to that charge without regard to wealth, birth, or other accidental conditions or circumstances.[2]

Thomas Jefferson's first quote speaks to the importance of an educated citizenry as necessary for constitutional democracy and the second displays the sentiment still

[1] Jefferson (1975).

[2] Jefferson (1950) Volume 1, Chapter 18, Document 11.

J. McGregor (✉)
Arizona State University, Tempe, AZ, USA
e-mail: J.mcgregor@asu.edu

G. A. Babst et al. (eds.), *Liberal Constitutionalism and its Contemporary Challenges*, AMINTAPHIL: The Philosophical Foundations of Law and Justice 12, https://doi.org/10.1007/978-3-031-53602-1_8

shared by Americans that those who go on to higher education should be those who merit it, those with talents, intellect, drive, and virtue not based on accidental conditions such wealth or social position. We removed barriers such as *de jure* school racial segregation to ensure that accidental conditions such as skin color didn't get in the way of achievement. Nevertheless, more than a half century after the landmark desegregation case was decided by the United States Supreme Court, schools in many states are as segregated on the basis of race as they were before the *Brown* decision.[3] Most of those segregated schools send few if any students on to institutions of higher learning.[4] Without advanced education, students from these communities will end up with lower incomes and fewer life prospects for themselves and their children. In America, Black, Latino, and Native Americans are consistently underrepresented in higher education and have substantially less wealth than whites.[5]

How do we account for the lack of Black, Latino, and Native Americans in higher education, particularly at the most selective schools? Why do those groups continue to be the most impoverished groups in the United States? And what effect does the absence of greater numbers from these groups in higher education and their relative lack of resources have on their role in democracy? If democracy requires that individuals stand as equals, not in roles of hierarchy, superior-inferior, what does this reality where many minorities find themselves excluded, at least in representative numbers, in universities and social positions of influences say about the state of our democracy? Can we achieve democratic equality with these inequalities in educational and economic achievement?

Essential to democracy are structures and institutions which ensure that individuals stand in relationships of equality to one another, wherein they are not in positions of inferiority or superiority. A basic tenet of democracy is citizens standing in positions of equality to one another. Consequently, an equalitarian theory of justice underlies liberal democratic theories; the basic premise is that all people are morally equal and deserving of respect. No one may be a subject of oppression. Historical forms of oppression include overt systems of racism and sexism and systems of hierarchy based upon income and family status. As Elizabeth Anderson argues, "Such unequal social relations generate, and were thought to justify, inequalities in the distribution of freedoms, resources, and welfare."[6] Egalitarianism repudiates the notion that some are worthier based on race, sex, inheritance, and so on. Given this, egalitarianism and democracy should be concerned when systems of hierarchy reproduce themselves as a result of the educational system. Positively, egalitarians think that competent adults "are equally moral agents: everyone equally has the power to develop and exercise moral responsibility, to cooperate with others

---

[3] https://www.gao.gov/products/gao-16-345.

[4] https://uncf.org/pages/k-12-disparity-facts-and-stats.

[5] https://www.brookings.edu/articles/unequal-opportunity-race-and-education/.

[6] Anderson (1999), p. 312.

according to principles of justice, to share and fill a conception of their good."[7] The point of democratic citizenship is to ensure the social conditions of freedom to guarantee equality in this sense. Egalitarianism should focus on these relationships of equality, argues Anderson, and not necessarily equality of resources. Critical to standing as equals is that groups are not relegated in inferior positions of power and status through no fault of their own. Universal public education was thought to be critical to a robust democracy, producing an informed and impowered citizenry who can make measured judgments about matters of the common good but also providing everyone equal opportunity to achieve merit required to access certain opportunities and positions. Universal public education was to eradicate the advantages of wealth and social status in the allocation of the benefits of society, e.g. positions in universities and resources in the market. What happened?

Many of the economic, social, and political advantages of our society are purportedly based on one's individual merit.[8] Which schools one gets admitted to and which positions of employment one gets are determined supposedly on the basis of one's merit. Hard work, effort, and innate intellectual and other talents and abilities that are developed are rewarded through your merit. Academic merit is determined on the basis of standardized test results, grades in competitive classes in secondary schools or other presumably neutral and objective measurements.

Is the lack of achievement on standardized tests and other measurements by BIPOC (black, indigenous, people of color) an illustration of these groups' lack of abilities and effort as our systems of merit assumes? How do we account for the lack of achievement of low-income and minority students (non-Asian minorities) and the differential distributional effects of that lack of achievement? The myth of America is that if you try hard enough, your hard work will permit you to succeed at the highest levels. That hard work will result in admission to institutions of higher education, lucrative occupations, and power and influence in society. It's your *choice* to succeed. With that description of the distribution of benefits in society, we are forced to conclude that the students who don't go on to college and end up without economic rewards just didn't try hard enough and/or didn't have the ability to succeed.[9] But the fact is social, economic, political inequities in and around the educational system put barriers in the way of low income and minority students that preclude most of them from achieving in the educational, and subsequently, the economic system. Consequently, they are then relegated to an inferior status in society. The educational system is reinforcing the system of hierarchy, not alleviating it.

[7] Anderson (1999), p. 312.

[8] Michael Sandel (2020) makes a very interesting argument about meritocracy in his recent book *The Tyranny of Merit*. He argues that our current system of merit justifies vast amounts of inequality in income, social status, and power. In this paper, I am not advocating a fairer version of meritocracy; rather I am arguing that the degree to which we do provide opportunities, positions, and incomes on the basis of merit (competence), those systems ought to be open to all on a fair basis .

[9] This is what Charles A. Murray in the infamous book *The Bell Curve* advanced.

The myth of America's meritocracy is that individuals are responsible for their own choices, their own success, and consequently those suffering from a lack of educational and economic success are merely suffering the consequences of their or their parents' bad choices. The school choice movement has been pushing this approach to solving the inequities in the educational system. These solutions are premised on the idea of "choice," and specifically that parents should have choices and those choices will result in better outcomes for their children. School choice has been the preferred solution to the problems of the educational crisis in states, such as Arizona. A second account of the lack of success of those suffering from the achievement gap is that they are merely suffering misfortunes. In terms of political philosophy, the first account, the choice account, aligns with libertarians' theories of justice and the second is endorsed by contemporary egalitarian theorists.

Rejecting both these accounts, I will argue that there are social structural impediments that limit individuals' capacities to simply "make better choices," and consequently the lack of achievement is not just a matter of misfortune and certainly not merely attributable to bad choices of the individuals in those communities. Building on the work of Iris Marion Young and Elizabeth Anderson on the nature of justice and responsibility,[10] I will argue that the inequalities in the educational system are perpetuated by unjust structural background conditions. Those unjust background conditions severely diminish the opportunities of some individuals and communities in our society. Those diminished opportunities in the current educational system result in harms to those who are mostly poor, and mostly people of color.[11] Inequalities of opportunities falling on some due to race, gender, and/or class are the subject of an egalitarian account of justice[12] and democracy. The subject of egalitarian justice, Anderson reminds us, is eradicating oppression which results from unequal opportunities. At minimum, egalitarian justice attempts to ensure that individuals have equal opportunities over essential capacities and to advocate the equal moral worth of person.[13] I want to argue that the differential educational achievement of low-income mostly minority students is a result of educational inequalities and differential treatment that result from structural injustices. What I will argue is that many suffer from inequalities of opportunity in the educational system that result from background structural conditions and that those structural conditions constitute injustices. That they are injustices is, sometimes difficult, if not impossible, to see. Often there is no obvious person or policy causing the limitations on their opportunities, and hence the limitations are without wrongdoers, specific individuals or groups, perpetrating them. Nevertheless, these structural injustices limit the opportunities in education and result in lower paying and lower influence careers in the economy, and a lesser voice in the democratic political processes. Therefore, this background structural system perpetuates academic inferiority for the poor and

[10] Young (2010) and Anderson (1999).

[11] Darling-Hammond (2001).

[12] Anderson (1999).

[13] Anderson (1999), p. 312.

minorities. It is important to emphasize that I don't deny that some of the harms or the lack of opportunities that any individual or community faces may result from specific government policies and practices and/or corporate agents. They do. But it is important to recognize that the limitations are a mix of those more explicit racist practices and more subtle ones that are harder to detect and trace, social norms about the expectations for certain groups or historical legacies from long ago of explicit racism, to mention some examples.

There are a number of harms that result from these structural injustices. One that is critical to democratic equality is a dignitary harm—the inability to stand up as an equal with other citizens who live without these limitations on them. Individuals who find themselves with these restricted opportunities, not because of their choices, which affect their economic, social, and ultimately political status in society, suffer a dignitary harm as a result. Because of the network of background circumstances limiting their "opportunity set",[14] they are not able to stand up as equals with other citizens who live without these limitations on the social conditions of freedom. Moreover, given that their restrictions often result from invisible background circumstances, their loss of agency is even more pernicious without obvious wrongdoers perpetrating wrong against them. This paper is focused not merely on the issue of structural injustice but on who should take responsibility, and why—this is the politics of responsibility. I argue that since these structural conditions are a result of social and political forces, they are all of our responsibility to eradicate them.

1 Educational [In]Justice and Responsibility

The disparities in educational attainment of the poor and minorities in the United States is widely recognized and met with concern but not necessarily regarded as an injustice. With the systems of merit admission to most institutions of higher learning in the United States, the assumption is that everyone is eligible to strive for these sought-after spots. The myth continues that everyone is in the position to achieve this merit, namely, high test scores on standardized tests, requisite advanced coursework including, for example, Advanced Placement courses and other opportunities. As part of this mythology there is the embedded notion that people are personally responsible for their choices and that their lack of ability to attain merit admission to institutions of higher learning and/or lucrative professions and influence in society is based on their own choices. This popular understanding of the problem of unequal educational attainment is the *personal responsibility model.* Under the personal responsibility account, individuals are responsible for their educational achievement and the resulting life outcomes. The assumption of the model is that we are all free actors with the same or roughly the same capacity to make better or worse choices, and consequently, it is no one's fault but the individual's if he or she

[14]Young (2010), p. 19.

make choices that lead to underachievement in education and in career. It is the behavior of individuals, it is argued, that puts them at relative disadvantage, or in harm's way, not, therefore, because of an injustice against them. Relying on the personal responsibility model, many educational reformers have successfully argued for school choice, lobbying for vouchers for private schools and funding for charter schools. These are supposed choices that the poor and minority communities can avail themselves of, and their decision not to do so makes them responsible for the outcomes.

Holding adults responsible for their decisions is a critical aspect of respect for individual agency and autonomy. The personal responsibility model can be seen as protecting that important value. States that do not value individuals' autonomy dictate what people do without regard to individuals' decisions and their own perceived interests. Treating adults as children as paternalism does—not competent to make choices, without real agency—is another way of not respecting autonomy. That said, it is only intelligible to hold individuals responsible when their decisions and options are to some extent in their control. To what extent does it make sense to claim low-income inner-city minorities, or rural farmworkers, or Native Americans living on remote reservations have the capacity to attain the measure of merit that the system rewards people for—do they actually have the choice? And, of course, the directly involved individuals are children, very young children who miss out on the scaffolding to reach these high levels of educational achievement and cannot recover no matter how hard they try.

As opposed to our partner industrialized countries in Europe and Asia where educational funding tends to be centralized and equal, in the United States the funding is radically unequal and substantially along racial lines.[15] In the US "the wealthiest 10% of school districts in the United States spend nearly 10 times more than the poorest 10%, and spending ratios of 3 to 1 are common within states."[16] Minority students are concentrated in the poorest schools whereas most white suburban schools are more highly funded.[17] But beyond merely the funding disparity there are other structural obstacles in the way of minority children's achievement. Consider some of these findings, all found in a recent study:

1. Schools serving more students of Color are less likely to offer advanced courses and GATE programs than schools serving mostly White populations. Additionally, students of Color are less likely than their White peers to be enrolled in those courses and programs within schools that have those offerings.
2. Preschool teachers are more likely to look for signs of challenging behavior of young Black children—especially young Black boys than young White boys.
3. Black children are disproportionately likely to be suspended from preschool than their White peers.

[15] https://edbuild.org/content/23-billion.

[16] Darling-Hammond (2001), p. 1.

[17] https://edbuild.org/content/23-billion.

4. Black students with high math performance in fifth grade are unlikely to be placed in algebra in eighth grade.
5. Students of Color in schools located in disinvested communities are less likely to receive course work targeted at grade appropriate standards, reflect higher-level cognitive demand and are meaningfully engaging and relevant (Santos and Haycock 2016).
6. Black and Latinx students are provided less rigorous feedback about their work from classroom teachers than White students (Harper et al. 2012).
7. Schools serving mostly students of Color are more likely to be taught by out-of-field and novice teachers (Bromberg and Christina 2016).
8. The provision of a stable teacher workforce is less likely to occur in schools with the highest enrollments of students of Color.
9. Schools serving mostly students of Color have lower quality or fewer resources than schools serving largely White populations, even within the same district.
10. Students of Color are more likely to attend school where more than 50% of teachers were absent for more than 10 days.
11. Students of Color are more likely to attend a school with an SRO, but not a school counselor, than White students.
12. Although Black students are more likely to be disciplined for harassment or bullying in schools than their White peers, Black students are disproportionately likely to be victims of harassment or bullying in school on the basis on their race, sex or disability than their White peers.
13. Predominantly White and middle-class students enrolled in private and suburban public high schools are being awarded higher grades—critical in the competition for college admission—more than their urban public-school counterparts with no less talent or potential (The Hechinger Report).[18]

Across a number of metrics, from school funding, teacher quality, teacher pay, quality curriculum, facilities, advanced programs, higher pay for teachers, to smaller class sizes, the better infrastructure are all concentrated in mostly white higher income neighborhoods.

This is not to say that the parents and students have no agency, but even if there are free alternative public schools that they could choose, there is no guarantee that those options would be better in their neighborhoods. Additionally, where there are options there is not always transportation to and from those schools. For parents without their own transportation or with long hours of work, it is all but impossible for them to get students to these alternative schools. Data on district funding across the country has confirmed that high-poverty schools receive less money than more

[18] From 24 Examples of Systemic Inequities Experienced by Students of Color and Students from Under-Resourced Communities in U.S. Schools.

affluent schools even within the same district and across districts.[19] Since the schools tend to be funded on the basis of property taxes, all the schools in areas with lower property values will be underfunded relative to the higher property tax areas. These parents are not in the same "choice" situation as middle-class suburbanites with better funded schools and more educational options. The topology of harms that low-income and minority students suffer includes the educational harms that come from not having a resourced school, precluding them from educational and occupational attainment; the psychological harms that result from the feelings of helplessness about lack of opportunities—the harm of lack of agency; the economic harm of a life without economic rewards that follow students who achieve at higher levels; the dignitary harm that comes from knowing that one is viewed as inferior to others in society who have more opportunities for themselves and their children. And finally, there is the psychic harm of society blaming them for their lack of achievement.

2 Bad Luck, Injustice, and Responsibility

It is disingenuous and demeaning to claim that students straddled with all these obstacles are personally responsible for their educational achievement and their life prospects that result. Since it is widely accepted that individuals should only be responsible for choices and outcomes that are in their control, it is not fair that individuals be blamed for conditions outside their control. Being in control or not is, of course, a matter of degree. Nevertheless, we can recognize when something is clearly in one's control and not in one's control. The harms of the educational system, particularly for low-income minorities living in underfunded and under-resourced schools, cannot justifiably be attributed to the individuals suffering those outcomes. They are not responsible for those harms.

Another approach to understanding the inequalities of the educational system and their differential impact on some groups is to conceive of those harms as matters of bad luck. Elements of individuals' situations that disadvantage them but are not in their control should, according to liberal egalitarian theorists, be compensated—they are injustices since they disadvantage vis-à-vis others in society. Egalitarian theorists, such as Ronald Dworkin and others, argue that those attributes or characteristics that disadvantage individuals and are not in their control are matters of bad luck. The poor and minorities are stuck in communities without good schools, investments in public infrastructures such as libraries, economic development, and even unequal goods are unlucky. Another approach to their misfortune is to ignore those differences and to suggest that these individuals are unlucky to not have attributes that would allow them to succeed on the standards of merit in this society. This argument would say it isn't their fault that they don't score higher on

[19] Bireda and Chait (2011); Equity and Excellence Commission (2013); Hall and Ushomirsky (2010).

the SAT or ACT and they shouldn't be radically disadvantaged because of that trait or attribute. It is no fault of their own as the personal responsibility model would suggest; it is, rather, a matter of bad luck that they find themselves in these circumstances or without attributes that the society rewards. Being a member of a minority group or even being female are characteristics that can disadvantage individuals, making them "unlucky" in the social system, and thereby receiving fewer "goods" than others. Luck egalitarians focus on the characteristics or attributes of persons to explain why they are disadvantaged, and the injustice is in terms of the unequal distribution of goods. Their disadvantage might be through disability or not having characteristics that are valued in the social system, e.g., being intelligent, attractive, athletic. According to Dworkin and other luck egalitarians, being disadvantaged in the social system by attributes beyond one's control is unjust.[20]

This account of the harms as products of misfortune is also flawed. At least it does not blame the harms on the victims as the personal responsibility model does. But does it make sense to focus on characteristics or attributes of individuals that work to their disadvantage and then compensate them for those characteristics or attributes as the luck egalitarian supposes? On this account, the poor and minorities are unfortunate to live in areas without good schools and other amenities requisite for advancement and achievement; and/or they are unfortunate for not having the attributes to do well on standardized tests and other measurement that this society values. This view conceives of egalitarian justice as essentially about how goods are distributed in society, how much goods people have in relation to others. Anderson in "What is the Point of Equality?" rightly objects to this approach to egalitarian justice focusing on attributes and distributions, since it looks like justice is a matter of "taking pity" on persons with the "bad luck" attributes that disadvantage them. Anderson argues that egalitarianism should be interested in how those distributions affect social relations, making some inferior to others and affecting their opportunities. Luck egalitarians suppose that the point of egalitarianism is to ensure that "losers in the natural lottery" not be disadvantaged by those features that are outside their control. Furthermore, it assumes that the "unlucky" attributes will disadvantage, whatever the social situation.

Starting with the second point, that unlucky attributes will disadvantage and limit one's capabilities, whatever the social situation, Anderson points out that "[o]ne's capabilities are a function not just of one's fixed personal traits and divisible resources, but of one's mutable traits, social relations and norms, and the structure of opportunities, public goods, and public spaces"[21] Focusing on the attributes as fixed traits that "inevitably" affect one's capacities misses how these other factors can and do affect individuals' capacities. Capacities are a measurement of what one is free to do, what it is accessible for one to do and be, and what opportunities are open to one. For example, consider many disabilities that do not fix individuals' capabilities in the way Dworkin implies. Being wheelchair bound can be

[20] Dworkin (1981).

[21] Anderson (1999), p. 319.

ameliorated by ramps and elevators, and laws and norms requiring nondiscrimination. Or alternatively, social and environmental structures can negatively impact wheelchair bound persons' lives by limiting their physical opportunities to get access to workplaces and schools and by not prohibiting discrimination of the disabled. Being a Black child in the educational system that conceives Black children's misbehavior as signs of social deviancy leads to over policing that behavior. This reaction has to do with norms about race and social relationship of superiority and inferiority—it isn't fixed in the structure. The background social structures can make an attribute, such as being a Black child, a disadvantage or not. Moreover, as Iris Marion Young rightly notes, Dworkin fails to distinguish "between the causes of relative disadvantage," those that are simply misfortune, and "those that result from social organizations and processes."[22] Many attributes that disadvantage individuals are a result of social organizations and processes; race and gender, for instance, are not immutably disadvantaging. They are attributes which for a variety of social/historical reasons make persons disadvantaged under the current social system. Race and gender are not simply misfortunes as having a serious and extremely debilitating genetic disorder can be.

Another related case to be addressed is that of social norms. Given social norms about gender roles of caregiving and appropriate career choices, women are disadvantaged, both from the facts that certain roles are gendered (for example caregiving), and are thereby low paying. Pitying women for their disadvantage and compensating them, by giving them SNAP benefits, for instance, does nothing to change the social system that limits them and limits their capacities, nor does it change the position of inferiority they experience in society. Just having a little more money does not change one's capacity to achieve: what is needed is changing the background conditions that one might access higher education and the social mobility that goes with it. Nor does having more resources affect the social norms, negative stereotypes about a group's abilities, that often trap minorities in inferior roles in society.

The second objection to luck egalitarianism is its focus solely on the distribution of goods. Egalitarian justice, according to Anderson, focuses on disrupting hierarchical systems of people, some superior and some inferior, that lead to oppression, and on the positive side, seeking social orders where people can "stand in relation of equality".[23] On this view of egalitarian justice, it is about destroying systems of privilege and ensuring that everyone has the social conditions for freedom. Just conceiving the problem as one of minorities, or the poor not getting as many goods, doesn't change all the background limitations on individuals. It should matter that people can stand in relations of equality, not oppressed, or marginalized or exploited. As discussed earlier, one critical way in which individuals can experience inferiority is when they do not have the same opportunities as others to seek higher education and the careers and power that education opens up. Where there is unequal

[22] Young (2010), p. 28.

[23] Anderson (1999), p. 313.

access to quality schools, libraries, outdoor public spaces for one's children, healthy food, those affected do not have the same social conditions of freedom as others in wealthy neighborhoods with that access. These conditions marginalize the communities who suffer these deficits. Dworkin's framing of the target misses the social structure and institutional contexts, the social norms within which the distributional inequality occurs and does nothing to change those social conditions. Seeing people as having traits that inhibit what capabilities they have in society and then compensating them, treating them as objects of pity or misfortune, does not address the sources of their incapacity, nor does it allow them to stand up as equals. Many of the obstacles to individuals' opportunities are structured in the background conditions in which people find themselves. They are "trapped" in relationships of inequality vis-à-vis those with more opportunities who don't face the same structural barriers. Just providing individuals with compensation, but not addressing the social structures that enable and perpetrate these disadvantages, is to perpetuate the cycle of inferiority or inequality in relation to those who do not face those limitations on their opportunities.

The luck egalitarian's answer to responsibility for harms of the educational system focuses on the wrong source of inequality—unlucky characteristics—and the wrong target for rectifying the inequality—distribution of goods. Neither focus tackles the social structural conditions that perpetuate unequal outcomes and limit the individuals' capacities to be and do things that others in society can.

3 Structural Injustice and Responsibility

What affects the ability of low income and minority students to achieve at the same level of more well-off white students? Who or what is responsible for their situation? Looking at the characteristics of schools, neighborhoods, and people where none of the students go on to institutions of higher education and others where all students do, shows a distinct pattern. From unequal funding, ill-equipped and untrained teachers, inferior curriculum, over-disciplining, crumbling buildings, to schools in communities without grocery stores, to higher levels of toxins in the environment, minority communities have many obstacles to contend with. Low-income minorities are oppressed by these social structures; namely, the background practices, policies, norms, and institutions which have perpetuated patterns of underachievement for those students in those communities. Given these practices, policies, and institutions, these students are relegated to an inferior position in relation to the white students who do not have those obstacles. Since these conditions are not necessarily caused by specific individuals or policies, they are difficult to see as injustices. Unlike race-based segregation where the impetus of school segregation and the funding discrepancies were based on explicit racist ideology on the part of legislators for example, these other background social structures are harder to trace and determine their pedigree, and harder to detect. But the harms from this *de facto* segregation of schools and neighborhoods results from human-created and maintained societal arrangements and, therefore, constitute social/political wrongs.

"Social structures" include the background conditions, rules, policies, practices, and norms which govern individual actions, collective actions, and government actions. When social structures unfairly constrain or limit some people's opportunities and their capabilities *vis à vis* others in society, they create structural injustices. "Capabilities" refers to the set of valuable functioning—e.g., being well-nourished, having control over some property, being educated—that a person can effectively access. Mere freedom to consider these functionings is not sufficient; the key is effective freedom to choose among them and thereby to choose the life that one values.[24]

Egalitarian justice on this account is concerned with equality of capabilities. Of course, egalitarian justice doesn't require that there must be equality of all capabilities. The capacity to race cars, be an expert skier, or take vacations to exotic lands are not ones that egalitarians are obligated to ensure. Following Anderson, "[P]eople are entitled to whatever capabilities are necessary to enable them to avoid or escape entanglement in oppressive social relationships…[and] they are entitled to the capabilities necessary for functioning as an equal citizen in a democratic state."[25] For Anderson this does cover a wide range of capabilities. She asks us to consider three aspects of individual functioning: "as a human being, as a participant in a system of cooperative production, and as a citizen of a democratic state"[26] One's capacity to function in these ways can be constrained not only by the distribution of resources but by "social relations and norms, and the structure of opportunities, public goods, and public spaces."[27] These constitute the social structure in which individuals function. Racist norms, for instance, can relegate groups both by others, teachers and administrators, and by the members themselves with internal obstacles undermining self-confidence to under achieve.[28] Historical racism can result in minority children internalizing norms of group inabilities to do, for example, academic work. Implicit bias on the part of teachers may lead them to over discipline and police Black boys, thereby setting them up for more discipline and punishment in the future. Background structures, which include institutionalizing historical discrimination, redlining or lending disparities, shape the current structure of opportunities for minorities to create wealth and stand up as equals with others not facing these obstacles.

Government policies and practices have shaped many of the background conditions in which public schools either flourish or languish. Laws that base school funding predominately on property taxes sounds neutral on their face. That is, it doesn't sound like a racist policy. But since there is a higher concentration of minorities in lower income and property value neighborhoods, it has the effect of giving

---

[24] Nussbaum (2003).

[25] Anderson (1999), p. 316.

[26] Anderson (1999), p. 317.

[27] Anderson (1999), p. 319.

[28] Kendi (2019), pp. 81–90.

less funds to schools in lower income minority neighborhoods. One of the central reasons that minority neighborhood property values are lower is the history of redlining and underinvestment by governments and private industries. There are multiple converging background conditions that create the current unjust social structure within which people function. Changing how schools are funded, not on the basis of property taxes, is an example of a policy that could start to ensure that all schools have the resources to secure equality of capacities. That alone, nevertheless, is not sufficient.

Nor can we suggest that the reasons for the composition of the neighborhoods are merely products of market forces and personal choices as they are often characterized. Segregated urban communities grew up in the 1940s when the government, through the FHA and VA, provided white middle-class families with home loans, enabling them to move to the suburbs of cities. Richard Rothstein in *The Color of Law* details how the FHA subsidized builders creating suburbs with the requirement that no houses be sold to African Americans.[29] "African American families" according to an ACLU study "were unable to access the same low-interest home loans as white families due to government sanctioned redlining, restrictive housing covenants, and discrimination, and were left stranded in the cities."[30] With the white flight to the suburbs, the city property values fell even more, creating a vicious cycle of devaluation. By 1970, the demographics of the country had drastically changed, and the typical northern African American was "more likely to live with other blacks than with whites." It is important to highlight that the "segregated living patterns are not a natural consequence of private choices but have been significantly influenced by government policies."[31]

The personal responsibility model and the luck egalitarian accounts of the discrepancies of the educational system ignore these background conditions, created by government policies, corporate practices, and other social practices, within which people act, and how those conditions limit the "opportunity set" of individuals, and how that affects individuals' abilities to stand as equals with others in society. Agency is having the capacity to act, not merely to overcome physical obstacles in one's way but having the physical, financial, geographical, and emotional resources to act in a particular way. The government does have complicity in creating and sustaining an unequal educational system but there are other forces at work as well. Corporations support discriminatory patterns of housing and the financial models for financing schools. Social norms maintain support for the notion that some kids can't succeed, and these norms are internalized by the communities themselves.

The social structures which encompass the background rules, policies, practices, and norms of society more severely limit the poor and members of minority groups' freedoms with lack of access and resources. The practical reality is that the

[29] Rothstein (2017).

[30] ACLU (2010).

[31] ACLU (2010).

existence of under-resourced schools, the declining income of low skill workers, the lack of social mobility, and the on-going racism all have a greater impact on poor minorities. The assumption that we are all free actors, with the same opportunity sets, voluntarily making informed choices in markets free from unjust background social structures is belied by the facts about the circumstances in which we act. Considering the above facts about why people live where they do, why some schools get much less resources than other schools, and why people in those communities "choose" the schools they do, *it is **simply** not accurate to suggest that those people are fully responsible for their educational achievement, and hence it is unjust to claim that they aren't meritorious*. When prescriptions for the problems of the educational system are focused on individuals taking personal responsibility, there is no recognition of the unjust structural conditions which limit and manipulate a person's range of choices. Nor is it adequate to suggest that people, minorities and the poor, who find themselves in these restricted circumstances, are just unlucky, and we should only compensate them for their bad luck but not change the structural conditions in which they act. These are human created and maintained structures, and people's standing in society will not be changed until the structures are changed.

4 Responsibility for Structural Injustices

Both of the earlier considered accounts of responsibility for harm, namely the personal responsibility and the luck egalitarian account, miss the essential focus on the background social structures that perpetuate some individuals' disadvantage in exercising their capacities to function as equals, such as to excel academically and move on into higher education and lucrative careers. The alternative account that I am advancing here is that the disadvantages to low-income and minority students in the educational system are the result of the social structures which put barriers (which are complex and varied) in individuals' option networks, closing off or not even providing certain options. Structural injustices are created by social structures—laws, rules, policies, practices, and social norms—that are largely products of human creation and maintenance.[32] The COVID-19 virus was a natural occurrence, but the responses to the pandemic, for example, which groups were most likely to get sick and who got treatment, are products of social institutions. The fact that low income and minority populations were disproportionately affected had to do with a number of social and political conditions: the fact that those populations are more likely to be in "essential services" roles (often low paid front line work) and were not able to work from home; that they didn't have ready access to medical treatment early on and medical professionals treated them differently from white patients; that they are more likely to live in multigenerational households; and that they are more likely to have co-morbidities, such as type-2 diabetes (a product of

[32] Haslanger (2012).

food deserts and other food injustices), all combined to make them more susceptible to serious outcomes of the disease.

Social structures can harm individuals in particular groups by narrowing the opportunities open to them, limiting their capacities to do and be various things.[33] The social structures, however, do not affect everyone the same way. The social structures we have noted here, such as, the policies that lead to red-lining and now the historical legacy of those practices, the undervalued properties in neighborhoods with high concentrations of minorities, the funding discrepancies among schools, and the over policing of minority children, only affect some, mostly poor and minority populations. Students in these neighborhoods without schools with quality teachers, advanced classes, and the other ingredients for achieving the measurements for meritorious success, can't achieve or at the least must struggle enormously to do so. All these background conditions limit the opportunities for students, making them unequal to others in society who are not limited by these social structures. Their capacities are diminished because of the social structures. The inequalities among individuals in society are socially created and maintained, and they relegate minorities to an inferior position. The constrained positions are products of social collective arrangements, even if they are historical byproducts of prior racism. Unlike being born with an unknown genetic disorder that affects one's opportunities (such a condition is bad luck, let's say), living in a historically redlined neighborhood with unequal funding is a product of social processes and could be reformed.

Although it is correct that individuals do make choices in these constrained circumstances, they are not, for example, coerced, but given their circumstances circumscribed by the background conditions not of their choosing, they are significantly constrained vis-à-vis others in their society. External conditions, for example, poorly funded schools and underpaid teachers, inadequate transportation, and internal conditions, (for example, racist norms about abilities) put constraints on their capacities to function. Those structural obstacles can undermine their agency and their ability to stand as equals in society. This has an effect on them to stand as equals in the democracy. The limited opportunity set that results constrains their essential capacities because these people do not have access to sufficient levels of functionings; hence they do not have the social conditions of freedom. Injustice in this sense concerns more than simply the fact that people suffer fates they do not deserve. It concerns how institutional rules and social interactions conspire to narrow the options that many have. Quoting Iris Young:

> Social structures do not constrain in the form of direct coercion of some individuals over others; they constrain more indirectly and cumulatively as blocking possibilities. Part of the difficulty of seeing structure, moreover, is that we do not experience particular institutions, particular material facts, or particular rules as themselves sources of constraint; the constraints occur through the joint action of individuals within institutions and given physical conditions as they affect our possibilities.[34]

[33] Sen (1992).

[34] Young (2010), p. 55.

These constraints are injustices as opposed to disadvantages that are entitled to be redressed. Egalitarian justice requires not that those individuals have the same resources, but that individuals have the social conditions of freedom to function as equal citizens in the democracy. When there are social and political structural barriers, particularly when those barriers are the result of governmental policies and other collective arrangements that prevent people from having the social conditions of freedoms, those limitations on their opportunities are injustices. Social structures are unjust when they limit opportunities, limit capabilities and result in perpetuating patterns of unequal distribution of harms. Those structures also result in some being inferior to others since they don't have the same capacities to live the life they value. When the capabilities we are addressing are the ones required to "merit" entrance into higher education and professions which are well-compensated the harm is particularly egregious. The narrative in society is that all who are meritorious can succeed when in fact many, particularly low income and minorities, are barred from achieving.

Those injustices, however, are not necessarily perpetrated by individual wrongdoers but rather by the collective arrangements of society. Many of the actions of individuals and even the government are not aimed at limiting opportunities or harming groups, they are working within the practices and norms of that structure. This is one of the reasons that it is not always possible to point out specific intentions of racists, for example, when heavy concentrations of pollutants end up in minority communities. The company siting a waste may well act within the guidelines laid out for the processes of picking a waste site, for instance, and not with specific racist intent. The social structures are the largely invisible framework in which we act. The background social structures, however, are products of human agency; for instance, racist motivation led to redlining and disinvestment in inner city minority neighborhoods. And, patriarchy supported gendered occupations and the low pay that went with them. Nevertheless, many of these background social conditions are not now necessarily supported by active racist or sexist actors. Redlined neighborhoods are no longer redlined but the legacy of those historical injustices persists, including the fact that minority families have much less wealth and so less wealth to pass on across generations than white families, due to the consequences of not providing housing loans to black families and investment in minority neighborhoods. Further, there are other government policies permitting the unequal funding of schools, and though the policy is facially neutral has a disproportionate impact on the poor and minorities.[35] The policy may not have been supported on a racist basis and in that way, they differ from directly racist or sexist policies—de jure segregation, for example. But the policy does have a differential impact on the poor and minorities that leads to injustices.

[35] Garcia and Aportela (2016).

5 Responsibility for Wrongs

Most theories of responsibility look for specific agents or collectives to hold responsible for the harm. As noted above, with these harms that result from the social structures, there are not necessarily identifiable wrongdoers who we can hold responsible for these injustices. There is not one identifiable person or group of persons who did some action that resulted in the harm and are thereby blameworthy for the harm. Many accounts of responsibility, particularly in the legal framework of criminal or tort law, are what are known as "liability" models.[36] There is a causal connection between someone doing or failing to do something that results in a harm to another person, which makes someone liable for blame for the harm. Who can we blame for all these minority students' poor scores on standardized tests? Students in particular communities don't attend higher education and find it difficult in the current economy to find jobs to live middle-class lifestyles. Who is responsible for the economic system's changes that no longer permit high school graduates the opportunity for decent employment? Who is to blame for the underinvestment in these neighborhoods, executives of banks and insurance companies who perpetrated redlining but are now long gone? These harms are not necessarily caused by any agents' intentional actions, consequently there is no individual or group responsible to hold accountable. If your theory of justice and responsibility only pertains to individual wrongdoings, then these structural cases go unaccounted for.

Theories of responsibility that focus on the guilty party who caused the harm or is liable for harm are backward-looking, assigning blame based on fault or liability to harm. But we also talk about "taking responsibility" for the future to ensure that harm or injustices do not occur. That approach doesn't ask whether anyone intended harm or injustice. Accounts of this type of responsibility are offered by Young, what she calls the "social connection model",[37] and what Darrel Moellendorf calls "social responsibility".[38] Both require us, as members of a political order, to collectively assume responsibility for changing the social structures that produce and reproduce these unjust outcomes. This is a shared responsibility of citizens to make these changes. As Young says:

> The social connection model finds that all those who contribute by their actions to structural processes with some unjust outcomes share responsibility for the injustice.... Being responsible in relation to structural injustice means that one has an obligation to join with others who share that responsibility in order to transform the structural processes to make their outcomes less unjust.[39]

This sense of responsibility doesn't replace the liability model, but is in addition to it. Living in a political society in which injustices occur because of social processes of society, whether they result from rules or practices or even norms, means that we

---

[36] Young (2010), p. 97.

[37] Young (2010), p. 96.

[38] Moellendorf (2014), p. 152-ff.

[39] Young (2010), p. 9.

are collectively responsible for those harms. Collectively through our institutions we maintain these processes, and we can change those that are contributing to inequalities.

Solving the problems of injustices inherent in the educational system requires that we change the background conditions that structure the relationships in society and not focus merely on individual bad actors. Again, quoting Young: "[P]romoting justice in social structure and their consequences implies restructuring institutions and relationships to *prevent* these threats to people's basic well-being."[40] With structural injustices the bad outcomes are a result of many social structures that function to oppress certain groups of people. In many of these students' cases they find themselves caught in a network of social structures that grossly disadvantage them, leaving them without the basic opportunities that others in society have—they result in them being oppressed by the social structure. If we acknowledge that those social structures oppress some groups in society, and if we are committed to a political theory that requires that everyone have the social conditions of freedom in terms of basic capabilities for well-being,[41] then we are collectively responsible to change those social structures that result in some people not having those social conditions for freedom. This is true whether we are personally benefiting from the injustices suffered by some groups. Society may not have to guarantee equality of resources, according to egalitarian justice, but society is obligated to ensure that people's basic capacities are roughly the same (at least for those capacities necessary for human well-being). There is a particular responsibility for redress if there are limitations on freedom that are a result of social arrangements created and sustained by the economic and political system.

The social system can be changed; as John Rawls noted "The social system is not an unchangeable order beyond human control but a pattern of human action."[42] Through structural reform we can change institutional rules, social practices, structural relationships, and the social background conditions that lead to limited opportunity sets, such as those we see in the educational system. We are responsible for preventing those injustices that are a product of our social structures even if we do not intend those oppressive outcomes. Changing the social structure so it does not produce unfair outcomes in one domain will have effects in others. For example, expanding capacities to participate in processes where decisions are made, having access to political power, education, and other opportunities that lead to wealth, will change the distributional outcomes, and provide agency to those with the expanded capacities. Changing the policies for magnet schools (higher resourced schools that attract students from all over) and incentives for highly qualified teachers, ensuring every school has an academically challenging curriculum and access to standardized testing preparations, and combating the stereotypes about certain groups and their abilities, are some of the changes to the social structure particularly in regard

---

[40] Young (2010), p. 34.

[41] Anderson (1999), p. 316.

[42] Rawls (1999), p. 88.

to the government's role that would make significant changes to children's ability to achieve. Larger societal changes around alleviating gross income inequality, lack of affordable housing and childcare, and so on would also greatly impact the opportunities of families in low income and minorities neighborhoods.

6 Summary and Conclusion

Acknowledging that harms perpetrated by the background social structure within which individuals act in relation to the educational system are wrongful matters of justice is to identify them as violations against what people are owed, what they deserve. People deserve equality, meaning, among other things, that they deserve equal opportunities for developing their capabilities to live good lives. Egalitarian justice of this sort is not so concerned about equality of resources. Rather the questions are whether individuals have the capacities to live meaningful lives or whether their opportunities are constrained by our collective human arrangements. I have focused to a large extent on the background conditions which limit people's opportunities and abilities, which result in these wrongful differential impacts.

Importantly, I pointed out that these harms are not all the result of bad actors, racists trying to perpetrate harm on certain populations, for example. They are wrongs without wrongdoers. Rather, many, maybe most, are products of agents within the processes of the social structure advancing their own interests. Indeed, some of those unwittingly perpetrating harms are acting within systems which are products of historical structural injustices in society that cause populations to be vulnerable to these abuses. Again, the actors themselves did not create those injustices. These injustices result from the social structures within which actors act. Individuals who find themselves with these unequal capacities, vis-à-vis other actors in society, are oppressed by these circumstances. These circumstances affect their agency, which in turn affects their moral standing in society; they cannot stand as equal citizens to others. That is critical to democracy that citizens stand as equal to one another. All these effects result in dignity harm to the victims. Egalitarian theories of justice are concerned with ensuring that individuals can stand up as equals with one another. These limitations on individuals' capacities make that difficult or impossible.

Claims of injustice are linked with calls for responsibility, determining who owes the debt or treatment to another. If we acknowledge that the current patterns of distribution of burdens, opportunities, and powers are unfair, who is responsible for ensuring that the wrongful harms are not perpetrated going forward? Because so much of the structural injustices are not products of individual action, attributions of responsibility are resisted. There is not necessarily someone in particular or some single, identifiable government policy at fault for the unfair treatment of the poor and minorities. Traditionally, theories of responsibility have focused on the guilty party who caused the harm or is liable for harm. Accounts of responsibility are often backward-looking, assigning blame based on fault or liability to harm. Here I argued for a notion of collective responsibility for "taking responsibility" to prevent injustices going forward. This account of responsibility is to collectively assume responsibility for changing the social structures that produce and reproduce these unjust outcomes. It is the shared responsibility of citizens in a democracy to make these changes.

References

24 Examples of Systemic Inequities Experienced by Students of Color and Students from Under-Resourced Communities in U.S. Schools. Great Lakes Equity Center

ACLU (2010) Unshared bounty: how structural racism contributes to the creation and persistence of food deserts. https://digitalcommons.nyls.edu/cgi/viewcontent.cgi?article=1002&context=racial_justice_project. Accessed 8/20

Anderson E (1999) What's the point of equality? Ethics 109(2):287–337

Bireda S, Chait R (2011) Increasing teacher diversity: strategies to improve the teacher workforce. Center for American Progress

Bromberg, Marni and Christina Theorkas (2016) Meandering toward graduation: transcript outcomes of high school graduates. MeanderingTowardGraduation_EdTrust_April2016.pdf

Darling-Hammond L (2001) Inequality in teaching and schooling: how opportunity is rationed to students of color in America. In: Smedley BD, Stith AY, Colburn L et al, Institute of Medicine (US) (eds) The right thing to do, the smart thing to do: enhancing diversity in the health professions: summary of the symposium on diversity in health professions in honor of Herbert W. Nickens, M.D. National Academies Press (US), Washington (DC). Available from: https://www.ncbi.nlm.nih.gov/books/NBK223640/

Dworkin R (1981) What is equality? II. Equality of resources. Philos Public Aff 30(10):283–345

Equity and Excellence Commission (2013). https://oese.ed.gov/files/2020/10/equity-excellence-commissionreport.pdf

For Each and Every Child 2020. https://oese.ed.gov/files/2020/10/equity-excellence-commission-report.pdf

Garcia D, Aportela A (2016) State of Latino Arizona: sparking a community conversation about school funding. https://outreach.asu.edu/sites/default/files/State_of_Latino_AZ_2016.pdf

Hall D, Ushomirsky N (2010) Close the hidden funding gaps in our schools. K-12 Policy. Education Trust. https://eric.ed.gov/?id=ED511871

Harper K et al (2012) Students' race and Teachers' social support affect the positive feedback bias in public schools. J Educ Psychol 104(4):1149

Haslanger S (2012) Resisting reality: social construction and social critique. Oxford University Press

https://edbuild.org/content/23-billion

https://www.phoenixnewtimes.com/news/segregation-phoenix-schools-separate-and-unequal-10295728

Jefferson T (1950) 79. A bill for the more general diffusion of knowledge, 18 June 1779. In: Boyd JP (ed) The Papers of Thomas Jefferson, vol. 2, 1777 – 18 June 1779. Princeton University Press, Princeton, NJ, pp 526–535

Jefferson T (1975) Letters of Thomas Jefferson. Sanbornton Bridge Press

Kendi IX (2019) How to be an antiracist. One World, New York

Moellendorf D (2014) The moral challenge of dangerous climate change. Cambridge University Press, Cambridge

Nussbaum M (2003) Capabilities as fundamental entitlements: Sen and social justice. Fem Econ 9(2–3):33–59

Rawls J (1999) A theory of justice, Revised ed. Harvard University Press, Cambridge

Rothstein R (2017) The color of law. Norton and Company, New York

Sandel M (2020) The tyranny of merit. Farrar, Straus and Giroux, New York
Santos JL, Haycock K (2016) Fixing america's college attainment problems: it's about more than affordability critical considerations for any new federal-state partnership. Education Trust
Sen A (1992) Inequality reexamined. Harvard University Press, Cambridge
Young IM (2010) Responsibility for justice. Oxford University Press, Cambridge

Joan McGregor is a professor of philosophy and head of the Philosophy faculty in the School of Historical, Philosophical and Religious Studies at Arizona State University and a Senior Sustainability Scholar in the Julie Ann Wrigley Global Institute of Sustainability. McGregor researches and publishes in legal philosophy, bioethics, and social and political philosophy.

The Black Scare

Eric Smaw

Abstract Recently, many conservative politicians have launched state propaganda campaigns against college and university professors who articulate and defend liberal positions, accusing them of teaching Critical Race Theory (CRT) in an effort to demonize "White" people and make European American students feel ashamed of being "White." While there is no evidence of such a cabal, many Republican state legislatures have passed prohibitions against teaching Critical Race Theory in K-12 public schools and in public colleges and universities. Like the loyalty laws during the Red Scare, the anti-CRT laws violate academic free speech and freedom of association. In what follows, I argue that college and university professors ought to sue states that pass anti-CRT laws. The case of *Pernell et al v. Florida Board of Governors* in which college students and professors sued the state of Florida successfully gives me reason to think that such an approach will be successful. However, in light of the Supreme Court's willingness to overturn fifty years of precedent in the case of *Dobbs v. Jackson Women's Health Organization*, professors cannot simply rely on the courts to protect academic free speech and freedom of academic association. In fact, I think lawsuits are just an immediate remedy. A long term solution, I argue, is for college students and professors to become civically engaged, organized, and pressure Congress to pass bills protecting academic free speech and freedom of academic association. This will ensure that college and university professors are not punished or fired for what they teach, lecture on, or publish.

E. Smaw (✉)
Rollins College, Winter Park, and Florida State University, School of Medicine, Orlando Campus, Orlando, FL, USA
e-mail: esmaw@rollins.edu

G. A. Babst et al. (eds.), *Liberal Constitutionalism and its Contemporary Challenges*, AMINTAPHIL: The Philosophical Foundations of Law and Justice 12, https://doi.org/10.1007/978-3-031-53602-1_9

1 Introduction

President John F. Kennedy taught us that "the great enemy of truth is very often not the lie--deliberate, contrived and dishonest--but the myth--persistent, persuasive, and unrealistic. Too often we hold fast to the cliches of our forebears. We subject all facts to a prefabricated set of interpretations. We enjoy the comfort of opinion without the discomfort of thought" (Kennedy 1962). Of course, Kennedy was not referring to the benign myths we find in fairytales, wherein the knight slays the dragon and the people of the town live happily ever after, but to the dangerous myths that gave rise to the Salem Witch Trials, the Red Scare, and the Lavender Scare. Of course, it can be trying for Americans to learn that such atrocities occurred in the United States, both before and after we established ourselves as a liberal democracy. But, although they are hard, such lessons must be learned. For, they teach us that a strong democracy requires a liberally educated and civically engaged citizenry, and this lesson is well worth the small discomfort that comes from learning it. President John Adams explained why in the "Thoughts on Government," he wrote: "Laws for the liberal education of youth, especially of the lower class of people, are so extremely wise and useful, that, to a humane and generous mind, no expense for this purpose would be thought extravagant" (Adams 1776, p. 85). He continues: a country founded on a liberal education

> introduces knowledge among the people, and inspires them with a conscious dignity becoming freemen; a general emulation takes place, which causes good humor, sociability, good manners, and good morals to be general. That elevation of sentiment inspired by such a government, makes the common people brave and enterprising. That ambition which is inspired by it makes them sober, industrious, and frugal. You will find among them some elegance, perhaps, but more solidity; a little pleasure, but a great deal of business; some politeness, but more civility ...when you compare such a country with the regions of domination, whether monarchical or aristocratical, you will fancy yourself in Arcadia or Elysium (Adams 1776, p. 85).

I concur with Kennedy and Adams. Liberal education is essential for elevating the minds of the citizenry and thereby helping them to see the importance of the checks and balances that protect democracy from the tyrannical impulses of demagogues. By liberal education, I mean the habitual practice of truth-seeking and knowledge acquisition, subject to enlightenment skepticism and re-examination guided by the principles of logic and critical thinking. Such an education is valuable in its own right, for example, when one studies philosophy, and when it is pursued for practical purposes, for example, when one studies medicine. Either way, those who internalize a liberal education are less likely to be seduced by the propaganda that motivated the Salem Witch Trials, the Red Scare, and the Lavender Scare, much less persecute others based on unsubstantiated falsehoods. In what follows, I offer historical analyses of state propaganda campaigns against college and university professors who articulated and defended liberal positions during the Red Scare of the 1940s and 50s. I argue that the purposes of the Red Scare propaganda were to stigmatize college and university professors, force them out of American colleges and universities, and prosecute them in courts and congresses. I show that the propaganda campaigns during the Red Scare resulted in serious violations of academic free speech and freedom of association, which, of course, are necessary for providing a liberal education and pursuing individual and societal progress. Fortunately, state and federal courts have reached similar conclusions.

Unfortunately, however, many Republican politicians have not learned the lessons of the past. Some have launched state propaganda campaigns similar to those used during the Red Scare, only this time the myth is that college and university professors are teaching Critical Race Theory in an effort to demonize "White" people and make European American students feel ashamed of being "White." While there is no evidence of such a cabal, some Republican state legislatures have passed prohibitions against teaching Critical Race Theory in K-12 public schools and in colleges and universities. Like the loyalty laws during the Red Scare, the anti-CRT laws violate academic free speech and freedom of academic association. By academic speech, I simply mean the intellectual discourse that is necessary for educating students in college classrooms, publishing articles in academic journals, and presenting research at academic conferences. By academic association, I mean professional organizations and affinity groups that college and university professors join to enhance and advance their research and careers within colleges and universities. I argue that academic speech and academic association ought to be free from state censorship as long as they do not present a "clear and imminent danger" to others (Holmes 1919, *Abrams v US*). When academic speech and academic association are allowed without state censorship, they are free. Conversely, when the state restricts academic speech and academic association without first demonstrating that the speech in question has resulted in actual harm or will result in imminent harm, it violates the rights of college professors and students. For this reason, I argue that college and university professors ought to sue states that pass anti-CRT laws. The case of *Pernell et al v. Florida Board of Governors* in which college students and professors sued the state of Florida successfully gives me reason to think that such an approach will be successful, at least in the short term. However, in light of the Supreme Court's willingness to overturn fifty years of precedent in the case of *Dobbs v. Jackson Women's Health Organization*, professors cannot simply rely on the courts to protect academic free speech and freedom of academic association. For this reason, I conclude that college and university professors must become civically engaged, organized, and pressure Congress to pass bills protecting academic free speech and freedom of academic association. This will ensure that professors are not punished or fired for what they teach, lecture on, or publish.

2 The Red Scare: Red-ucators in American Colleges and Universities

In 1940, Bertrand Russell received an appointment letter offering him a professorship in mathematics at the City College of New York. This was a big deal because Russell was a renowned philosopher and public intellectual with writings on communism, religion, sexual liberation, marriage, and other matters of public interest.

Paradoxically, Russell's notoriety was also the reason why his appointment letter was rescinded. After all, when word of Russell's appointment offer spread to New York's religious conservatives, they fulminated against him in the press, calling his public scholarship a "Hitler-Stalin program of anti-religion" (Schrecker 1986, p. 76). Despite the backlash, Bertrand Russell was confirmed by the New York City Board of Education shortly after receiving his appointment letter; but the controversy was not over, not by a long shot.

After his confirmation, Jean Kay sued New York's Board of Education on the grounds that Russell's confirmation was illegal because his teachings were salacious and his character immoral, among other things (*Kay v. Bd. of Higher Education* 1940, p. 1). In an astonishing opinion, Judge J.E. McGeehan agreed, ruling that "there are certain basic principles upon which this government is founded. If a teacher, who is a person of [bad] moral character [and] is appointed by any authority, the appointment violates these essential prerequisites. One of the prerequisites of a teacher is good moral character" (*Kay v. Bd. of Higher Education* 1940, p. 3). McGeehan continues: the claim that "Mr. Russell has taught in his books immoral and salacious doctrines is amply sustained by the books concededly to be the writings of Bertrand Russell, which were offered in evidence. It is not necessary to detail here the filth which is contained in the books" (*Kay v. Bd. of Higher Education* 1940, p. 4). Rather, Judge McGeehan was satisfied by simply highlighting passages in which Russell challenged commonly held views on marriage and sex (Russell 1957, pp. 165–166), and sexual orientation (Russell 1932, p. 119). McGeehan concluded:

> the board of higher education of the city of New York in appointing Dr. Russell to the department of philosophy of the City College... to be paid by public funds, is in effect establishing a chair of indecency and in doing so has acted arbitrarily, capriciously and in direct violation of the public health, safety and morals of the people and of the petitioner's rights herein, and the petitioner is entitled to an order revoking the appointment of the said Bertrand Russell and discharging him from his said position (*Kay v. Bd. of Higher Education* 1940, p. 7).

Following the Russell controversy, the New York State Legislature charged the Rapp-Coudert Committee with discovering "the extent to which, if any, subversive activities may have been permitted to be carried on in the schools and colleges" in the state of New York (Schrecker 1986, p. 76). Immediately after receiving the charge, the Committee began looking for potential informants in the ranks of the faculty at City College, particularly those who would be willing to accuse their colleagues of participating in a communist plot to overthrow the U.S. government. They found the perfect informant in William Martin Canning, a history instructor and member of the Catholic Church. Since Canning was Catholic and presumably conservative, the Committee believed that he would be helpful to their investigation. Others had much harsher suspicions about Canning, calling him "a willing tool" who would testify against his "colleagues" and coworkers (Feffer 2019, pp. 177–178). The Committee's supposition about Canning's usefulness was correct. During his testimony, Canning accused "fifty-four" faculty of being members of the Communist Party (Schrecker 1986, p. 79). Not surprisingly, most of them denied the accusation. This part of their testimony was false, at least for some of them, but one can understand why they lied. After all, just ten days after Canning accused them of being communists, "the Board of Higher Education issued a resolution declaring that it would not retain" faculty who were "members of any Communist, Fascist, or Nazi group" (Schrecker 1986, pp. 79–80). Subsequently, it "suspended all the professors named by Canning… and prepared formal charges… in anticipation of the trials" to come (Schrecker 1986, p. 81).

New York was not the only state in which professors came under scrutiny, particularly after Congress passed the *Smith Act*. In short, the *Smith Act* made it illegal to teach, advocate, or to be a member of a group that advocated for the violent overthrowal of the United States government (*Smith Act* 1940, 54 Stat. 670, 671, title I, §§2-3). Thus, under the auspices of ridding American colleges and universities of communist subversives many states followed New York's lead. For example, in 1946, the Washington state legislature established the Canwell Committee to smoke out and expel communist professors from the faculty at the University of Washington. During its investigation, the Canwell Committee accused eleven professors of being communists. Some professors denied the accusation while others admitted they were communists but denied that they were part of a plot to attack the U.S. government. Either way, the outcome was the same, those who testified were fired for lying and subterfuge (Schrecker 1986, p. 98).

The three professors who refused to testify, Joseph Butterworth, Herbert Phillips, and Ralph Gundlach, were cited for contempt and threatened with imprisonment. After some legal wrangling, the state prosecutor declined to charge Joseph Butterworth. This did not matter to the university because he was fired immediately after the charges were dropped. Unlike Joseph Butterworth, Herbert Phillips was charged, tried, and acquitted in court. This didn't matter either. Phillips was fired shortly after he was acquitted. After they were both fired, a university spokesman explained that Butterworth and Phillips had "displayed dishonesty and incompetence because they had consistently followed the… 'party line,' that is to say, instructions emanating from Moscow, and they had neglected their duty to the university by spending their time at political meetings" (Schrecker 1986, p. 98). Unlike Butterworth and Phillips, Ralph Gundlach was charged, tried, convicted, and sentenced to thirty days in jail (Schrecker 1986, p. 96). This made it easy for the university administration to fire him.

Similar scenarios played out in many states throughout the country despite the fact that "faculty radicalism… simply did not exist in any organized form after the Second World War" (Schrecker 1986, p. 93). In fact, in *Bad Faith: Teachers, Liberalism, and the Origins of McCarthyism*, Andrew Feffer points out that "there had been no substantial evidence of incitement or indoctrination" in college and university classrooms (Feffer 2019, p. 47). Ironically, there was great organization and incitement on the other side. As Timothy Cain points out in "Little Red Schoolhouses?" "beginning in 1938, …both the Teachers Alliance of New York City and the American Education Association organized conservative teachers in opposition to their liberal and leftist colleagues" (Cain 2014, p. 127). Like Canning, many conservative educators accused their colleagues of being Communists, testified against them, and called for their books and articles to be banned from school curriculums (Cain 2014, p. 130). These activities are strikingly similar to the actions of groups like Moms for Liberty in the present day.

Recently, some colleges and universities have issued apologies and offered restitution to former faculty who lost their jobs during the Red Scare (Roberts 2017). This is not surprising because much of the "evidence" presented against them was based on remarkably dubious witness testimony. For example, some of the witnesses made wild and unsubstantiated accusations against reputable politicians, college presidents, and Supreme Court justices. For example, Elizabeth Dilling, a staunch anti-communist witness and author of *The Red Network: A "Who's Who" and Handbook of Radicalism for Patriots*, testified that Supreme Court Justice Louis Brandeis and Senator William Borah were communists (Schrecker 1986, p. 70). Similarly, J.P. Matthews testified that "Dwight Eisenhower, then President of Columbia University, was secretly harboring Communists" at the university (Schrecker 1986, p. 96). In recent years, evidence has emerged revealing that William Canning was coached by the Chair of the Rapp-Coudert Committee in order to bolster the "myth of classroom indoctrination" (Feffer 2019, p. 189).

Still, unlike some colleges and universities, Congress and state legislatures have not offered any apologies or restitution to those harmed by federal and state un-American activities committees. In fact, Florida State Senator Lauren Book is one of a small number of elected officials who are willing to apologize and give restitution. In March 2021, she introduced *SCR 244* in the Florida state legislature to get an acknowledgement of the "injustices perpetrated against the targets of the Florida Legislative Investigation Committee between 1956 and 1965 and to offer a formal and heartfelt apology to those whose lives, well-being, and livelihoods were damaged or destroyed by" the Committee (Book 2021, p. 4). The harms perpetrated by members of the Florida Legislative Investigation Committee included, targeting, intimidating, harassing, surveilling, and smearing the reputations of professors at the University of Florida, Florida A&M University, and the University of South Florida, and forcing more than thirty-five of them to resigned, be fired, and, in some case, face criminal prosecutions (Book 2021, p. 4). Despite this, the Florida state legislature stopped Senator Book's Bill in the Governmental Oversight and Accountability Committee. How ironic?

3 The Black Scare: Critical Race Theory in American Colleges and Universities

Even worse, the Florida state legislature has passed laws similar to the loyalty laws we saw during the Red Scare of the 1940s and 50s. For example, in April 2021, the Florida state legislature passed *HB 233* which requires the state Board of Education and Board of Governors to conduct an annual survey of professors at public colleges and universities in an effort to determine their political views. A year later, in March

2022, the Florida state legislature passed *HB 7* which prohibits Florida's K-12 public school teachers and public college and university professors from teaching anything deemed "Critical Race Theory" because it makes "White" students "feel guilt, anguish, and other forms of psychological distress" (Avila 2022, p. 4). Notice, however, that the philosopher J.S. Mill draws an important distinction between offense and harm. Offense occurs when one is annoyed, embarrassed, disgusted, distressed, or insulted by what another says or does. In *On Liberty*, Mill writes: "when a person disables himself, by conduct purely self-regarding, from the performance of some [normative] duty incumbent on him to the public, he is guilty of a social offense," and "no person ought to be punished" by law for social offenses [Mill 1859, p. 1094]. By contrast, harm occurs when one is injured, physically or reputationally, or loses rights or income by what another says or does. For example, we do not allow people to slander others because those who are slandered will suffer reputational damage and lose their jobs, incomes, or freedom as a result. More importantly, notice that feelings of guilt, anguish, embarrassment, disgust, insult, annoyance, distress, etc... are emotional responses to speech that one does not like. However, emotional responses to speech that one does not like do not rise to the level of harm. For, there are no economic or reputational damages, or loss of freedom.

Nevertheless, parents who believe that a professor has violated *HB 7* may bring a claim against him (*Pernell v Florida Board of Governors* 2022, p. 5). More importantly, if an investigation finds that a professor's

> instruction or training is inconsistent with the law, the Board of Governors commands state universities to take prompt action to correct the violation by mandating that the employee responsible for the instruction or training modify it to be consistent with the law, issuing disciplinary measures where appropriate and remove, by termination if appropriate, the employee if he fails or refuses to comply (*Pernell v Florida Board* 2022, p. 5).

Obviously, these bills are designed to suppress academic free speech because many professors will simply avoid teaching anything related to race, diversity, or equity. In fact, this is already happening. For example, in August of 2022, University of Central Florida Assistant Professor Jonathan Cox cancelled two of his sociology courses, *Race and Social Media*, and *Race and Ethnicity*. Not surprisingly, Dr. Cox was worried that *HB 7* "effectively banned him from discussing his ideas in class, and that teaching the courses could cost him his livelihood," especially since he does not have tenure (Golden 2022a, b). Professor Cox explained "it's not worth the risk… I'm completely unprotected…. Somebody who's not even in the class could come after me. Somebody sees the course catalog, complains to a legislator--next thing I know, I'm out of a job" (Golden 2022a, b).

Dr. Cox has good reason to be worried. In 2021, Professor Nicole Hannah-Jones, an African American female professor of Journalism and author of the *1619 Project*, was denied tenure by the Board of Trustees at the University of North Carolina (Robertson 2021). The Board's decision came as a shock to the academic community because Dr. Hannah-Jones is among the most recognized, accomplished, and celebrated professors in the country. For example, in 2017, she received a *MacArthur*

Foundation Fellowship; in 2019, she was awarded the *University of North Carolina Distinguished Professor Award*; in 2020, she received a *Pulitzer Prize* for her *1619 Project*; and, in 2022, she received the *NAACP Image Award*. These and other professional accomplishments coupled with the fact that Dr. Hannah-Jones was recommended for tenure and promotion by the Faculty Evaluation Committee at the University of North Carolina demonstrate that the Board's failure to approve her was motivated by something other than her qualifications (Robertson 2021).

Even worse, Dr. Hannah-Jones is not the only professor who has been denied tenure under suspicious circumstances. For example, in April 2023, "five professors at the New College of Florida were denied tenure--even though they had already received approvals at every other point in the process" of being awarded tenure (Moody 2023). The denial of their tenure is a result of conspicuous political appointments made to the Board of Trustees and Presidency of Florida New College. For example, in January of 2023, Governor Ron DeSantis appointed Chris Rufo, a conservative activist and the architect of the anti-CRT propaganda, to the Board of Florida New College. DeSantis also fired President Patricia Okker and installed Richard Corcoran, a former Republican member of the Florida House of Representatives, as President of the college. DeSantis has boasted that these changes are designed to make Florida New College the "Hillsdale College of the South" (Moody 2023). Additionally, Jeremy Redfern, a spokesman for Governor DeSantis, argued that DeSantis's policies "protects the open exchange of ideas by prohibiting teachers from forcing discriminatory concepts on students" (Golden 2022a, b). How Orwellian?

Florida politicians are not alone in passing policies to suppress academic free speech. Twenty-eight states have either passed or are in the process of passing similar anti-CRT legislation (Greene 2022). As a result, college and university administrators worried about running afoul of the law have cancelled courses that address race, diversity, and equity. For example, after the Oklahoma state legislature passed *HB 1775*, the administration at Oklahoma City Community College canceled a course on race and ethnicity that had been taught for six years without controversy (Lati 2021). A spokesman for the College explained the decision by arguing that "HB 1775 essentially revokes any ability to teach critical race theory, including discussions of white privilege, from required courses in Oklahoma," and therefore, "substantial changes to the [syllabus] for the class" must be made before it can be reintroduced into the curriculum (Lati 2021).

Even college administrators have found themselves in the crosshairs of anti-CRT conservatives. For example, in November 2022, a group of parents, alumni, and students at Grove City Christian College (GCCC) in Pennsylvania signed a petition "raising concerns that critical race theory… was threatening the academic and spiritual foundations that make the school distinctly Christian" (Post 2022). As evidence of the threat of Critical Race Theory to the college, the petitioners cited

> a fall 2020 chapel presentation by Jemar Tisby, a historian and author who writes on race and religion; a chapel presentation that included a pre-recorded TED talk by Bryan Stevenson, the Equal Justice Initiative founder and criminal justice reform advocate; a Resident Assistant training that included the concepts of white privilege and white guilt;

> and several books used in an education studies class and in focus groups, including Ibram X. Kendi's "How to be an Antiracist" and Wheaton professor Esau McCaulley's "Reading While Black (Post 2022).

After receiving the petition, the President of the college issued a letter reiterating the school's mission to "equip students to pursue their unique callings through a Christ-centered, academically excellent, and affordable learning and living experience;" denouncing Critical Race Theory as an "improper framework for examining and understanding the real challenges faced in our fallen world;" addressing what he saw as misinformation in the petition; and encouraging all Grove City Christian College members to elevate themselves above the innuendos, hearsay, and rumors found on the internet (McNulty 2021).

This wasn't enough. A group of faculty members at Grove City sent an anonymous letter to the Board of Trustees accusing the President of "publicly rebuking parents for raising concerns about the education of their sons and daughters" and claiming to have "heard him negatively characterize the parents behind closed doors in faculty meetings" (Anonymous Faculty at GCCC 2021). They called for an investigation into the "President's handling of the situation" and suggested that professors who teach courses that are not aligned with the religious mission and conservative values of the college seek employment elsewhere (Anonymous Faculty at GCCC 2021). Finally, they closed by defending their anonymity, arguing that, "in the context of… the campus atmosphere… we believe that revealing our identity could result in reprisals from senior administrators, perhaps even non-renewal of our annual faculty contracts" (Anonymous Faculty at GCCC 2021).

In response, the Board of Trustees established a special committee to investigate and offer recommendations for resolving the controversy. Among other things, the special committee recommended that (a) *Education 290*, the course at the center of the controversy, be replaced with a course that "considers the controversial issue (Critical Race Theory) in light of the College's vision, mission, and values," (b) the Office of Multicultural Education and Initiatives, the office that chose the books for co-curricular discussion groups, be reconstituted and renamed, and (c) that the President be empowered to take "action" against any faculty, staff, or administrators who demonstrate misalignment with the college's mission (Special Committee 2022). While the special committee did not specify what counts as misalignment with the college's mission or the kinds of remedial actions the President should be empowered to take, it is clear that the special committee's recommendations were designed to suppress academic free speech, particularly the academic free speech of the professor who taught *Education 290*.

4 Essential for a Strong Democracy: The Case for Academic Free Speech

Laws prohibiting public college and university professors from teaching Critical Race Theory run afoul of current legal precedents, both on the issue of political pedigree tests for employment, raised by *HB 233*, and on the questions of academic free speech and who has the right to place limits on academic free speech, raised by *HB 7*. The attempt to establish political pedigree tests for employment is not a new strategy for suppressing speech. In fact, during the Red Scare of the 1940s and 50s, New York's *Feinberg Law* prohibited anyone deemed subversive from being hired in public employment (Twohy 1950, pp. 202–203). Other New York public employment laws required candidates to take loyalty oaths, which included candidates for employment at public colleges and universities. Not surprisingly, this did not sit well with many professors. In fact, several professors at the State University of New York at Buffalo refused to sign documents swearing that they were not members of the Communist Party. They were fired. In response, they sued the New York Board of Regents on the grounds that it violated their *First Amendment Right* to freedom of academic association. Upon review, in the case of *Keyishian v. Board of Regents of University of the State of New York*, the Supreme Court determined that loyalty oaths violate the *First Amendment* right to freedom of academic association, (*Keyishian v. Bd. of Regents*, 1967).) and therefore, the New York Board of Regents acted illegally when it fired professors at the State University of New York at Buffalo for refusing to sign documents declaring that they were not members of the Communist Party. In short, the Court was worried that New York's law was so broad and vague that it prohibited professors from joining controversial organizations that aligned with their academic interests and research agendas without illustrating that those organizations had a specific intent to overthrow the government or cause harm to others.

Similarly, attempts to define professors as subversives as a way of suppressing academic free speech are not new either. In fact, in 1951, the New Hampshire State Legislature passed the *Subversive Activities Act* which empowered the state Attorney General to investigate subversive organizations and persons. Three years later, Professor Paul Sweezy gave a speech at the University of New Hampshire on socialism and communism. The state attorney general summoned Professor Sweezy to an interview to be questioned about his political beliefs and associations. During his interview, Dr. Sweezy refused to answer any questions about his political beliefs or the substance of his speech at the University of New Hampshire. Subsequently, he was charged with contempt and ordered to be held in custody until he answered the Attorney General's questions.

Professor Sweezy sued the state of New Hampshire on the grounds that the *Subversive Activities Act* violated his *First Amendment* right to academic free speech. Upon review, in the case of *Sweezy v. New Hampshire*, the Supreme Court determined that "there unquestionably was an invasion of petitioner's liberties in the area of academic freedom" and thereby reversed the contempt order against him

(*Sweezy v. New Hampshire*, (1957), p. 354). Most importantly, the Court found that colleges and universities possess four essential freedoms: to determine (1) who may teach, (2) what may be taught, (3) how it shall be taught, and (4) who may be admitted to study at the college or university (*Sweezy v. New Hampshire*, (1957), p. 354). It thereby settled the question of who has the right to establish limits on academic free speech.

Finally, in August of 2022, the American Civil Liberties Union filed a lawsuit on behalf of a group of Florida professors and students, challenging *HB 7* on the grounds that it violated their *First Amendment* rights to academic free speech. In this case, the plaintiffs "asked the Court to enjoin enforcement of the challenged provisions, citing the Supreme Court's long history of shielding academic freedom from government encroachment" and "intolerance towards government attempts to cast a pall of orthodoxy over the classroom" (*Pernell et al v. Florida Board of Governors* (2022), p. 8). Judge Mark Walker began his ruling by quoting George Orwell's *1984*,

> "It was a bright cold day in April, and the clocks were striking thirteen," and the powers in charge of Florida's public university system have declared the State has unfettered authority to muzzle its professors in the name of "freedom." To confront certain viewpoints that offend the powers that be, the State of Florida passed the so-called "Stop W.O.K.E." Act in 2022--redubbed (in line with the State's doublespeak) the "Individual Freedom Act." The law officially bans professors from expressing disfavored viewpoints in university classrooms while permitting unfettered expression of the opposite viewpoints. Defendants argue that, under this Act, professors enjoy "academic freedom" so long as they express only those viewpoints of which the State approves. This is positively dystopian (*Pernell et al v. Florida Board of Governors* (2022), p. 2).

After taking great pains to weigh the arguments, Judge Walker ruled that "the Plaintiffs have carried their burden as to… the preliminary injunction," and concluded that "they are entitled to a preliminary injunction" (*Pernell et al v. Florida Board of Governors* (2022), p. 8). He therefore stopped the provisions of *HB 7* that place restrictions on the academic speech of public college and university professors from going into effect. Hence, in light of *Keyishian v. Bd. of Regents*, *Sweezy v. New Hampshire*, and *Pernell et al v. Florida Board of Governors*, I conclude that college and university professors ought to sue states that have passed anti-CRT legislation on the grounds that such legislation violates their *First Amendment* rights to academic free speech and freedom of academic association.

Beyond jurisprudence, the United States is a liberal democracy. Colleges and universities play a vital role in educating and developing students to become full-fledged members of our free society. Or, to put it in another way, colleges and universities are incubators for reproducing free democratic citizens. Ronald Daniels, Grant Shreve, and Phillip Spector make this case in *What Universities Owe Democracy*. Quoting John Dewey, they write: "democracy has to be born anew every generation and education is its midwife" (Daniels et al. 2021, p. 89). More importantly, the Supreme Court recognized the essential relation between academic free speech and democracy in *Sweezy v. New Hampshire*. Chief Justice Warren writes:

> The essentiality of freedom in the community of American universities is almost self-evident. No one should underestimate the vital role in a democracy that is played by those

> who guide and train our youth. To impose any strait jacket upon the intellectual leaders in our colleges and universities would imperil the future of our Nation. No field of education is so thoroughly comprehended by man that new discoveries cannot yet be made. Particularly is that true in the social sciences, where few, if any, principles are accepted as absolutes. Scholarship cannot flourish in an atmosphere of suspicion and distrust. Teachers and students must always remain free to inquire, to study and to evaluate, to gain new maturity and understanding; otherwise, our civilization will stagnate and die (*Sweezy v. New Hampshire*, (1957), p. 354).

I concur with Chief Justice Warren. For, if we make the mistake of prohibiting free inquiry into and discourse about controversial ideas, like Critical Race Theory, particularly on college and university campuses, students will simply assume that the prohibited ideas are incorrect, and the accepted ideas are correct. Even worse, professors will not be able to challenge the unjustified assumptions of their students because they will be prohibited by the state from inquiring into and discussing controversial ideas. After a few decades have passed, it will not matter whether the prohibited ideas or the accepted ideas are correct. Effectively, American colleges and universities will become theological seminaries, "educational" institutions wherein professors preach doctrine instead of teaching students how to engage in habitual truth-seeking and knowledge acquisition, subject to enlightenment skepticism and re-examination guided by the principles of logic and critical thinking. At best, this will hamper the pursuit of knowledge, but what's more likely is that it will undermine American colleges and universities altogether.

Before long, American democracy will wither and die. For, the ideas that are accepted as common sense today were once investigated, scrutinized, and debated intensely among the intelligentsia, including the heliocentric model of the universe, the theory of evolution, women suffrage, and interracial marriage. In the early stages, ideas are often controversial and threatening to the status quo. As the investigations and debates lead the intelligentsia toward truth or justice, they began to make the case for those ideas in courts, congresses, and college classrooms. For example, after evolution was accepted largely by the intelligentsia, Clarence Darrow made the case for teaching evolution in public schools in the Scopes Monkey Trial (*Tennessee v. Scopes* 1925). After evolution was adjudicated in court, and as time passed, what was once controversial ripened into common sense. This is how progress is made in a liberal democracy.

Given that college and university professors make up a great portion of the intelligentsia, and the intelligentsia who are not members of the academy are invited to college and university campuses to engage in discourse with professors, many, if not most, of the investigations and debates into controversial ideas take place on college and university campuses. Thus, one can see why academic free speech is vital for college and university professors. More importantly, however, without academic free speech most, if not all, of the controversial investigations and debates would cease. Ideas in the status quo will become entrenched and blindly recycled generation after generation, producing what John Stuart Mill called "dead dogma," (Mill 1859, p. 1065). For this reason, I conclude that academic free speech is necessary for a strong liberal democracy.

5 Civic Engagement

In the end, college and university professors cannot simply rely on the courts to protect academic free speech and freedom of academic association. After all, despite the legal victories in court, classes are still being cancelled (Wagner 2023), professors are being denied tenure (Robertson 2021), and professors are being fired (Kim and Payne 2023). Therefore, liberals must avoid making the same mistake they made regarding *Roe v. Wade*, namely, assuming that because the Supreme Court had consistently ruled in their favor they would always do so. Indeed, *Dobbs v. Jackson Women's Health Organization* has taught us otherwise. In fact, the current Supreme Court could rely on a selective reading of the nation's history and traditions to overturn nearly any precedent. In fact, Justice Thomas expressed interest in re-examining the rights to contraception and marriage equality in his concurring opinion in *Dobbs*. He wrote: "I agree that nothing in [the Court's] opinion should be understood to cast doubt on precedents that do not concern abortion. For that reason, in future cases, we should reconsider all this Court's substantive due process precedents, including *Griswold*, *Lawrence*, and *Obergefell*" (*Dobbs v. Jackson Women's Health Organization*, 2022). Thus, I see no reason why the Court could not rely on a selective reading of America's history and traditions to undermine academic free speech and uphold state laws prohibiting the teaching Critical Race Theory. After all, in *Bonnell v. Lorenzo*, a federal appeals court determined that *academic free speech is not always protected by the Constitution*, particularly when "a college professor is speaking to a captive audience of students who cannot effectively avoid further bombardment of their sensibilities simply by averting their ears" (*Bonnell v. Lorenzo* 2001, pp. 820–821). This could be the opening the Court needs to undermine academic free speech.

Therefore, professors must become civically engaged. First, professors ought to teach student organizations how to establish online petitions, motivate their friends to sign them, and forward the signed petitions to Congress, demanding that they pass federal legislation establishing academic free speech and freedom of academic association for all college and university professors and students. This would be an excellent civics lesson and good educational project for student groups like the Democracy Project. More importantly, it would ensure that professors are not punished or fired for what they teach, lecture on, or publish. Secondly, colleges and universities must return to teaching civics. The state of our democracy demonstrates that professors can no longer "blithely assume our students have an understanding of democratic citizenship" or knowledge of the importance of voting (Daniels et al. 2021, p. 87). Third, professors must come down from their ivory towers and participate in public discourse. This requires professors to take off their academic robes, exercise patience, understanding that most people are not members of the intelligentsia, and engage with everyday people in everyday language. This will help us overcome anti-intellectualism and reduce the chances of everyday people being manipulated by propaganda, especially if we can gain the trust of our fellow citizens. Finally, more professors must run for public office. After all, few people understand the how vital academic free speech and freedom of academic association are to education and democracy like college professors. This suggestion is not as unusual as it might sound. Stephanie Murphy was a professor at Rollins College before becoming a member of the U.S. House of Representatives; Ben Sasse was the President of Midland Lutheran College before becoming a U.S. Senator; and Dwight Eisenhower was the President of Columbia University before becoming the President of the United States (Sara Jerde 2014 College Professors who served in Congress Chronicle of Higher Education). This suggestion will ensure that some congressional representatives understand and can articulate the importance of academic free speech and freedom of academic association—and other interests of the academy like tenure—to those in power.

6 Conclusion

In this paper, I have demonstrated that conservative state legislatures are passing prohibitions against teaching Critical Race Theory based on the myth that professors are teaching CRT to demonize "White" people. I have argued that such prohibitions violate academic free speech and freedom of academic association. I have demonstrated that *Keyishian v. Bd. of Regents*, *Sweezy v. New Hampshire*, and *Pernell et al v. Florida Board of Governors* provide a blueprint for how professors might respond to these prohibitions, at least in the short term. However, given the Supreme Court's willingness to overturn fifty years of precedent in *Dobbs v. Jackson*, I have concluded that professors cannot simply rely on the courts to protect academic free speech and freedom of academic association in the long term. Instead, I have concluded that professors must become civically engaged and pressure Congress to pass legislation protecting academic interests like academic free speech and freedom of academic association.

References

Adams J (2021) [1776] Thoughts on education. In: Founding America: documents from the revolution to the bill of rights. Barnes and Nobles Publishing, New York, pp 79–86

Anonymous Faculty at GCCC (2021) An open letter to the Grove City College Board of Trustees. In: GCC Webpage. https://www.gcc.edu/Home/Our-Story/Leadership-Teams/Office-of-the-President/A-Response-to-the-CRT-Petition

Avila B (2022) HB 7, Individual Freedom ACT. https://www.flsenate.gov/Session/Bill/2022/7/BillText/Filed/PDF

Bonnell v. Lorenzo, 241 F.3d 800, 820-21 (6th Cir. 2001). https://casetext.com/case/bonnell-v-lorenzo-2

Book L (2021) SCR 244, Florida Legislative Investigation Committee. https://www.myfloridahouse.gov/Sections/Bills/billsdetail.aspx?BillId=69925

Cain TR (2014) Little red schoolhouses? Anti-communists and education in an 'age of conflicts'. In: Goldstein RJ (ed) Little 'Red Scares': anti-communists and political repression in the United States 1921-1946. Routledge, New York, pp 105–133

Daniels RJ, Shreve G, Spector P (2021) What universities owe democracy. Johns Hopkins Press, Baltimore

Dobbs v. Jackson Women's Health Organization, 597 US _ (2022). https://supreme.justia.com/cases/federal/us/597/19-1392/#tab-opinion-4600818

Feffer A (2019) Bad faith: teachers, liberalism, and the origins of McCarthyism. Fordham University Press, New York

Golden D (2022a) IT'S MAKING US MORE IGNORANT' Governor Ron DeSantis's anti-critical-race-theory legislation is already changing how professors in Florida teach. In: The Atlantic, January 3, 2022. https://www.theatlantic.com/ideas/archive/2023/01/ron-desantis-florida-critical-race-theory-professors/672507/

Golden D (2022b) Muzzled by DeSantis, critical race theory professors cancel courses or modify their teaching. In: ProPublica, January 3, 2022. https://www.propublica.org/article/desantis-critical-race-theory-florida-college-professors

Greene P (2022) Teacher anti-CRT bills coast to coast: a state by state guide. In: Forbes, February 16, 2022. https://www.forbes.com/sites/petergreene/2022/02/16/teacher-anti-crt-bills-coast-to-coast-a-state-by-state-guide/?sh=1baa27e54ff6

Kay v. Bd. of Higher Education, N.Y. City, 173 Misc. 943 (N.Y. Misc. 1940) 18 N.Y.S.2d 821. https://casetext.com/case/matter-of-kay-v-bd-of-higher-education-ny-city-1

Kennedy JF (1962) Commencement address at Yale University. https://www.jfklibrary.org/archives/other-resources/john-f-kennedy-speeches/yale-university-19620611

Keyishian v. Bd. of Regents, 385 U.S. 589 (1967). 385 U. S. 591. https://supreme.justia.com/cases/federal/us/385/589/

Kim J, Payne K (2023) A Florida professor says his contract was terminated for teaching about racial justice. In: NPR, March 18, 2023. https://www.npr.org/2023/03/18/1164530319/florida-professor-fired-racial-justice-woke

Lati M (2021) What is critical race theory, and why do Republicans want to ban it in schools? In: The Washington Post, May 29, 2021. https://www.washingtonpost.com/education/2021/05/29/critical-race-theory-bans-schools/

McNulty PJ (2021) A response to the CRT petition. In: GCC Webpage. https://www.gcc.edu/Home/Our-Story/Leadership-Teams/Office-of-the-President/A-Response-to-the-CRT-Petition

Mill JS (1992) [1859] On liberty. In: Morgan ML (ed) Classics of moral and political theory. Hackett Pub., Indianapolis, pp 1043–1115

Moody J (2023) New college board denies tenure for 5 professors. In: Inside Higher Education, April 27, 2023. https://www.insidehighered.com/news/governance/trustees-regents/2023/04/27/new-college-board-denies-tenure-5-professors

Orwell G (1950) 1984. Signet, New York

Pernell et al v. Florida Board of Governors of the State University System et al, No. 4:2022cv00304 - Document 63 (N.D. Fla. 2022), p 5. https://law.justia.com/cases/federal/district-courts/florida/flndce/4:2022cv00304/442797/63/

Post K (2022) Grove City College caught in crossfire of evangelical CRT battles. In: Religious News Service, March 11, 2022. https://religionnews.com/2022/03/11/faculty-students-alumni-push-back-after-grove-city-college-rejects-critical-race-theory/

Roberts S (2017) Vera Shlakman, professor fired during the Red Scare, dies of 108. In: The New York Times, November 27, 2017. https://www.nytimes.com/2017/11/27/obituaries/vera-shlakman-professor-fired-during-red-scare-dies-at-108.htmlmes

Robertson K (2021) Nikole Hannah-Jones Denied Tenure at University of North Carolina. In: The New York Times, May 19, 2021. https://www.nytimes.com/2021/05/19/business/media/nikole-hannah-jones-unc.html

Russell B (1932) Education and the modern world. W. W. Norton Co., New York

Russell B (1957) Marriage and morals. Liveright Co., New York

Schrecker E (1986) No ivory tower: McCarthyism and the universities. Oxford University Press, Oxford

Smith Act of 1940, 54 Stat. 670, 671, title I, §§2–3. chrome-extension://efaidnbmnnnibpcajpcglclefindmkaj/http://homepages.gac.edu/~arosenth/395/Smith_Act_of_1940

Special Committee (2022) Report and Recommendation of the Special Committee. In: GCC Webpage. https://www.gcc.edu/Home/Our-Story/Leadership-Teams/Office-of-the-President/A-Response-to-the-CRT-Petition

Sweezy v. New Hampshire, 354 U.S. 234 (1957). p 354 U. S. 251. https://supreme.justia.com/cases/federal/us/354/234/

Tennessee v. Scopes 289 SW 363 (1925). https://casetext.com/case/scopes-v-state-1

Twohy J (1950) The Feinberg Law. St. John's Law Rev 24(2):202–203

Wagner A (2023) Florida student's 'discomfort' causes cancellation of civil rights class. In: MSNBC March 24, 2023. https://www.msnbc.com/alex-wagner-tonight/watch/florida-student-s-discomfort-causes-cancellation-of-civil-rights-class-166822981602

Eric Smaw is a Professor of Philosophy in the Department of Philosophy and Religion at Rollins College, and Clinical Ethicist at Florida State University, College of Medicine, Orlando Campus.

Representative Democracy, the Right to Vote and the Weighting of Votes

Alistair M. Macleod

Abstract My aim in this paper is to explore the contours of the right to vote in a properly functioning representative democracy. I begin by noting that in all the roles voting can play—whether in non-democratic societies or, in democratic societies, in the service of a variety of democracy-independent goals—the right to vote is both an individual and a collective right. I then argue that its primary function in a representative democracy is to facilitate the participation of its members, through the election of their representatives in the society's legislature(s), in the making of the major political decisions that help to shape the framework in which they all have to live their lives.

The right to vote in a properly functioning representative democracy is a complex right, a right that comprises three distinguishable rights.

(1) The first of these is the right of all the (adult) members of a society to cast ballots in the regularly recurring elections that determine the composition of a society's legislature(s). This is the right to a universal franchise.
(2) The second is the right to have all the votes that have been cast in legally permissible ways counted and certified accurately.
(3) The third is the right to have all accurately tabulated and confirmed votes count towards the election of legislatures that are reasonably representative of all who have voted.

Breaches of all three rights can occur in societies that are widely regarded as representative democracies. Thus. breaches of the first right can occur if, for example, ex-felons are excluded from voting lists, or if the right to vote is denied to certain permanent residents in disregard of the fact that they are full participants in the economic and social life of a country. The second right can be breached if, whether because of inefficiency in the structuring of vote tabulation arrangements or—a more sinister possibility—because of politically-motivated attempts to interfere

A. M. Macleod (✉)
Department of Philosophy, Queen's University, Kingston, ON, Canada
e-mail: alistair.macleod@queensu.ca

G. A. Babst et al. (eds.), *Liberal Constitutionalism and its Contemporary Challenges*, AMINTAPHIL: The Philosophical Foundations of Law and Justice 12, https://doi.org/10.1007/978-3-031-53602-1_10

with these arrangements, not all legally cast votes form part of final election tallies. The third right can be breached if not all the votes that have been correctly tallied are allowed to contribute to the election of a legislature that fairly represents the most important of the political preferences and priorities of all voting members of the electorate.

While examples can easily be provided of breaches of the first two kinds that continue to occur, I focus in the paper on a sometimes-overlooked breach of the third sort that is generated by a familiar and widely endorsed electoral system. I argue that the first-past-the-post (or "single-member-constituency") system—henceforth FPTP for short—has structural features that make it inevitable that many members of FPTP electorates don't have a democratically defensible version of the right to vote.

For one thing, the representation in a legislature that voters hope to secure by the votes they cast as members of an electorate can be obtained, under FPTP rules, only by those voters who vote for the winning candidate in the only electoral contest—viz. the contest at local constituency level—in which the system permits them to cast ballots. The many voters in all such contests who vote for any of the losing candidates are consequently deprived of representation in the legislature. Since the right of members of the electorate to participate indirectly in the making of political decisions is facilitated in a properly functioning representative democracy by the election of members of a legislature who reflect to some reasonable degree their major political preferences and priorities, the fact that the FPTP system permits the election to a legislature of only those candidates who win constituency-level electoral contests means that the many voters in all such contests who vote for any of the losing candidates are deprived of representation in the legislature.

Moreover, the fact that all the votes cast in these local elections—including the votes cast for losing candidates—contribute to the jurisdiction-wide popular vote does nothing to alter the seat distribution in a legislature, simply because under FPTP the popular vote is allowed to play absolutely no role in determining election outcomes. Voters who support losing candidates in constituency-level electoral contests and who are consequently deprived of representation in the legislature cannot take comfort in the thought that at least their losing votes add to the jurisdiction-wide popular vote for the political parties they favor in the popular vote. Yes; their losing votes in constituency-level electoral contests help to boost the jurisdiction-wide popular vote secured by the political party that sponsored the local candidate they supported. But No; contributing to the jurisdiction-wide popular vote of the political party they favor makes absolutely no difference to the party's seat-count in the legislature. The jurisdiction-wide popular vote is permitted by FPTP to play no constitutionally recognized role in determining this seat-count.

The conclusion to be drawn is that the version of the right to vote that is conferred on the members of a society by the first-past-the-post electoral system is deficient in a way that threatens the democratic credentials of the representative democracies (like Canada, the UK, and the USA) in which this system is established and maintained.

1 Preliminary Commonplaces About Voting

(1) Voting practices aren't necessarily related to democratic political arrangements. The early history of these practices in societies that have eventually developed democratic institutions is replete with examples of the role voting has played in the exercise of power in decidedly non-democratic regimes.[1]

(2) Voting practices aren't necessarily linked to a society's political arrangements, whether or not these happen to be democratic. Within non-political groups and organizations of many different kinds—social, religious, cultural, recreational, educational—collective decisions can be made by members through exercise of their right to vote.[2]

(3) The right to vote must be regarded, not merely as an individual right, but also as a group right.[3] Individuals couldn't have the right to vote as individuals unless by voting they could be seen to be participating in the making of a group decision of some sort—that is, unless their right to vote were also correctly describable as a right to contribute to the making of a group decision. Equally, their right to vote couldn't be correctly described as a group right unless they were in a position to exercise the right by deciding, as individual members of a group, how to cast their vote. This means that there is a necessary connection between the practice of voting in the many forms it can take and the making of collective decisions.[4] The tightness of the connection between the right to vote, when

[1] Within the so-called "Parliamentary" tradition in England, not only were members of Parliament elected (when they weren't simply appointed) by narrow swaths of the general public but their votes were allowed to influence government decisions only on carefully delimited issues and even on these issues their votes were not infrequently a mere formality, under the control of the aristocrats to whom they owed their Parliamentary seats. As for the United States, its "founding fathers" were members of an elite whose constitutional deliberations, while nominally "democratic", established electoral arrangements with a severely restricted franchise, a franchise that excluded not only all women but also all men who didn't hold property of specified kinds.

[2] For example, many of the rules governing such groups as tennis clubs and tenant associations are adopted and revised by the votes cast by their members. Again, some of the activities of religious or cultural organizations can be decided on by the votes of members. Yet again, many of the policies adopted by school boards are voted on by board members. And so on.

[3] There are, of course, individual rights that aren't also group rights (the right to the public expression of political opinions being an example), and group rights that aren't also individual rights (the right of a union of municipal employees to merge with a union of provincial employees being an example), but the right to vote has to be described, and classified, differently. It is both an individual right and a group right, and it's both as a matter of conceptual necessity.

[4] Decisions of many kinds can of course be made by individuals all on their own—that is, when they make decisions just **as** individuals. But it's logically impossible for them to arrive at these decisions by "voting" to do so. An individual can make a personal decision to take the bus into town or to place a phone call to a friend—where a "personal" decision is, at least roughly, a decision reached without others being necessarily involved in the making of the decision—and the reasons for the decision can be of an indefinitely large number of different sorts, but that individual cannot (logically, cannot) make the decision by "voting" to make it. For an individual to be in a position to cast a "vote" for the making of some decision (D1, say), D1 has to be, not a "personal"

described as a right that individuals have, and the right to vote, when described as a group (or collective) right, is robbed of its mystery as soon as it's noted that the right can be possessed only by individuals in their capacity **as members of a group**.

(4) The fact that the right to vote is correctly describable—correctly describable, that is, on conceptual grounds—both as an individual and as a collective right, does not imply that it's essential to enjoyment of the right to vote for some uniform weight to be assigned the votes that contribute to the making of collective decisions. It consequently can't be taken for granted, for example, that it's a condition of the making of a group decision by the casting of votes by members of the group that equal weight is assignable to the votes the members have a right to cast. On the contrary, whether an equal weighting rule is in fact a built-in feature of the voting practices of any particular group is an empirical question, and whether it's a desirable feature of such practices is a normative question. Neither of these questions can be answered by merely noting that, conceptually, the right to vote is necessarily both an individual right and a group right.

2 Two Assumptions

In broaching questions about the relationship between democracy and the right to vote, it's important to begin by acknowledging a couple of background assumptions that circumscribe the scope of the discussion.

(1) **Normative and non-normative understandings of "democracy" and "right to vote"**

The first of these assumptions is that a distinction can be drawn between normative and non-normative understandings of both "democracy" and "the right to vote." Thus, (a) there can be merely descriptive understandings of these terms, (b) there can be expressly normative understandings, and (c) the terms can also be understood, in many familiar contexts, both descriptively and normatively.

(a) The terms "democracy" and "right to vote" must sometimes be taken to be **merely** descriptive terms. This is the case when their use involves the application

decision (in the sense explained), but a collective or group decision, and that individual must be a voting member of the group. Thus, if A is member of a poker club and the members have to decide, collectively, how frequently to meet for poker sessions, A may be able to contribute to the decision of the group by casting a vote for (say) weekly meetings. In all such contexts, voters must be **members of the group** in question. It's only **qua** members (members of a school board, a tennis club, a tenant association, and so on) that they have the right to vote. The right to vote is the form taken by the right to participate in (and thereby contribute to) the making of a group decision. An account of the right to vote is consequently quite mistaken if it fails to give recognition to the fact that whenever individuals cast a vote they are acting as members of some group.

of **empirically verifiable** criteria of the appropriate sort but **without** any suggestion (or implication) that these criteria can be taken to have evaluative force of some kind **as well**. Thus, the expression "right to vote" must be understood non-normatively—that is, as a merely descriptive expression—when there are empirically specifiable criteria for determining whether or not the right exists and absolutely no assessment is simultaneously being made (even tacitly) about the defensibility of the right. The right may, for example, be grounded in a society's existing laws and conventions with no judgment being made or presupposed about whether these laws and conventions are defensible or indefensible. Critics of frequent resort to referenda for the settlement of political disagreements consider the casting of votes in most referenda by members of the public at large to be an undesirable practice, but they nevertheless agree that the term "voting" correctly describes this kind of decision-making process and that, when a referendum is called (even if, in their view, indefensibly), those who participate may correctly be said to be exercising their "right to vote."

(b) There can also be **expressly normative understandings** of "democracy" and "right to vote" in contexts in which evaluative considerations of some sort must be satisfied (at least to some degree) if a society's institutional arrangements are to qualify as "democratic" and if a society's members are to be said to have a "right to vote" under these arrangements. The normative judgments in question may of course be controversial because of standing disagreements about what justifies democratic institutions and about the right to vote that is underpinned by these institutions.

(c) In many familiar situations, the terms "democracy" and "right to vote" have to be understood both descriptively and normatively. After all, the right to vote is only one of the many possible specifications of the (abstract) "right **to X**" and it's a commonplace that judgments about the existence or non-existence of a "right to X" may have to be construed, simultaneously, as expressing both empirical and normatively-toned judgments. For example, a society's pension arrangements can be the subject of judgments of both sorts. The question what the laws and policies governing a society's pension arrangements **in fact are** at any given time is an empirical question, and the question whether these laws and policies are **defensible** (desirable, fair, just, etc.) is a normative question—and it's common for questions of both kinds to be asked and answered at one and the same time.

(2) **Not all democratic rights involve voting**

Even when it is assumed, however, that questions about democracy and the right to vote are to be taken to be normative (and not merely descriptive) questions, there's a second background assumption that needs to be noted—viz. that the right to vote isn't the only right members of democratic societies typically have to participate in their society's political decision-making processes. The right to freedom of speech, for example, enables citizens to express their political views publicly; the right to freedom of association gives them the opportunity to join forces with other like-minded citizens in pressing governments to adopt certain policies; the right to freedom of the press is crucial to the provision, for the members of a society, of the many kinds of information that underpin the political judgments they make; and so on. Importantly though all these rights contribute to the rights members of a democratic society have to participate in political decision-making processes, none of them involves the casting of votes. The right to vote is thus only one of several political rights the members of a democratic society should have even when the focus is on (what can be taken to be) the general political right under which all these rights fall—viz. the right to **participate** in the making of decisions that shape the institutional framework for individual and social life. It then remains to be determined how the democratic right to vote is to be understood and how it is to be distinguished from other political rights the members of a democratic society should have.

3 Direct and Indirect Participation in Democratic Decision-Making

However, before the distinction between voting and non-voting political rights in a democracy can be usefully discussed, another (partially overlapping) distinction needs to be drawn. This is the distinction between "direct" and "indirect" political rights. The question whether political rights are direct or indirect is a different question from the question whether they involve the casting of votes. Yet they are partially overlapping questions because "direct" and "indirect" political rights can take the form either of voting or of non-voting rights.

Thus, (i) in a democratically organized society, a clear example of a "direct" political right that does **not** involve exercise of the right to vote is the right individual members have to give public expression to their support for (or their criticism of) the law- or policy-making proposals of the government: the views they express may or may not have any influence on the government's legislative or policy decisions, but either way expressing such views doesn't take the form of casting a vote of any kind.

(ii) A clear example of a "direct" political right that **does** involve the casting of a vote is the right the elected members of a legislature have to express their opinion of legislative or policy proposals by casting votes in favor of or against these proposals.

(iii) A clear example of an "indirect" political right that involves the casting of votes is the right to vote citizens exercise when, as members of the electorate, they cast ballots, in an election, for the members of a legislature. This sort of vote is indirect because it is only through their representatives in a legislature that members of the electorate can hope to contribute to the decisions a government makes.

(iv) A clear example of an "indirect" political right that does not involve the casting of a vote is the right the members of a society have to support a political party of their choice, whether (for example) by donating to the party or by signing party petitions, and so on.[5]

4 Voting Rights in a Representative Democracy

Virtually all democratic societies nowadays are organized as **representative** democracies because it is recognized to be neither feasible nor desirable for all the members of any society to be direct participants in processes for the making of decisions about its laws, public policies and institutions. Their direct participation isn't feasible because of the size and complexity of these societies, and it isn't desirable partly because the information that underpins political judgments can't in practice be made available to everyone and partly because defensible use of relevant information often calls for technical expertise. The Indirect participation in these processes that is needed is facilitated by the establishment of an electoral system of some kind, a system that enables the members of a society to vote for their representatives in a legislature and thus participate—indirectly—in political decision-making through the votes these representatives cast when matters of law and public policy have to be decided.

However, even when voting is acknowledged to be involved in this sort of indirect participation in a democratic society's political decision-making processes, and even when attention is focused on the right to vote the members of a society's electorate exercise when they vote for their representatives in a legislature, it would be a mistake to suppose that voting rights in a representative democracy can be characterized—summarily, and compendiously—as indirect political rights. Indeed, such a characterization provides a misleadingly partial account. The reason is that it's an **indirect** voting right that couldn't so much as exist without the existence of a voting right that plays a **direct** role in the making of a society's political decisions—viz. the right the elected members of a legislature have to vote for or against a government's law- and policy-making proposals.

Any accurate account of the voting arrangements needed in a properly functioning representative democracy to facilitate the appointment of the members of a legislature by the society's electorate must consequently give recognition to at least **two kinds of voting rights**—the right that all members of a society's electorate have to vote for representatives in a legislature, and the right that those representatives have to vote for or against the political agenda of the government. To bring out the complexity of the contribution these rights make to the structure of a

[5]These are all examples of ways in which citizens can support a political party without casting a ballot of any sort. There is, of course, one kind of party support that does involve voting—viz. voting, in a local election, for the candidate sponsored by a political party.

representative democracy, notice has to be taken not only of the respects in which they are similar and the respects in which they differ but also of their interconnections.[6]

(a) **Similarities.** There are at least two respects in which the right to vote for their representatives in a legislature that the members of a society's electorate have [henceforth to be dubbed **E-rights**] and the right that the elected members of a legislature have to vote for or against the legislative/policy proposals of a government [henceforth to be dubbed **L-rights**] are similar. (i) The first similarity is that, by casting their votes, those who have either E-rights or L-rights are contributing to a collective decision-making process. This similarity is, of course, entirely to be expected because—as was noted earlier—the right to vote is both an individual and a collective right. Since this is the case as a matter of conceptual necessity, it follows that both E-rights and L-rights are rights to participate in a collective decision-making process. (ii) Second, in both cases the contribution to the making of a collective decision is a **direct** contribution. The casting of E-votes by the members of a democratic electorate contributes directly to the composition of a legislature, and the L-votes cast by the elected members of a legislature contribute directly to the adoption or rejection of the laws and policies proposed by a government.
(b) **Differences**. There are also at least three differences between the voting rights of members of an electorate and the voting rights of the elected members of a legislature. (i) The first is that while both, as already noted, contribute to the settlement of collective decision-making processes, the processes in question are different. In the case of E-votes, the collective processes are **electoral** processes of a special sort—viz. processes that determine the composition of a legislature. In the case of L-votes, the processes are **legislative** processes—viz. processes that result in the adoption or rejection of specific law- or policy-making proposals. (ii) The second difference is that whereas an E-right is a right to vote that **all** the members of a democratic society's electorate have, an L-right is a voting right enjoyed by **only a small proportion** of a society's members—viz. those who have been duly elected to a legislature. (iii) A third difference is that whereas an L-right is a right to participate **directly** in a collective decision-making process—by voting for or against legislative and policy measures a government is contemplating adopting—an E-right is **both a direct and an indirect** participatory right. It's a direct right in that it enables the members of an electorate, by casting their votes, to determine the composition of a

[6] In the discussion of these three sets of questions in this paper, consideration is restricted to voting rights that can be exercised in two contexts: first, the context in which the members of a society's electorate vote for their representatives in a legislature, and second, the context in which the elected members of a legislature vote for or against a government's legislative or policy proposals. There will be no discussion, consequently, of the role voting can play in the mounting of referenda, or in the making of political decisions at either lower (for example, municipal) or higher (for example, cabinet) levels, or in judicial contexts (whether in the appointment of judges or in the making of collective decisions by courts of appeal).

legislature. But it's also an indirect right in that, it enables them, through the votes cast by their representatives in a legislature, to participate to some extent in the control these representatives have over the legislative and policy decisions a government makes.

(c) **Interconnections**

Despite the differences there are between E-rights and L-rights, it would be a mistake to regard them as simply existing alongside one another within the institutional arrangements a representative democracy requires. On the contrary, while both are crucial to the very existence of a representative democracy, they couldn't play this role if they were not **essentially interconnected** rights. Neither right can exist without the other. L-rights depend for their existence on E-rights, and E-rights depend for their existence on L-rights.[7]

(A) Consider, first, the dependence of L-rights on E-rights in a properly functioning representative democracy. The members of a legislature wouldn't have the right to play a direct role in political decision-making processes—which is precisely what their having an L-right amounts to—if they hadn't been elected to the legislature by the members of a society's electorate through the exercise of their E-rights. This sort of link between L-rights and E-rights—a link, to repeat, that marks the dependence of L-rights on E-rights—is important because the (legislative and policy-related) decisions to which the members of a legislature contribute when they exercise their L-rights owe whatever democratic authority they have to the electoral decisions members of a democratic society's electorate make when they exercise their E-rights.

(B) Consider now the dependence of E-rights on L-rights. A link of this second sort is important because the only thing that gives an E-right its democratic credentials is the role its exercise plays in enabling all members of an electorate to participate indirectly, through their representatives in a legislature, in political decision-making processes.

---

[7]When the link between E-rights and L-rights is severed completely—as it is in a society in which laws are enacted and policies adopted without even the semblance of "input" from its rank-and-file members—the society doesn't qualify as a "democratic" society at all. However, even in societies that are widely regarded as democratic, the government's democratic authority can be impaired when the connection is frayed without being severed. This sort of fraying can occur in two importantly different ways. (i) On the one hand, the democratic authority of a government can be impaired because—somewhat paradoxically—some **E-votes** don't contribute at all to the election of the members of a legislature despite the fact that the society has a universal franchise and the votes in question have been cast in a legally permissible way by members of the electorate in exercise of their E-rights. (This sort of deficiency in a government's democratic authority is generated by a defect of a specific sort in the structure of the society's electoral system.) On the other hand, the democratic authority of a government can be impaired even if the E-votes of all members of an electorate are allowed by an electoral system to contribute to the election of the members of a legislature—that is, even if the electoral system doesn't suffer from any democracy-undermining structural deficiency. For example, the problem may be that the duly-elected legislators are insufficiently responsive when exercising their L-rights to the preferences and priorities of the members of the electorate to whom they owe their very membership in the legislature.

If exercise of E-rights didn't enable the members of a society to participate indirectly in the decisions their representatives make when, in exercising their L-rights, they play a direct role in the making of governmental decisions, then an E-right would cease to double as an indirect right to participate in political decision-making processes. It would consequently lose its significance as an indispensable **democratic** right.

5 The Right to Vote and the Electoral System

As noted in the previous section, the voting rights members of a properly functioning representative democracy enjoy are facilitated by the establishment of an electoral system. However, in order to play this crucial role, the system must contribute to preservation of appropriate linkages between E-rights and L-rights. Unfortunately, an electoral system can have structural features that make it impossible for these linkages to be properly maintained. When this is the case, the democratic credentials of the system are undermined. I want in this section to show that and how certain structural deficiencies in a familiar electoral system—viz. the first-past-the-post (or "single-member-constituency") system—are a standing threat to the maintenance of genuinely democratic arrangements in a representative democracy.

That there can be such deficiencies points to the fact that an electoral system must satisfy certain conditions if its democratic credentials are to be defended. Only when these conditions are met can the E-rights it confers on a society's members qualify as genuinely democratic rights.

What, then, are the conditions that must be satisfied by an electoral system if its democratic credentials are to be maintained?

At least three conditions must be satisfied, as can be confirmed by noting three general ways in which E-rights can fail to qualify as genuinely democratic rights.

For one thing, E-rights don't count as democratic rights unless they are enjoyed by **all** the (adult) members of a society: all members must belong to a society's electorate. Again, E-rights don't qualify as genuinely democratic rights unless all the votes cast by the members of an electorate are accurately tabulated and certified. Yet again, E-rights aren't bona fide democratic rights unless all accurately tabulated and certified votes are allowed to contribute to the conferment of L-rights on the elected members of a legislature.

This means—to express the main point in a somewhat different way—that an electoral system can pass muster as a crucial ingredient in the institutional arrangements needed by a representative democracy only if the E-rights it confers satisfy at least three conditions. These are (what might be dubbed) the "three C's" of truly democratic E-rights.

(1) The first C is the right to **Cast** a ballot. **All** the (adult) members of a society must have **a right to cast ballots** in electoral contests that determine the

fundamental conditions under which they have to live their lives. This is the Universal Franchise requirement.

(2) The second C is the right to have all ballots **Counted** and **Certified.** All the ballots cast by voters must be accurately counted and certified.

(3) The third C is the right to have all ballots **Count**. All the ballots that are cast, counted, and certified must also count—where "count" means (roughly) "contribute to representation in the legislature of all who have cast E-votes."

Unfortunately, it's not uncommon for one or more of these requirements to be breached in societies that purport to be democratic. Indeed, such breaches often go unrecognized—or unacknowledged.

Thus—apropos **the first requirement**—it's true that **explicit** restriction of the franchise on (say) religious or racial grounds is no longer typically attempted in contemporary democratic societies, largely because it is widely acknowledged to be a flagrant breach of the democratic ideal. However, subtler violations of the right to cast a ballot are not uncommon, even though the violations are often denied by irrelevant appeals to the need to prevent fraudulent voting. Voting rolls can be trimmed by the unjustified exclusion of whole classes of potential voters: for example, law breakers who have already served their sentences can be excluded and the vote can be denied to certain permanent residents in disregard of the fact that they are full participants in the economic and social life of a society. Again, unnecessarily demanding voter registration procedures can be adopted. Yet again, balloting stations can be located in difficult-to-access places, and burdensome rules about when and how ballots are to be cast can be imposed.[8]

The second requirement—the requirement that calls for all votes that are cast to be counted and certified—is sometimes breached by irregularities in the tallying (or in the certification) of votes. While such breaches can be inadvertent—evidence, at most, of inefficiency in the establishment or execution of counting procedures—and while miscounts can sometimes be traced to the malfunction of technologically complex voting-machines, there is also a more sinister possibility—viz. the engineering or concealment of miscounts by officials who are trying to facilitate the election, corruptly, of political candidates or parties. Another sinister possibility is the refusal of politicians or political parties to certify votes that have been correctly tallied, as the effort by Trump loyalists to do so after the 2020 US Presidential Election ominously demonstrated.

[8]Voting laws that have been enacted very recently in such US states as Georgia, Texas, and Florida provide evidence of renewed attempts to restrict the franchise in these indirect ways by politicians who haven't fully accepted the universality of the franchise but who recognize that there is no longer popular support for any direct assault on the universal franchise laws that were enacted in the mid-1960s. Defenders of the restrictions imposed under these new laws typically claim that they are needed to prevent electoral fraud. However, as critics of this claim have rightly pointed out, not only is electoral fraud quite rare in most US electoral contests, but most of the restrictions imposed by the new laws—on the number and location of voting stations, or on the shortening of periods for the casting or counting of votes, for example—are unrelated to the prevention of fraudulent voting.

However, it is breaches of **the third requirement** that are nowadays the most important of the challenges to the democratic credentials of the right to vote. In democratic jurisdictions like Canada, the UK and the USA, the source of this challenge is the structure of the electoral system that gives determinate content in these societies to the right to vote—viz. the "first-past-the-post" or "single member constituency" system.

6 The First-Past-the-Post System and the Representation Deficit

Two defining features of an FPTP system are responsible for the most egregious violations of the requirement that all votes that are **counted** (in the sense of correctly calculated or tabulated) should also **count** (in the sense of contribute to the election of the members of a legislature).

(1) The first of these features is that because the first-past-the-post system subdivides electoral jurisdictions (whether country-wide or regional) into a large number of manageably small single-member constituencies (or "ridings", or "electoral districts"), and because each of these constituencies is entitled to elect a single member to the relevant legislature, the criterion for determining which candidate in a constituency-level electoral contest gets to occupy that seat in the legislature is a version of the so-called "winner-take-all" principle. What this means is that the single seat in the legislature for which all the candidates for election in a particular constituency are competing goes to the candidate who gets at least one vote more **in that constituency** than any other candidate.

(2) The second structural feature of the First-Past-the-Post electoral system is that the **only** electoral contests in which the right to vote can be exercised by the members of an electorate are the **constituency-level** elections, in each of which, as already noted, the single seat for which all the local candidates are competing is won by the candidate who secures the support of the largest sub-group of voters in that constituency. An obvious corollary is that no constitutional role (no role, specifically, in helping to determine the composition of a legislature) is assigned by the system to the jurisdiction-wide popular vote. While votes cast in constituency-level elections can of course be added up to determine both the jurisdiction-wide popular vote and the share of the popular vote secured by the political parties that sponsor candidates in constituency-level elections, these calculations have no bearing on the securing of seats in a legislature. Thus, while all votes cast at constituency level, whether for winning or losing candidates, can be **counted** (in the sense of tabulated) in the calculation of the jurisdiction-wide popular vote, under First-Past-the-Post electoral rules these duly-tabulated votes aren't allowed to **count**: they have no impact on the seat-count in a legislature.

> These features of the First-Past-the-Post electoral system undermine the democratic credentials of the right to vote members of a society enjoy under the system's rules because they guarantee that many of the ballots cast by voters—viz. all the votes cast for **losing** candidates—play **no role at all** in helping to shape the laws, policies, and institutions that provide the framework for individual and social life.

How so?

Take the "winner-take-all" feature that determines the outcome of any local (constituency-level) election. In such an election, the only voters whose votes contribute to the election of a legislature representative are the voters who vote for the winning candidate, the candidate who secures at least one vote more than any of the other candidates. This means that all the voters in these constituency-level elections who vote for any of the losing candidates are deprived of representation in the legislature. They cast their votes hoping thereby to be represented in the legislature by a member through whom they can play a role (indirect though it can only be) in the political decisions made by the legislature—but the fact that their vote was cast for a losing candidate means that, in the event, they have to settle for being totally unrepresented in the legislature.

Consider, now, the second structural feature of the First-Past-the-Post system—viz. that no constitutional role (specifically in determining the composition of a legislature) can be played by the jurisdiction-wide popular vote.

This vote—both the total vote and the share of the vote won by the political parties whose candidates are running in the constituency-level elections—can of course be calculated, and the calculations are easy to make. For example, to determine the total (jurisdiction-wide) popular vote, all that has to be done is add up all the votes cast in constituency-level elections, it being irrelevant to this calculation whether they are winning or losing votes and irrelevant too which political parties the votes are designed to support. Again, to determine the shares of the total popular vote secured by the political parties that sponsor candidates in the constituency-level elections, only two simple calculations need to be conducted. First, the votes cast in these local elections for the candidates sponsored by each of the political parties have to be added up—and for this calculation it's immaterial whether the votes are winning or losing votes. Second, the shares of the total vote secured by the various political parties contesting the election can then be calculated by determining what fraction of the total vote the electorate-wide vote for each of the political parties represents.

However, given the constitutional irrelevance of the electorate-wide popular vote under First-Past-the-Post, the shares of this vote secured by the competing political parties have absolutely no impact on the party-political distribution of seats in the legislature. The seat-count secured by any political party is **wholly** determined by its performance in the electoral contests at individual constituency level. This means that voters who failed in these contests to secure the representation in the legislature for which they had voted—failed to achieve this objective, of course, because they cast their votes for losing candidates—cannot console themselves with the thought that their losing vote might nevertheless have an impact on the seat-count in the legislature through its (mathematically determinable) contribution to the share of the jurisdiction-wide popular vote secured by the party whose local candidate they voted for. No such consolation is available. Since the electorate-wide popular vote isn't permitted by First-Past-the-Post rules to help determine the seat-count in the legislature, the representation voters are unable to secure through the losing vote they cast in the constituency-level election can't be secured through the contribution even their losing votes make to the jurisdiction-wide popular vote for the party they support. Yes, their losing votes can boost their party's share of the popular vote; but No, these votes can't do anything to provide them with the representation in the legislature that they fail entirely to secure when their votes in constituency-level elections are losing votes.

The upshot is that the First-Past-the-Post electoral system suffers from structural deficiencies that contribute to a representation deficit for the many members of the electorate who cast votes for losing candidates in the only electoral contests—viz. local constituency-level contests—that the system permits. Precisely because the deficiencies are structural, the only available remedy is abandonment of the system or (if such a change proves feasible) its radical transformation. Since the representation deficit the system generates is incompatible with the existence of a defensible version of the right to vote, the democratic credentials of representative democracies with voting systems indebted to the first-past-the-post electoral system will continue to be threatened for as long as the system is allowed to survive.

7 A Residual Issue: The Weighting of Votes in a Representative Democracy?

(1) Even if the third of the 3 C's that must be satisfied if the right to vote is to conform to the requirements of representative democracy can be appropriately dealt with[9]—the third C being, it will be recalled, the right to have all ballots **Count**, where "count" means (roughly) "contribute to representation in the legislature of all who have cast E-votes"—there is a fourth question that must be faced. What if the requirement that all the votes that are cast by voters do indeed **count** (in the sense that they help determine the outcome of an election) but aren't assigned the same weight in the calculation of the result? For example, what if some votes are weighted more heavily than others? Or what if some voters are allowed to cast more votes than one?

Should it be assumed, once these further issues are taken up, that having all votes count **equally** is the preferred—the default—answer?

A complication that must be borne in mind in tackling this supplementary question arises from the fact (noted earlier in the paper) that the right to vote is

[9] Presumably through abandonment of the FPTP approach to the structuring of an electoral system and adoption of a preferable approach.

both an individual and a collective right. This means that at least **two** questions have to be distinguished. (a) On the one hand, there's the question whether the right to vote, when identified as an **individual** right, is a right to which, in the relevant electoral context, the same weight should be assigned for all voters. (b) However, there's also a question about how the **collective** voting rights which all individual voters are also exercising when they cast their individual votes are to be weighted.

(a) The most plausible answer to the first of these questions is that all individual votes must be assigned **equal** weight. From the standpoint of the democratic ideal, it is uncontroversial that, when the focus is on the weighting of the individual votes cast in some electoral contest by the members of the relevant electorate, each of these votes must be assigned the same weight: the "one person one vote" rule is what the democratic ideal requires.

(b) However, the same "equal weight" answer is almost always unavailable when the focus is on the "shares" of the vote secured in some election by competing **groups of voters**. Except in the case where competing groups happen to receive the support of exactly the same number of votes—a highly unusual case, especially when the electorate has many members—the "shares" of the total vote received by competing groups will be **unequal**. Indeed, the larger the electorate and/or the larger the number of candidates in an electoral contest, the less likely the contest is to yield an "equal shares" result for the competing groups and the greater the likelihood is consequently that the **shares** of the vote secured by these groups will be **unequal**.[10]

(2) But although these two questions—the question whether "equal weight" should be given to all the votes cast by **individual** voters in an election and the question how "shares" of the total vote should be weighted among competing **groups**—are different questions, it shouldn't be assumed that the questions are unrelated. For example, perhaps the answer to the second question should be "proportionally" if the answer to the first is "equally." How so? Well … if the preferred answer to the first of the weighting questions is that all individual votes cast should be assigned equal weight in the calculation of the total vote, the preferred

[10] For example, in an electoral contest with a very small electorate—an electorate, say, of only 6—there can be only 3 "unequal share" outcomes when all 6 members cast votes and there are only 2 candidates—viz. 6-0, 5-1, and 4-2. However, the number of such outcomes will be much larger when the electorate is large and when all members cast votes. Thus, in an election with (say) a 120-member electorate and where all 120 cast votes, ruling out "equal shares" leaves open many more "unequal share" outcomes than the 3 that are left open when an electorate has only 6 voting members. For example, in a 2-candidate contest, this means that ruling out the 60-60 outcome leaves open a great many possible uneven electoral outcomes—from 59-61, 58-62, 57-63 at one end of the spectrum to 2-118. 1-119, and 0-120 at the other end. Again, if it's a 3-candidate contest, ruling out the "equal shares" result—40-40-40—leaves open a large number of possible "unequal share" results. 39-40-41, 38-40-42, and 37-40-43 are just three of these many "unequal vote" results.

answer to the second question is that the various shares of the total vote should be assigned a weight that is "proportional" to their size.[11] This might mean, for example, that if the Green Party's share of the popular vote in an election is (say) twice the share secured by the Libertarian Party, then the obvious way of arranging for all the **individual** votes cast for the Green Party and all the **individual** votes for the Libertarian Party to be assigned **equal** weight would be to assign **twice as much weight** to the Green Party's **share** of the vote as to the Libertarian Party's **share**.

Attention to the "weighting of votes" problem thus points to the need for substitution of a "proportional representation" approach to the structuring of a democratically defensible electoral system for the First-Past-the-Post approach.

8 Conclusion

I have argued in this paper that the right to vote in a properly functioning representative democracy is a complex right. Indeed, it is best seen as comprising three distinguishable rights: the right to cast a vote in periodic elections, the right to have votes that have been cast accurately counted and certified, and the right to have all the votes that have been accurately counted and certified help to bring about the election of a legislature that faithfully represents voting members of the electorate. The first of these rights calls for the establishment and protection of a universal franchise: all the adult members of a representative democracy must be part of the society's electorate and have the right as members of the electorate to cast their votes for representation in the relevant (national, provincial, state) legislatures. The second right requires reliable procedures to be established and maintained for the accurate tabulation and certification of all the votes that have been cast in legally permissible ways in all the electoral contests that determine the composition of a legislature. The third right is fully enjoyed only when all the votes for representation in a legislature that have been cast, counted and certified actually count towards the election of a reasonably representative legislature.

While I cite some examples of breaches of the first two rights that still occur, much of the focus of the paper is on a sometimes-overlooked breach of the third

[11] A competing answer that is sometimes proposed is that decisive political authority should be vested in the party that secures a **majority** of the popular vote. This cannot be right, however; and for at least two reasons. First, with the exception of electoral contests in which there are only two competitors (and such contests are virtually non-existent in modern democratic societies), it is something of a rarity in multi-party democracies for any of the competing parties to secure a majority—which means that insistence on the securing of a majority would almost always result in inconclusive elections, elections in which none of the competing parties would be entitled to form the government. Second, giving decisive governmental authority to a party that happened to secure a majority of the popular vote would leave the parties that secured only a minority of the popular vote with no democratic basis for loyalty to the government.

right. I argue that the First-Past-the-Post (or "single-member-constituency") system has structural features that result in many members of electorates in First-Past-the-Post jurisdictions not having a democratically defensible version of the right to vote.

I also argue, in the final section, that, even when all three parts of the right to vote are protected, a properly functioning democracy must have a satisfactory approach to the **weighting** of the votes cast by the members of the electorate. This weighting problem has two parts. While the votes cast by **individual** members must be **equally** weighted to be defensible, the **political power** of competing political parties must be **unequally** distributed whenever this corresponds to the unequal shares of the popular vote they may have received. Inequality of political power can therefore be justified in a representative democracy, but only when it is proportional to electoral support.

Alistair M. Macleod teaches moral and political philosophy in the philosophy graduate program at Queen's University (Canada). He is the author of *Social Justice, Progressive Politics, and Taxes* and a book on Paul Tillich's ontology (reissued by Routledge in 2017). Some recent publications are on such topics as the moral foundation for human rights, the diversity of concepts of privacy, and undemocratic electoral systems.

The Importance of Condorcet Consistency in Preserving Democracy

Robbie Robinette and Nicolaus Tideman

Abstract This paper explores optimal candidate strategy in partisan primaries, under Condorcet-consistent voting rules and under Instant Runoff. We suggest that a good voting rule rewards candidates for finding compromises among the desires of their electorates rather than for placing their party (or faction) ahead of their country. We conclude that Instant Runoff often yields results with the same problems as those that occur under plurality with a partisan primary, because voters choose candidates who support their factions. Condorcet-consistent voting rules, on the other hand, to which we give the name "Consensus Voting," lead candidates to centrist strategies, by rewarding candidates who propose compromises over voters' desires.

1 Introduction

Competitive poker has been developing in a direction that sheds light on competitive politics. Game theory and neural networks are now used to derive optimal strategies for poker. The result is called "game theory optimal" poker, or GTO poker. Players who win now almost invariably play GTO poker, while those who do not play GTO poker lose. Like poker, politics is a strategic game where the strategies are primarily positions on which to run. Which endorsements to seek and which ads to run are also strategic decisions, but the complexity they add would not illuminate the points made in this paper, so they play no role in the analysis that follows.

From a game theory perspective, politics is a simpler game than poker, making it all the more likely that winning politicians will play GTO politics. In this paper we

R. Robinette
Better Choices, Austin, TX, USA

N. Tideman (✉)
Virginia Tech, Blacksburg, VA, USA
e-mail: ntideman@vt.edu

G. A. Babst et al. (eds.), *Liberal Constitutionalism and its Contemporary Challenges*, AMINTAPHIL: The Philosophical Foundations of Law and Justice 12, https://doi.org/10.1007/978-3-031-53602-1_11

show that under existing rules, GTO politics leads to polarization. Instant runoff voting (IRV) is supposed to reduce polarization, but GTO calculations show that it can be expected to do so only slightly. On the other hand, GTO politics under Condorcet-consistent voting rules (Condorcet 1785) leads to the elimination of polarization. We therefore suggest that Condorcet-consistent voting, newly branded as "Consensus Voting," should be endorsed by those who would like to see a less polarized politics.

2 The Deeper Purpose of Elections

The superficial purpose of an election is to select a candidate to fill a role in government. However, the deeper, more important function that elections fulfill is to shape the behavior of candidates by rewarding and penalizing certain types of behavior. Choosing the correct winner is a Pyrrhic victory for democracy if all candidates must be divisive to be viable. Conversely, any candidate is acceptable if all candidates must be representative to be viable. In Federalist 10, James Madison declared factions to be the bane of early democracies and cited factions for making democracies "as short in their lives as they are violent in their deaths." Yet most American states filter candidates for factional purity through partisan primaries. The result is candidates whose first duty is to their faction and not their nation. Changing the voting rule alters optimal candidate strategy.

The proper choice of a winner is of less value if the election rule rewards divisive and unrepresentative tactics and all viable candidates are divisive. Similarly, if all candidates must adopt highly representative tactics to be competitive, the selection of any such candidate may be acceptable. The behavior that an election rule rewards is more important than aggregating the votes properly to ensure the selection of the proper winner from among the viable candidates.

This influence of incentives generated by election rules extends beyond the election, into the behavior of candidates while in office, as they anticipate the next election cycle.

This shaping of behavior is related to but distinct from the choice of a winner. Disparate election systems may agree on which candidate wins when the behavior and tactics of the candidates, and the consequent votes of voters, are held constant across systems, but that is not relevant to the evaluation of election systems. The optimal candidate strategy varies with the election process and governs candidate behavior. When a society chooses an election system, it also chooses the type of candidate behavior it will promote.

An election system that rewards candidates who adopt divisive tactics has a profoundly different impact on society than an election system that rewards representative tactics, even though they often choose the same winner for a fixed set of votes. Election systems must be judged on the combination of the behavior they reward and the winners they choose.

3 Madison's Republic

> AMONG the numerous advantages promised by a well-constructed Union, none deserves to be more accurately developed than its tendency to break and control the violence of faction. James Madison—Federalist 10

Madison opens Federalist 10 by stating that the most important advantage of a well-constructed union is its ability to "control the violence of faction."

> By a faction, I understand a number of citizens, whether amounting to a majority or a minority of the whole, who are united and actuated by some common impulse of passion, or of interest, adversed to the rights of other citizens, or to the permanent and aggregate interests of the community.

> If the impulse and the opportunity be suffered to coincide, we well know that neither moral nor religious motives can be relied on as an adequate control.

Earlier attempts at democracy had failed because a majority faction with some "common passion or interest" abused the rights of the minority "in almost every case." The result was that early democracies had been "as short in their lives as they have been violent in their deaths." Democracy had a terrible reputation. To secure the adoption of the new constitution Madison needed to make the case that the new republic would be different.

> The effect of the first difference is, on the one hand, to refine and enlarge the public views, by passing them through the medium of a chosen body of citizens, whose wisdom may best discern the true interest of their country, and whose patriotism and love of justice will be least likely to sacrifice it to temporary or partial considerations.

Madison acknowledges that factions are inherent in human nature but argues that they can be controlled by passing the "public views" through "a chosen body of citizens, whose wisdom may best discern the true interest of their country." To Madison, it is essential that this chosen body of citizens place the good of the country above factional interests. If they were nothing more than pure representatives of the various factions then, ultimately, all the problems of direct democracy would simply be recreated with a smaller number of people.

> Does the advantage consist in the substitution of representatives whose enlightened views and virtuous sentiments render them superior to local prejudices and schemes of injustice? It will not be denied that the representation of the Union will be most likely to possess these requisite endowments.

Madison's rousing conclusion is a vote of confidence in the virtuous sentiments of the soon-to-be representatives. There are many other important aspects of Federalist 10, but it is these, concerning the need for representatives in the new government to be capable of placing the "public good" ahead of "temporary or partial considerations," that we want to focus on.

We make an argument that Madison did not. The problem with direct democracies is not so much that they are direct, but that, being direct, they are vulnerable to "the mischief of factions." This is important because it is not only direct democracy that is susceptible to the dangers of factions, but republics as well.

4 Game Theory and Elections

> Ambition must be made to counter ambition. James Madison—Federalist 51

Game theory would not be invented for another 150 years, but Madison appears to have understood the basic principle, though he did not anticipate how game theory would apply to elections. Winning an election requires a candidate to assemble sufficient support from some set of voters. These voters may be voters from a single party but often also include independents. It is rare for such a set of voters to include voters from both parties. Let us call these voters, whose support a candidate must have to win an election, the candidate's *core voters*. A candidate cannot contradict these supporting voters without risk of defeat by a competitor who defends them.

Candidates who say, "my voters," generally mean their core voters only. They do not mean the entire electorates they represent. Voters who are unlikely to support a candidate are ignored and are vulnerable to abuse.

> There are 47% of the people who will vote for the president no matter what ... who are dependent upon government, who believe that they are victims. ... These are people who pay no income tax. ... and so my job is not to worry about those people. Mitt Romney, New York Times, 2012

Romney's comment was a strategic blunder and a direct statement about the game theory of elections. In the quote, Romney clearly states that he does not represent the 47% of people who aren't going to vote for him. He also attacks the 47% to further motivate his core voters. The only surprising thing about the comment is that Romney made it in a semi-public setting. Romney would certainly assert that the policy he would implement would be in the best interest of the 47%, even though they might not agree with him.

In any democracy, candidates are accountable exclusively to the set of voters required to win election. The set of voters required varies depending on the election system and the candidate, but voters not in a candidate's set of core voters are not represented by that candidate.

Much of the prior analysis of outcomes from alternative voting methods has involved choosing candidates with positions drawn randomly from the same distribution as the population. Drawing candidate positions randomly from the population is equivalent to assuming that they have no capacity to choose positions. In fact, candidates are adept at choosing policy positions that maximize their chances of winning elections.

5 Game Theory *vs.* Madison

Madison's argument for a republic hinges on the premise that elected leaders will not sacrifice the "common good" to "temporary or partial considerations". Conversely, the game theory of elections demands that candidates represent only their core voters and not the “common good”. Candidates who attempt to prioritize the common good ahead of the narrow interests of the voters required to elect them risk defeat. On its face, the conflict seems irreconcilable, and Madison’s vision for a republic appears doomed because “enlightened views and virtuous sentiments” are handicaps in a partisan primary.

6 How Has Our Democracy Survived?

In the 1950s, American politics was at a peak of cooperation, compromise, and progress. Both parties tried to recruit Eisenhower, and though he ran and served as a Republican, he governed straight down the middle. Anthony Downs (1957) argued that our two-party system was ultimately stable. This was highly influential, and the conclusions seemed self-evident at the time. In the 1950s, neither party met Madison’s definition of a faction in *Federalist 10* because neither Democrats nor Republicans were united in their policy goals, and each party had a diversity of opinion within its caucus.

The important thing is not the behavior of individual representatives, but rather the resulting policy. Each party had representatives who were accountable to voters with different priorities, and the parties themselves did not have rigidly defined ideologies. This allowed representatives to compromise. The resulting policy reflected priorities of a spectrum of voters and respected the rights of minorities.

In “Breaking the Two-Party Doom Loop,” Lee Drutman (2020) details the chronology of the sorting of the parties into two distinct camps starting in 1960 and finishing in 2010. On issue after issue, Republicans chose what we now call the conservative side while Democrats chose the liberal side. This sorting eroded the diversity within each party, and they each became the factions that the founders dreaded.

These parties now meet the definition of the founders of “a number of citizens … united by a common impulse or passion.” A less pejorative description of a faction is a group of people united by a shared sense of justice. When either party gains control, its leaders declare that the voters have spoken, that they have a mandate, and they proceed to govern according to their faction’s concept of justice. Each party denies governing “adversed to the rights of other citizens.” They each argue that their priorities are in the best interest of all citizens, even though citizens in the minority vehemently disagree. Their actions are a transparently false justification for governing solely according to the sense of justice of the voters who elected them, while disregarding the views of the minority. Except for a few politicians who seem to take particular glee in goading their opponents, neither the parties nor individual politicians deserve blame. They must play by the rules of GTO politics or lose to opponents who do. To change this behavior, we must change the rules.

7 Understanding Candidate Strategy

Our focus is on strategies that winning candidates employ under different voting rules and on the implied sets of core voters. Who do these candidates represent and who do they not represent? To understand this, we choose a spatial model for voter preference, in some unspecified number of dimensions. The illustrations and examples are presented in a two-dimensional ideological space, but the strategies can easily be expanded to any number of dimensions. In an actual election, candidates take a series of actions, which define their place in the ideological spatial model. It is these positions in ideological space that we wish to analyze.

We model voters as preferring to stay within their party. Voters who identify with a party will prefer a candidate who matches their party, given two candidates who are equidistant from them. Voters without a party affiliation do not consider party when evaluating candidates.

Finally, we assume some uncertainty in the voters' knowledge of the ideology and quality of the candidates. Each voter will have seen different media and have different life experiences, which influence their opinions of the candidates. The lines demarking voter preference are perfect but should be thought of as "this voter is most likely to vote for this candidate" instead of "this voter will always vote for this candidate".

Importantly, we show some illustrations that were created using simulation, but we do not rest our case on simulation results. While we are confident in our simulation results, personal experience has shown that simulation is not an effective tool for persuading a skeptical audience. For many people, simulation is an untrusted black box, and detailed explanation of the mechanics of the simulation does not change that. Instead, we rely on simple explanations of likely scenarios where the outcome can be clearly understood without simulation.

We present two scenarios for each election system we discuss: a balanced district and a district with enough lean to be uncompetitive. As of April 11, 2022 The Cook Political Report lists 45 out of 435 out of U.S. House of Representative seats as competitive and 9 out of the 35 Senate seats in play in 2024 as being competitive. This corresponds to 10% of House seats and 25% of Senate seats as being competitive. This makes the outcomes in non-competitive seats more important than those for competitive seats.

The non-competitive races are presented in a district dominated by the Republican Party, but the arguments are symmetric, and the labels could be swapped.

8 Optimal Strategy and Core Voters Under Current Rules

The current election system is the only system for which there is hard data on the relationship between candidate ideology and voter ideology. This allows us to supplement the hypothetical model for the outcomes and strategy with actual results and observations (Fig. 1).

Of the 435 seats in the U.S. House of Representatives, the Cook Political Report considers 43 to be competitive. For the remaining seats, the dominant party chooses their candidate with no consideration of electability in the general election or of the views of voters in the minority party. Having 55% rather than 70% of the electorate has very little impact on the candidate chosen.

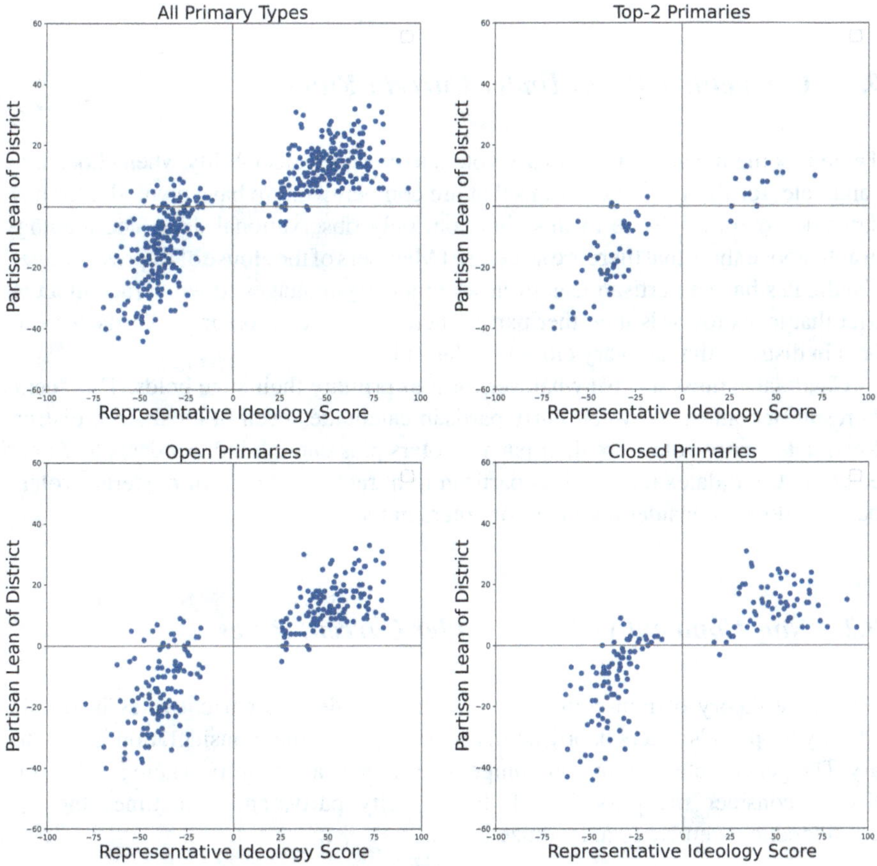

Fig. 1 Relationship between District Lean and Representative Ideology. Partisan lean vs representative ideology score for the United States House of Representatives, 117th Congress. Partisan lean is taken from the Cook Political Report. Representative Ideology is the DWNominate Dim1 (*100)

9 The Primary Electorate

There is an open question about the distinction between primary voters and general election voters for the same party. Are primary voters more partisan? Abramowitz (2008) and Sides et al. (2018) both conclude that the primary electorate is no more partisan than the voters in the same party in the general election. Drutman (2021) cites Sides et al. and other sources and concludes that the accepted wisdom that primary voters are more partisan is not well supported.

We consider the question to be unsettled, but we will assume that the primary electorate is substantially like the general electorate for a competitive primary. More competitive primaries have higher turnout, which causes the primary electorate to move toward the general electorate as turnout increases. In cases where the primary electorate does differ from the general electorate, candidates need to alter their strategy to match that change.

9.1 Competitive Races Under Current Rules

There is some incentive for primary voters to consider electability when choosing a candidate, for the 10% of elections that are competitive. We have no model for how strategic voters might be in this situation, only observational data. The ideology graphs above show that there are no centrist Members of the House of Representatives. Candidates have a partisan lean even when a party manages to win a race in a district that leans towards the other party. There are some surprisingly partisan members in districts that are very close to balanced.

Candidates must survive whatever form of primary their state holds. This seems to result in contests between fairly partisan candidates even in a balanced district. Candidates' core voters are their party's voters plus enough independents to win an election. Candidates may be less partisan to attract support from moderate voters, but they do not consider the views of voters in the other party.

9.2 Non-Competitive Races Under Current Rules

The game theory of non-competitive elections under the current rules is simple: Make your party's voters happy no matter what. Any other consideration is secondary. The general election in non-competitive races is a formality. There is no incentive to consider the priorities of the minority party, and sometimes there is considerable incentive to antagonize them.

9.3 *Current Rules Summary*

The primary process serves as a filter, to prevent any candidate who places the public good above the immediate interest of their primary voters from winning an election to Congress. Madison's "representatives whose enlightened views and virtuous sentiments render them superior to local prejudices and schemes of injustice" can't survive their parties' primaries.

10 Optimal Strategy Under Instant Runoff Voting

We treat an Instant Runoff-RCV contest as a contest among 5 candidates who qualify in a Top-5 multi-winner plurality primary, featuring candidates from all parties. The Top-5 candidates regardless of party advance to the general election, often with multiple candidates from each party advancing. For a congressional contest, it may well be that there are fewer than 6 well organized campaigns, and every serious candidate advances to the general election. Though we anticipate having five candidates, most examples show only three candidates, to make an illustration of a strategic point clearer. These examples can be considered to arise when five candidates have been whittled down to three.

10.1 *Instant Runoff-Ranked Choice Voting*

Instant Runoff Ranked Choice Voting (IRV) uses a ranked choice ballot, where voters list the candidates in their order of preference. We assume the best possible circumstances, where well informed voters submit complete and honest ballots showing their sincere preferences. If voters cannot expect a good outcome under such circumstances, it would seem unrealistic to expect a good outcome in the less ideal world of a real election.

Instant Runoff works by counting each ballot as a vote for the highest-ranked active candidate on that ballot. If a candidate has a majority, that candidate is the winner. If no candidate has a majority, the candidate with the fewest votes is eliminated, and each ballot that had counted for the eliminated candidate is transferred to highest-ranked candidate still active on that ballot. This process repeats until a candidate has a majority of the remaining ballots.

10.2 A Simplified Example with Three Candidates

We start with a simple example of Instant Runoff voting in Fig. 2, to illustrate the process of IRV and some problems. Consider an election in a Republican leaning district with three candidates, two Republicans (Juan and Anne) and a Democrat (Bob).

Democrats list Bob and then Anne on their ballots, Republican leaning voters list Juan or Anne first, with a majority of them listing Juan first. Those who list Juan first list Anne second. Among those who list Anne first, most list Juan second, but some list Bob second. Anne has the fewest first-round votes and is eliminated.

Voters who preferred Anne now have their votes transferred to the second choices on their ballots. Most of these votes go to Juan, who now has a majority of the votes and is the winner.

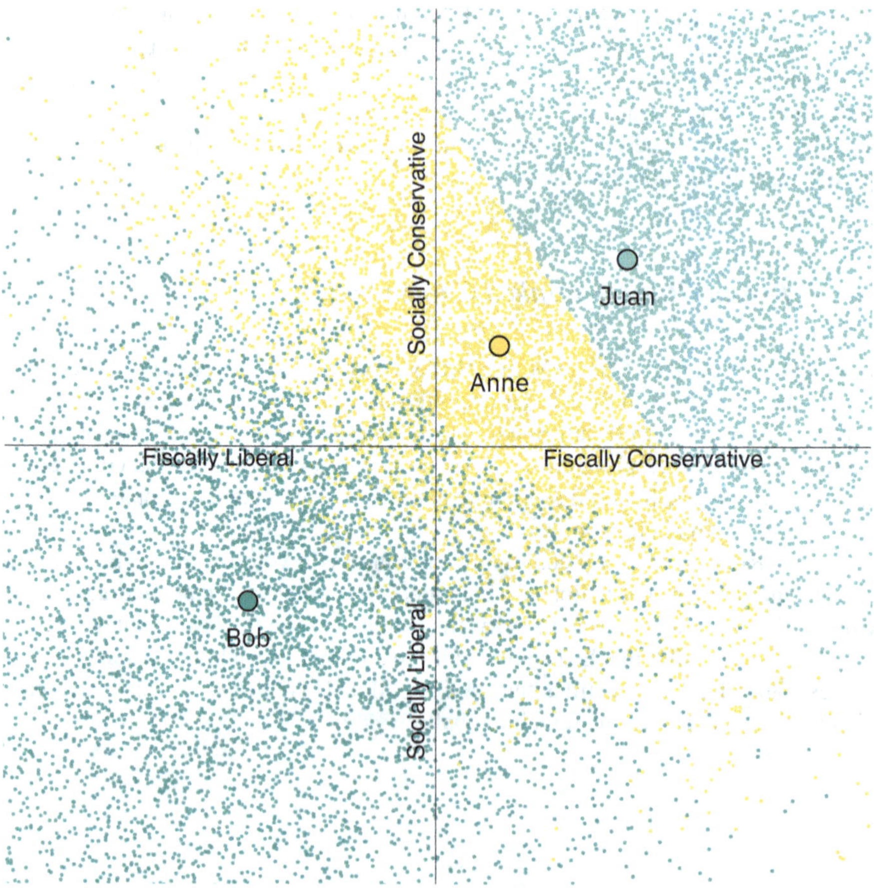

Fig. 2 A simplified example with three candidates

Democratic voters strongly preferred the more moderate Anne to Juan, but their preference was never considered because it was "covered" by their preference for their own party. The Republican voters alone chose which Republican would advance to the final round of Instant Runoff, much like they would have in a primary.

Juan's core voters are members of the Republican Party, and consequently GTO-politics demands that Juan must represent their interests alone. The fact that Democrats strongly preferred Anne was irrelevant. Anne's loss demonstrates the consequences of GTO politics. Her more moderate position representing the entire electorate was a liability and caused her to lose the election. This outcome is the same as the outcome under primaries, Republican-leaning voters chose a Republican in the first round of Instant Runoff, and the candidate motivations are the same.

10.3 Core Voters Under Instant Runoff

Estimates of the number of swing voters vary between 6% and 9% (Smidt 2015; Mayer 2008). These voters prefer the candidate closest to them ideologically, regardless of party. The remaining 91–94% of voters will choose candidates within their party before ranking a candidate from the other party.

Under Instant Runoff, a ballot counts towards the highest ranked candidate still active on that ballot. For voters in one party, their preference for a less divisive candidate from the other party will be "covered" or "hidden" by their preference for their own party. The only way it can be uncovered is if the race comes down to two candidates from the same party.

There are 16 districts (3.7%) in the House of Representatives where the partisan lean is greater than 33%. In those 16 races it is possible that final round of IRV will be contest between two candidates from the same party. In those races—or other races where the minority party fields a particularly weak candidate—voters in the minority party get some say in their representation. It is ironic that having fewer voters would give the minority party greater representation.

In all other circumstances, the set of core voters under Instant Runoff is nearly identical to the core voters under our current election system. Any candidate who attempts to represent the entire electorate risks elimination in the early rounds, when partisan voters on each side determine which candidates survive to the final round.

10.4 Adding More Candidates

Adding more candidates does not change the dynamic. Voters who prefer Democrats will determine which Democrat survives to the final round while voters who prefer Republicans will determine the surviving Republican. Voters on each side will have no say on which candidate from the other party survives to the final round. The GTO

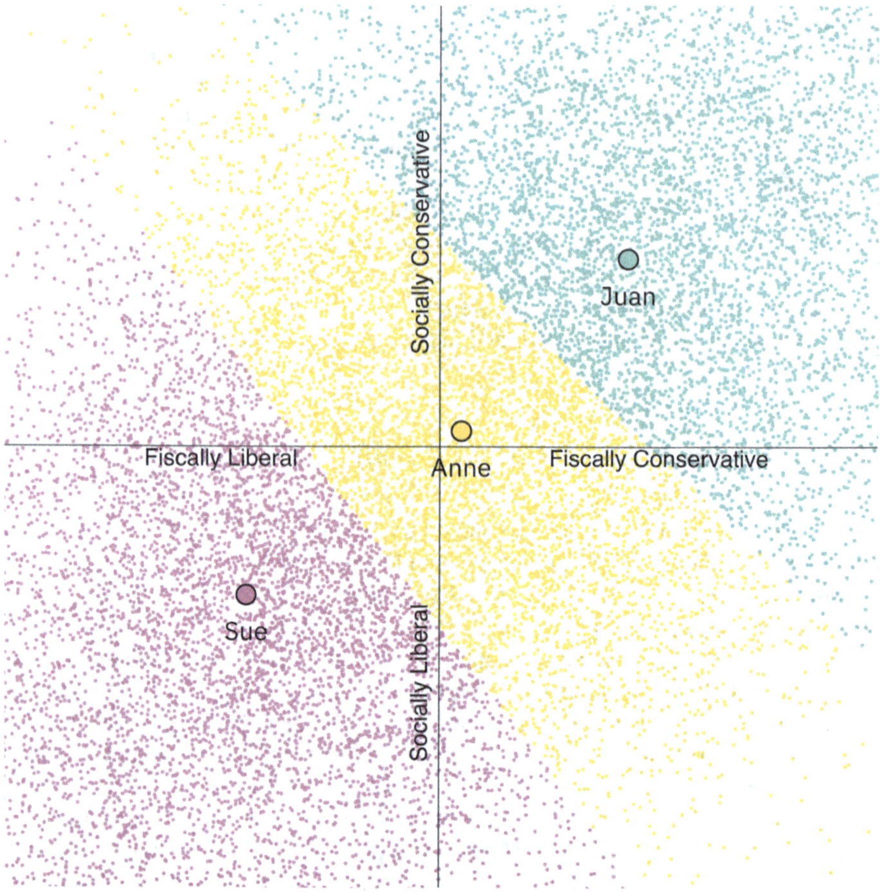

Fig. 3 An example in a balanced district

strategy in such a race is very clear: candidates must make their party's voters happy to survive to the final round of IRV.

10.5 An Example in a Balanced District

For the balanced race in Fig. 3, we start with a candidate (Anne) near the median voter (geometric median when the number of dimensions is greater than one) and a partisan candidate (Sue) who will receive more than 1/3 of the vote. A partisan (Juan) on the opposite side ensures the defeat of the representative candidate and competes with the other partisan for the win.

Proponents of Instant Runoff contend that such a scenario is unlikely. There are numerous academic analyses also say that such a scenario is unlikely, but they are only correct under the assumption that candidates are chosen randomly and do not act strategically. In fact, candidates play GTO politics. Candidates are adept at analyzing the dynamics of elections, and they carefully calculate their ideological positions to maximize their chances of winning under the current system. They will continue to do so under any new system, IRV included.

There *is* something unlikely about this scenario. Because representative candidates cannot win against partisans, it is unlikely that they will run or be able to finance and operate successful campaigns when they do run.

10.6 IRV and Madison

Candidates must serve their core voters to be elected and reelected, regardless of the election process. The question is: Who are those core voters? Like what happens under the current system, under Instant Runoff, a candidate's core voters are the voters in the candidate's party. In a balanced district, this may extend to include enough moderate or swing voters to form a majority. It never includes voters from the opposition party.

Madison's representatives with "enlightened views," who place the public good above the needs of any faction, would never survive to the final, head-to-head contest between two candidates under Instant Runoff, because moderates get squeezed out under Instant Runoff.

11 Strategy and Core Voters Under Consensus Voting

Condorcet consistency, first proposed by the Marquis de Condorcet in 1785, is the condition that, if there is a candidate in an election who beats every other candidate in head-to-head comparisons, then that candidate wins the election. Recent evidence suggests that in large elections, there will be a Condorcet winner at least 99% of the time.

We chose Consensus Voting as a new public name for Condorcet-consistent voting systems. Just as Instant Runoff was chosen to describe the Hare method of voting, Consensus Voting is a more public-friendly way to refer to a Condorcet consistent voting system. Consensus does not mean to imply that all voters get exactly what they want. That is clearly impossible. Consensus means that the electorate prefers one candidate, by majority rule, to any other available candidate. Such a candidate is the Consensus Candidate (the Condorcet Candidate) and the winner under Consensus Voting.

To produce more representative results, voters must express a preference for less divisive candidates within the other party. If the general election has too many candidates, it becomes unlikely that a voter will rank deeply enough to register a preference among candidates from the other party. At the same time, a larger field provides

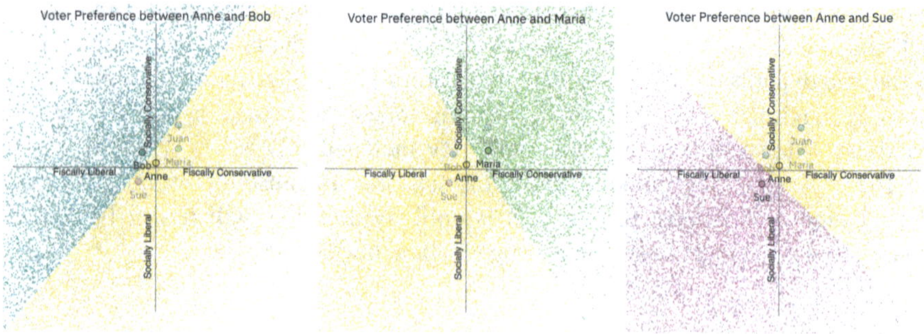

Fig. 4 Consensus voting in a balanced district

more choices for the voters and reduces the importance of the primary, when fewer voters may participate. To balance these competing priorities and manage the complexity of the election, Consensus Voting uses a Top-5 primary to select 5 candidates for the general election, using a simple plurality rule.[1]

11.1 Consensus Voting in a Balanced District

Anne wins this election because she does the best job of balancing the needs of the electorate. Figure 4 shows the outcome in a two-dimensional spatial model of voter preference, but the result is more general than that. The voters prefer Anne to each of the other candidates so therefore Anne is the best representative of the voters.

11.2 Consensus Voting in a Non-Competitive District

The ideal position for each candidate shifts with the median voter (see Fig. 5). Party preference will favor a candidate from the dominant party at the median voter over a candidate from the minority party at the same location. Even though her party dominates the election, Anne needs support from voters from the other party to defeat a candidate to her right. At the same time Anne needs support from voters to her right to defeat a candidate to her left. Anne wins because she satisfies the entire electorate, not just her party's voters.

[1] The argument for a primary that reduces the field to five candidates (for ranked choice IRV) is made by Gehl (forthcoming).

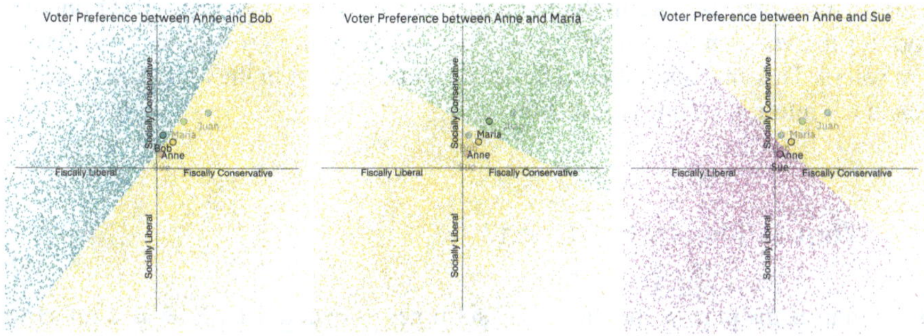

Fig. 5 Consensus voting in a non-competitive district

11.3 Why Consensus Works

What if a single party makes up 70% of the electorate? How does Consensus prevent them from choosing a candidate who ignores or even attacks the minority party? If all members of a faction or party had identical political views and opinions, they would vote as a block and any faction comprising a majority would be able to govern without respecting the rights of the minority, even in a Consensus election process. Fortunately, all political parties represent a spectrum of voters within their party. Though they may coalesce behind whichever candidate a party chooses in a primary or IRV process, some voters would prefer a more moderate candidate while others would prefer a more partisan candidate. When all voters from all parties get to participate in the choice between these two candidates, it can be expected that the more moderate candidate (relative to the given electorate) will prevail. Thus, the guarantee that a candidate who defeats each of the other candidates in a one-on-one comparison will be the winner creates an incentive for candidates to move towards the center of the distribution of the voters in the electorate.

11.4 Consensus Voting and Madison

Candidates need support from different areas of the electorate against different candidates. Every voter plays a role in that support (or lack thereof), depending on the opponent. A successful candidate must balance the needs of the entire electorate to win an election. This makes a candidate's core voters the entire electorate and not just one party's voters. Winning candidates must balance the priorities of a spectrum of voters.

Madison repeatedly cites the need for representatives who govern in the public good instead of the narrow interests of a faction. GTO politics requires that candidates serve exclusively the voters required to elect them; that cannot be changed. These seemingly irreconcilable statements can be combined by making every voter matter, even when they are in the minority. Consensus Voting makes GTO-politics work for the voters by making the entire electorate a part of a winning candidate's core voters. This enables and even forces candidates to act in the public good rather than in the interests of any one faction.

12 What Is This Public Good?

Madison uses the phrase "public good" six times in Federalist 10; he also refers to the "true interest" of the country, the "aggregate interest" of the community, and the "good of the whole". These terms all refer to the same concept, but Madison never defines exactly what it is. So, what is the public good in a democracy? There is no absolute yardstick for correct policy; it cannot be mathematically derived. How do we define the public good?

The most fundamental rule of a democracy is that, given two options, the one preferred by a majority of voters is more likely to be the better choice. The weakness of this is that it applies only to the case of two options. To define the public good, we invert this idea and state that we must not contradict it, if possible. In short, a democracy must seek to avoid violating majority rule.

13 Consensus RCV Rules to Choose Among

A wide variety of Condorcet consistent election rules have been proposed. Which one should Consensus Voting use? They all produce the same result from a given set of ballots, in the 99% or more of large elections in which there is a Condorcet winner. Still, none is perfect. Every voting rule for more than two candidates, the Gibbard-Satterthwaite theorem tells us, will sometimes offer an opportunity for some voters to obtain an outcome they like better by voting insincerely. The main bases for rejecting some of the Condorcet consistent rules are that they produce too many ties, they offer too great a temptation to insincere voting, and that they are too opaque. In the remainder of this section, we discuss the relative merits of four rules that we regard as acceptable.

13.1 Bottom Two Runoff

Bottom Two Runoff is similar to Instant Runoff, but instead of eliminating the candidate with the fewest first place votes, it compares the bottom two candidates, and the candidate listed higher on fewer ballots is eliminated. All choices are used on each ballot, so even if the two candidates being compared are third and fourth on a ballot, that ballot will count as a vote for the candidate ranked third. Because the

Condorcet winner can never be eliminated, the process is Condorcet consistent. Bottom-Two Runoff may be a good option because of its similarity to Instant Runoff. Voters may find it appealing as a small adjustment to a familiar process. Because it has not been as well studied as other systems, we are unsure how susceptible it is to insincere voting.

13.2 Condorcet-Hare

Condorcet-Hare is a family of four rules that share the Hare (and Instant Runoff) practice of eliminating the candidate with the fewest first-choice votes is undertaken only if there is a majority-rule cycle that needs to be broken (Green-Armytage 2011). All four versions of Condorcet-Hare treat a simple cycle among three candidates the same. Condorcet Hare has been well studied and is highly resistant to insincere voting (Green-Armytage et al. 2016). Condorcet-Hare can be described as a simple check that patches the potential problem with Instant Runoff (Hare), that it can fail to elect an available Condorcet winner. It is thus a minor change to an existing election rule that voters are familiar with. The impact on candidate behavior remains profound, as the vast majority of elections (those with Condorcet winners) will be resolved without resorting to Instant Runoff.

13.3 Ranked Pairs

Ranked pairs is a favorite among voting theorists. It takes each result between two candidates as a desideratum with importance equal to the margin of victory. Desiderata are incorporated into the election result sequentially, starting with the one with the greatest importance. If a new desideratum is inconsistent with others already in the result, then it is ignored. The winner is the candidate at the head of the one ranking that remains after all desiderata have been considered.

The principal drawback of Ranked Pairs is its complexity.

13.4 Minimax

Minimax is the rule that if no candidate is undefeated, the candidate whose worst defeat is smallest is the winner. It is simple to understand and to implement, though, unlike Bottom Two Runoff and Condorcet-Hare, it cannot be described as a variation on Instant Runoff. Minimax is somewhat more susceptible than Condorcet-Hare to insincere voting.

For all three-candidate cycles and most four-candidate cycles, Minimax produces the same result as Ranked Pairs. Minimax is quite easy to describe, and four-candidate cycles are extraordinarily rare. Thus, absent considerations of choosing a rule that can be described as amending IRV, Minimax may be the best balance of mathematical rigor and simplicity.

13.5 Summary

The choice of a system for resolving cycles is ultimately a political decision. The most important job of an election rule is to influence candidate behavior, and that can be accomplished with any Condorcet consistent system. Whichever Condorcet consistent system best suits the local conditions is to be preferred over any politically less feasible choice.

14 Conclusion

Elections should select candidates who best embody what voters want. The rules we have been using, as well as the emerging idea of the instant runoff version of ranked choice voting, give us polarization and not what we want, because they make partisanship the path to electoral victory. What voters want is best expressed as the result of Consensus Voting, the selection of the candidate who beats all others in head-to-head comparisons. We should adopt Consensus Voting.

References

Abramowitz A (2008) Don't blame primary voters for polarization. The Forum 5(4). https://doi.org/10.2202/1540-8884.1210

Condorcet, Marie Jean Antoine Nicolas de Caritat, Marquis de (1785) Essai sur l'Application de l'Analyse à la Probabilité des Décisions Rendues à la Pluralité des Voix. Paris

Downs A (1957) An economic theory of democracy

Drutman L (2020) Breaking the two-party doom loop: the case for multiparty democracy in America. Oxford University Press, USA

Drutman LD (2021, July 1) What we know about congressional primaries and congressional primary reform. New America. Retrieved April 8, 2022, from https://www.newamerica.org/political-reform/reports/what-we-know-about-congressional-primaries-and-congressional-primary-reform

Gehl K. The case for the five in final five voting. Constitutional Political Economy, forthcoming

Green-Armytage J (2011) Four Condorcet-Hare hybrid methods for single-winner elections. Voting Matters 29:1–14

Green-Armytage J, Tideman TN, Cosman R (2016) Statistical evaluation of voting rules. Soc Choice Welfare 46(1):183–212

Madison J. Federalist 10

Madison J. Federalist 51

Mayer WG (2008) The swing voter in American politics. Brookings Institution Press

New York Times, 9/19/2012 Transcript of Romney's Speech from Mother Jones Video. https://www.nytimes.com/2012/09/19/us/politics/mitt-romneys-speech-from-mother-jones-video.html

Sides J, Tausanovitch C, Vavreck L, Warshaw C (2018) On the representativeness of primary electorates. Br J Polit Sci 50(2):677–685. https://doi.org/10.1017/s000712341700062x

Smidt CD (2015) Polarization and the decline of the American floating voter. Am J Polit Sci 61(2):365–381. https://doi.org/10.1111/ajps.12218

Robbie Robinette lives in Austin, Texas. He had a career in machine learning and now devotes himself to expanding public awareness of how election rules shape society.

Nicolaus Tideman is a Professor of Economics at Virginia Tech. He received a B.A. from Reed College and a Ph.D. from the University of Chicago. Before moving to Virginia Tech, he was an Assistant Professor of Economics at Harvard University and a Senior Staff Economics at the President's Council of Economic Advisors.

Comprehensive Pluralism, Liberalism, and Religious Liberty

Emily R. Gill

Abstract Divisiveness over the meaning of the free exercise of religion has increased in recent years. Exemption requests and litigation have come not from religious minorities as much as from Christians. First, I explain comprehensive pluralism, a regime that legal scholar Michel Rosenfeld believes would provide a reduction of current tensions. Second, I explain why the current juridical emphasis on equal access and the reaction to it would render comprehensive pluralism unworkable. Finally, I explain why the rise of Christian nationalism renders comprehensive pluralism still more doubtful as a solution. Neither liberty nor democracy are protected when one interpretation of religious values seeks political ascendancy. This challenge merits particular attention at a time when the religious right seeks to realize its own priorities in public policy to the exclusion of other values.

1 Introduction

The twenty-first century has encompassed increasing divisiveness over the meaning of the free exercise of religion guaranteed by the First Amendment. Traditionally, requests for exemptions from generally applicable laws have originated with religious minorities whose freedom to worship or to live out commitments flowing from their beliefs has been stymied. During the last half of the twentieth century, litigation involved individuals seeking military draft exemptions who did not belong to peace churches or who subscribed to ethical beliefs that were areligious. Recently, however, requests and litigation have come from Christians, particular conservative Christians. These include, for example, individuals who refuse to provide goods for same-sex couples' weddings or commitment ceremonies, nonprofit entities that do

E. R. Gill (✉)
Bradley University, Peoria, IL, USA
e-mail: gill@fsmail.bradley.edu

G. A. Babst et al. (eds.), *Liberal Constitutionalism and its Contemporary Challenges*, AMINTAPHIL: The Philosophical Foundations of Law and Justice 12, https://doi.org/10.1007/978-3-031-53602-1_12

not want to work with same-sex couples seeking to foster children, and for-profit entities that decline to cover contraceptives in their health plans that they consider abortifacients. I have argued elsewhere that individuals living their lives should not be held hostage to the religious beliefs of others, most especially if these beliefs and ensuing practices are endorsed or supported by public authority through generous exemptions (Gill 2019). This paper will address and criticize a proposed solution to this problem.

Legal scholar Michel Rosenfeld stipulates that the United States is a regime of institutional secularism. That is, the public sphere is theoretically neutral toward religion, but the government grants exemptions as necessary to allow it to flourish in the private sphere. The expansion of the welfare state, however, has led to greater public activity in and regulation of the traditional private sphere, while religion has been deprivatized and repoliticized as religious individuals and institutions have sought to influence public policy, often successfully. Rosenfeld suggests that instead of secular liberalism, which prioritizes individual rights and disadvantages religion, we should promote what he terms comprehensive pluralism, which places all conceptions of the good, religious and secular, on an equal plane. He hopes that this approach will lead to a decrease in conscience-based conflicts (Rosenfeld 2018).

First, I shall explain why Rosenfeld believes that adhering to his conception of comprehensive pluralism would provide an improvement upon the present impasse. Next, I will take up the equal access justification for greater dissemination of publicly available benefits to religious individuals and institutions. Although its ascendancy has aided religion, at least some religionists discount it because it does not accord to religion a superior place in the polity. Finally, I shall discuss Christian nationalism, suggesting that because its adherents want to restore religion, specifically Christianity, to what they view as its rightful place in the U.S., the appeal of comprehensive pluralism is likely to be narrow to Christian nationalists as well as to many of their detractors. Although many methods for protecting democracy, liberty, and the common good are made in good faith, I believe that Rosenfeld's comprehensive pluralism would not be superior to our current treatment of religion. When some groups within the polity wish to use democracy to instantiate their own values as superior at the expense of those who differ, neither liberty nor the common good are well protected despite efforts at evenhandedness.

It bears mentioning at the outset that some liberal secularists adhere to comprehensive commitments that seem "religious" in nature to others (Lee 2022). Some conservative Christians, for example, regard a strict interpretation of the separation of church and state as a comprehensive commitment imposed upon those who do not share it. Even strict separationists, however, support the legitimacy of religious values in individuals' conduct of their own lives. Many conservative Christians, on the other hand, appear to subscribe to foundationalist integralism, which seeks "a share of political as well as social power; its goal is to give religion a controlling place in public arenas and public law," holding that "because of its truths, religion is the sole carrier of value" (Rosenblum 2000, p. 20). As put by Ann Pellegrini, the establishment of a secular state through the "disestablishment [of religion] … is the structuring condition for free exercise. Otherwise, those who are religiously different or not religious at all may well find their lives not simply less admired and valued than those who belong to the dominant religion; they may find they have diminished legal status" (Pellegrini 2015, p. 255; see also p. 260).

2 Comprehensive Pluralism

Although some classify religion as part of a broader conception of conscience (Nussbaum 2008, pp. 18–25, pp. 52–53; Maclure and Taylor 2011, p. 76), others view religion as the more encompassing term. "What in fact unites … disparate worldviews is a well-established and well-understood semantic practice of using the term 'religion' to signify them *and relevantly analogous beliefs and practices*" (Koppelman 2013, p. 7, emphasis added; see pp. 3–8). Either way, the state may not define religious truth without violating the establishment clause of the First Amendment, but it may not be inattentive to the claims of religion without violating the free exercise clause. Attentiveness may sometimes require religious exemptions, however religion may be defined. On Andrew Koppelman's view, American law maintains neutrality toward religion by treating religion as a good, but without specifying the character of this good. "The state is agnostic about religion, but it is an interested and sympathetic agnosticism" (p. 45; see pp. 42–45; Koppelman 2018, pp. 171–181).

Rosenfeld begins with democratic pluralism, which "prescribes peaceful accommodation of as many diverse and competing conceptions of the good as possible through deployment of majority rule subject to anti-majoritarian exceptions," which will themselves enhance the spread of pluralism (Rosenfeld 2018, p. 59). Liberalism, however, is to him itself a conception of the good, and it inscribes institutional secularism in the Constitution to the disadvantage of religion. Unlike Koppelman, he does not view liberalism as neutral, let alone as sympathetic toward religion. Historically, religion has retreated from the public sphere and has received protection for its beliefs and practices in the private sphere (p. 74). Broader claims of conscience must portray themselves as in some sense religious in order to receive this protection.

Comprehensive pluralism, however, "regards all conceptions of the good that count with adherents within the polity as *ex ante* equal in worth and dignity," mediating among conflicts "with the aim of achieving *ex post* the greatest possible peaceful coexistence among the greatest possible number of competing conceptions of the good" (Rosenfeld 2018, p. 67, italics original; see pp. 66–69). This may be achieved if the proponents of conflicting views each imagine from *within themselves* the conceptions they oppose, deciding in good faith what is negotiable and what is not. In contrast to liberalism, comprehensive pluralism does not privilege individual interests over communal ones. Instead, it grants greater scope to conceptions of the good that operate intra-communally, or within particular communities of conscience, as opposed to those that are intercommunal and affect the larger public as well. Most important, the respect and dignity afforded to secularism and liberalism are no more or less than that afforded to religion.

In many cases, Rosenfeld suggests, outcomes would be similar to those under liberalism, although justifications would be different. Marriage equality, for example, is an easy case as it can be justified either by the individual right to equal liberty (liberalism) or because no conception of the good, religious or secular, deserves priority (pluralism). Religious objectors are supreme only intra-communally. He argues that the grounds of conscientious objectors to military service should either be expanded to all types of conscience, or should be narrowed substantially so that both secular and religious objectors are treated equally. A Catholic physician working in a public hospital should be exempted from performing abortions, but a secular physician in a Catholic hospital should also receive an exemption allowing him/her to perform a legally entitled abortion on a patient whom it would benefit. Under institutional secularism, religion is both privileged and politically disempowered. Under comprehensive pluralism, religious claims are deprivileged compared to secularly based claims of conscience, which are equal to religious ones, while religion is implicitly re-empowered or repoliticized (Rosenfeld 2018, pp. 79–86, pp. 93–95).

This characterization initially appears alarming, but not for Rosenfeld. Under liberalism, religions legitimately seek public policies that protect their own faith communities. The problem is "that certain religions seek to subject the entire population of the polity to normative constraints emanating from their own faith-based imperatives, but not shared by many other religious and secular members of the polity" (p. 77). Under comprehensive pluralism, public policy concerning religion would apply only intra-communally; policy concerning secular ethics would presumably apply only to *its* own conscientious adherents. Rosenfeld asserts that conscience claims, both religious and nonreligious, would not be reduced to the level of ordinary policy claims, as they enjoy priority as long as they accord with the core norms of pluralism. "The priority in question would of course be limited, but only to the extent necessary to guarantee the equal liberties principle or to realize policy objectives that prove to be compelling in relation to the common good of the polity as the community of communities" (p. 94). Presumably both secular and religious arguments would determine the "policy objectives that prove to be compelling."

Many questions occur to the reader, such as possible conflict between claims of conscience and those of policy. Uppermost in my mind is the likely reaction of many religious adherents to the prospect of comprehensive pluralism. On one interpretation, religious conscience claims are only deprivileged in the sense that nonreligious claims are now treated equally. That is, they are leveled up. The current baseline, however, is one where religious claims are considered special. From this perspective, under comprehensive pluralism religion would be leveled down. Religion is treated no better than any other constellation of beliefs. At a time that the claims of religion are increasingly empowered in politics, many religionists will prefer their current special treatment in the private sphere in combination with their new political influence in the public sphere.

3 Equal Access

As we have seen, observers disagree about the meaning of neutrality in the context of the relationship of religion and government. A key difficulty, for example, is that to strict separationists, the government is neutral when it denies financial aid equally to all religious organizations while granting it to secular ones. To accommodationists or advocates of equal treatment, however, when organizations engage in activities that promote the public good such as schools or social services, neutrality means that the government cannot exclude them from generally available benefits based on their religious character. "Equal treatment theory would allow religious individuals and groups to participate fully and equally with their fellow citizens in America's public life, without being forced either to shed or disguise their religious convictions and character" (Esbeck 1998, p. 12; see pp. 12–14).

A classic example of equal access is *Widmar v. Vincent* (454 U.S. 263 [1981]), in which the Supreme Court ruled that because a state university allowed student organizations to meet in unused campus facilities, it must also allow religious student organizations equal access to these facilities. Specifically, because the university had established a limited public forum for student expression, it could not exclude religious expression (Esbeck 1998, pp. 14–15). A recent case touching upon the availability of public benefits with a secular purpose appears in *Trinity Lutheran Church v. Comer* (130 S. Ct. 2012 [2017]). Although Missouri's constitution forbids awarding public funds to churches, the Supreme Court overturned the exclusion of a Lutheran church's learning center because of its religious character from a competitive program using recycled tires to resurface school playgrounds for safety reasons. In another example, although Montana's constitution bars the use of public money for any sectarian purpose, the Supreme Court in *Espinoza v. Montana Department of Revenue* (140 S. Ct. 2246 [2020]) ruled that the exclusion of students in religious schools from eligibility for scholarships financed by a program affording tax credits to donors was unconstitutional, as the denial was based solely on the schools' religious status. This constituted unequal treatment and therefore violated the free exercise clause. Finally, in *Carson v. Makin* (596 U.S. ___ [2022]), the Supreme Court ruled that Maine must finance tuition at religious schools for students whose public school districts do not include secondary schools.

These examples all place religious practice on an equal plane with secular activity. This elevates the status of religion, but it does not treat it as special in any way. Some advocates of religious liberty, however, emphasize the way in which religion is different from any other types of belief or practice. For one scholar, religion is neither simply a species of belief nor a moral attitude, but a distinctive form of human activity oriented toward the transcendent. The ethical obligations of religion, unlike secular ones, are rooted in an agent's ultimate intention of honoring God (Chik 2020). For another, religious liberty is a special right because only religion seeks truth *about* truth (Finnis 2020). Yet another scholar argues that religion should be supported and set apart because it is a *public* good, as well as an aspect of self-definition within the private sphere of social life (Bradley 2020).

From one perspective, the equal treatment of religious and secular claims can be a positive development. In *West Virginia Board of Education v. Barnette* (319 U.S. 624 [1943]), for example, the Supreme Court could have granted a religious exemption to Jehovah's Witness school children protecting them from a forced salute of the American flag while reciting the Pledge of Allegiance. Instead, however, the court simply barred the enforcement of the flag salute, meaning that "all students have a right to refuse a state-compelled affirmation of political loyalty," whether for religious or nonreligious reasons (Lupu and Tuttle 2014, p. 187; see pp. 183–190). Secular claims may have moral force that is equal to that presented by religious claims, and they may simultaneously represent the liberal democratic commitment to free and equal citizenship (Gill 2019, pp. 56–57, pp. 141–142). Courts or legislatures need not determine whether a claim is truly a religious one, whether it is sincere, whether the practice or abstention in question is central to religion, or how these may balance against the state's competing interests (Lupu and Tuttle 2014, pp. 190–205). Both religious and nonreligious activity are protected in domains generally distinguished as outside state control; in other domains, the state can regulate activity whether or not it is religiously motivated or justified (p. 204; see also pp. 207–210; Eisgruber and Sager 2007, p. 6, pp. 8–14, pp. 54–56, p. 104).

Similar issues arise in *Church of the Lukumi Babalu Aye v. City of Hialeah* (508 U.S. 510 [1993]). Here the Supreme Court struck down a Hialeah ordinance forbidding the killing of animals in a ritual not primarily for consumption, which thereby forbade this Santeria church from the ritual sacrifice of animals that are then cooked and eaten. The court ruled that Hialeah was burdening a permitted practice—killing animals—because of its religious nature. It did not accord a benefit or exemption because the practice was religious, but simply treated Santeria adherents like others who kill and eat animals for secular reasons. The deciding factor was the city's hostility toward Santeria, as only the killing of animals for religious reasons was prohibited (Gill 2019, p. 42, p. 59). As put by Kent Greenawalt, "The free exercise clause … bars the government from prohibiting any activity *because* it is religious; the law cannot forbid an activity that is part of religious practice and leave unregulated identical or closely similar activities that are not religious" (Greenawalt 2012, p. 49, emphasis original). In *Barnette*, the protected activity was an abstention; in *Lukumi*, it was a practice. In both cases, however, the court's reasoning left religious and secular activity on the same plane. Religious claims were protected by treatment similar to that for secular claims. From this perspective, they should be textbook examples of equal access.

From a different perspective, however, equal access arguments disrespect the claims of religion, or more specifically, the cultural value of Christianity in the United States. Viewing religion—or in this case Christianity—as irrelevant is not neutral. "Indeed, in a society in which Christianity has had such overwhelming predominance, insisting on equality is tantamount to squelching Christianity" and its foundational role in American law and politics (DeGirolami 2020, p. 398; see pp. 413–419). More specifically, a number of religionists argue that religious justifications should not have to play second fiddle to secular ones.

Gerard Bradley, for example, deplores the fact that in *Barnette*, the Supreme Court on his view secularized our understanding of the Constitution. Instead of granting a religious exemption from saluting the flag to the Jehovah's Witness children involved, it released petitioners more generally from any endorsement of orthodoxy. Orthodoxy, he maintains, is a matter of mere opinion, convention, or stipulation, not of truth. Similarly, draft exemption cases such as *United States v. Seeger* (518 U.S. 515 [1965]) rendered religious claims as "opaque reports of someone's self-understanding" (Bradley 2020, p. 449; see pp. 433–450). To Bradley, these kinds of decisions represent moral agnosticism rather than moral truth. In sum, although he agrees with *Barnette*, he believes that it should have been decided on different grounds.

Similarly, Vincent Phillip Muñoz questions the nonreligious grounds for the Supreme Court's decision in *Lukumi*. Although he believes in the natural right to the free exercise of religion, he dislikes what he terms modern moral autonomy exemptionism. When the government rules on exemptions, it is taking authoritative notice of religion instead of remaining neutral toward or "noncognizant" of religion, and this increases its power. The right to disregard laws impeding one's religious obligations is not a constitutional right to an exemption. In *Lukumi*, the court ruled that the Hialeah ordinance was not neutral when it forbade a religious practice but not similar secular ones, absent a narrowly tailored prohibition designed to advance a compelling interest. For Muñoz, the outcome was not problematic, but it was the fact that the court balanced the natural right to the free exercise of religion against possibly competing state interests, instead of simply striking down the ordinance as a violation of a natural right outside the government's jurisdiction. In the latter case, Santeria would not have received an exemption, but would simply have regained exclusive sovereignty over its adherents' fulfillment of their religious obligations (Muñoz 2020, pp. 302–306). The court properly removed a burden on the permitted practice of killing and eating animals, rather than according a benefit to Santeria because of the practice's religious nature. But to Muñoz, the court should have based its decision on the natural right to the free exercise of religion.

These commentators and others are wary of arguments from equal access because these are framed in secular terms. Marc DeGirolami, for example, objects to the equal treatment rationale that grounded the Supreme Court's decision in *Trinity Lutheran*, mentioned above. "True, the church won the case, but its victory depended on the fact that Christian belief and exercise was [*sic*] completely irrelevant to its claim" for funding for playground resurfacing (DeGirolami 2020, p. 425; see pp. 419–427). Perhaps it is religion's and Christianity's loss of preeminence among an increasing diversity of belief systems that engenders this thought process. Yet the legal recognition of this diversity no more renders Christianity or religion in general irrelevant or obnoxious, in DeGirolami's terms (pp. 413–419), than the awarding of civil rights to people of color rendered white people irrelevant or obnoxious—although some white Christian nationalists would disagree. Under equal access, moreover, religious claims have been successful where they would have failed under the establishment clause of the First Amendment with strict separation. If religion is special, would it not be a positive development that they advance under equal access, even if this justification is the wrong one for some religious advocates?

There is a seldom-noticed downside to the equal access regime. Some court decisions have expanded generally available benefits to religious institutions or individuals on the basis of equal access to publicly funded benefits, as we have seen, while others have relied on the free speech clause. In *Rosenberger v. Rector of the University of Virginia* (115 S. Ct. 2510 [1995]), the Supreme Court ruled that because the university had funded other publications issued by private student groups, by refusing to fund a student religious group's publication it had engaged in viewpoint discrimination. Justice David Souter observed, however, that by addressing the issue as a free speech case despite the publication's evangelical message, the court had ignored the establishment clause, thereby detracting from the special position of religion under the Constitution. "The *Rosenberger* decision denies the power of religion by approving state subsidization for the preaching of the gospel. By *not denying* religion its place in the marketplace of ideas, the Court denies the special place held by religion in our constitutional framework" (Davis 1998, p. 141; emphasis added; see pp. 137–142).

Ironically, here Derek Davis is implying that to protect the special status of religion, in some circumstances we must disadvantage rather than facilitate religious practice. Underlying the equal access principle as well as the free speech defense is the free exercise clause. But under this rubric, "It is difficult to see what jurisdiction, if any, would remain to the establishment clause other than forbidding an official establishment of a government-sponsored religion, or the express preference of one religion over another" (Davis 1998, p. 146). Vigorous application of the establishment clause can dampen the free exercise of religion, but the reverse is also true. More specifically, "If equal treatment prevails, one's religious beliefs would be protected equally and at the same level as the right to attend a particular university, live in a certain neighborhood, or express a particular political opinion. In short, one's religious faith would be on a par with every other worldview and life belief" (p. 154; see pp. 145–157), a situation that Rosenfeld advocates but that a great many religionists would abhor.

Equal access then means that religious interests receive equal treatment under the establishment clause—but because courts *ignore* troubling establishment issues. When this is linked with special protections in free exercise cases, the combination does not promote equality, but instead "compound[s] the advantages already enjoyed by the religious viewpoints that are most widely shared and most politically potent in the United States" (Smith 1998, p. 183). Alternatively, by deciding *Rosenberger* as a free speech case, "there is no stopping point to support religion other than that such support is also available to non-religious causes" (Joppke 2015, p. 119; see pp. 118–120). Put differently, for religious interests equal treatment becomes a majoritarian cudgel against with wider society, deployed to enshrine its dominance.

According to Rosenfeld's comprehensive pluralism, secular conscience claims are leveled up and are on a par with religious ones. Under equal access, religious claims are leveled up to match the previous standing reserved to secular ones. Many religionists, as we have seen, want to preserve the superior status of religion.

Comprehensive pluralism would deny them this status. Equal access seems to constitute an improvement in outcomes, but does so only by denying religion's special status. Ultimately, many religionists desire not only equal access concerning particular claims but also political superiority in general.

4 The Lure of Christian Nationalism

Rosenfeld, as we have seen, objects that under liberalism, some religionists seek not only to protect the interests of their own faith communities, but also "seek to subject the entire population of the polity to normative constraints emanating from their own faith-based imperatives, but not shared by many other religious and secular members of the polity" (Rosenfeld 2018, p. 77). His comprehensive pluralism, he believes, would solve this problem by granting to religionists greater scope to apply and enforce their convictions within their own communities, but not intercommunally or across those borders to the larger public. I have thus far argued that under equal access, religionists have already won the right to partake of many available public benefits for their own communities that were previously foreclosed to them, but that some are dissatisfied that the justification for these victories has not been based upon the special status of religion. Here I shall argue that whether under liberalism or under comprehensive pluralism, some religionists in the twenty-first century will aim at nothing less than political superiority.

As argued by Zoë Robinson, religious liberty jurisprudence in the United States has historically reflected constitutional majoritarianism except for a period between 1960 and 1979. During this time, the Supreme Court removed some burdens under the free exercise clause and removed a number of benefits, such as prayers in public schools, under the establishment clause. Subsequently, the court generally limited the success of religious claims under the free exercise clause but broadened what was allowed under the establishment clause. Since 2005, religious decisions have been characterized by the rise of religious institutionalism or deference to the claims of religious institutions, often at the expense of individuals (*Hosanna-Tabor Evangelical Lutheran Church and School v. EEOC*, 565 U.S. 171 [2012]; *Burwell v. Hobby Lobby Stores*, 134 S. Ct. 275 [2014]; *Trinity Lutheran Church v. Comer*, 137 S. Ct. 2012 [2017]). Religious institutions have acquired a constitutional right to benefits that would previously violated the establishment clause. "Taken together, the contemporary establishment clause and free exercise clause cases indicate a model of religious liberty that reflects an asymmetrical form of unitary separationism, whereby religious institutions can avail themselves of the Constitution's protections in order to ensure that general law imposes no burdens, yet provides equal benefits" (Robinson 2020, p. 247; see also pp. 219–224). Altogether, these interpretations have tended to privilege the majority—which traditionally has been not only religious, but Christian. To put this differently, under equal access religious groups receive the same benefits as secular organizations, but also receive the additional benefit of exemptions from generally applicable laws for which secular entities are ineligible (Gill 2019, pp. 30–31; see also p. 7, pp. 21–22, pp. 69–73).

Although a great many religious institutionalists are not Christian nationalists, much current jurisprudence serendipitously supports the latter's desires for political supremacy. Powerful segments of the conservative religious community promote not pluralism, but rather a particular interpretation of Christianity rooted in a biblical worldview. This Christian nationalism "purports to derive its legitimacy from its claim to represent a specific identity unique to and representative of the American nation" (Stewart 2019, p. 5; see pp. 3–11). It is a political movement, not simply a social or cultural one. It treats Bible study as political advocacy, arguing that the bible mandates adherence to right-wing policy positions on deregulation, private property, flat-rate taxation, social welfare programs, male supremacy, and illegal immigration (pp. 48–51). It treats history not as something to be studied, but instead to be interpreted as a means to its own ends (p. 139). It identifies pastors and congregants who will vote on the basis of biblical values to the extent that it is political beliefs, not religious ones, that signify belonging. To put this differently, Christian nationalists prioritize Christian culture over political liberty, and Christian power over Christian principle (Miller 2022, pp. 77–86).

Many Christian nationalist principles reflect the influence of Rousas Rushdoony, born in 1916, whose Armenian immigrant family barely escaped the Armenian genocide. He believed that Christian Armenian culture was lost because Armenians were a non-Christian minority. For him, there could be no neutral ground. Christians needed to redeem the authentically Christian nation that he believed the Constitution was designed for from the godless humanism that was overtaking it. Christian schools, for example, must gain independence from what many conservatives call government schools, an agenda now being advanced through tax-supported vouchers to be used at private schools and by introducing Christian principles into lightly regulated charter schools (Stewart 2019, pp. 185–186, pp. 193–208, pp. 218–219, pp. 227–233). "Liberal education," lamented Rushdoony, "is inevitably pluralistic" (Stewart 2019, p. 118; see pp. 102–120). Christians need to take back education, law, and civil government to reconstruct a Bible-based order, according to influential conservative thinker Gary North, "which finally denies religious liberty to the enemies of God" (p. 119). This sort of thinking is the basis of Christian Reconstructionism (pp. 102–105).

To this end, conservative Christians have introduced religious freedom bills into state legislatures, aimed at areas such a contraceptive and abortion access and freedom to discriminate against disfavored groups such as LGBT individuals (Stewart 2019, pp. 152–168). According to Christian nationalists, this effort will return us to a time revered by dominionists, or those who believe "that right-thinking Christians should assume power in all spheres of life" (p. 123; see also pp. 123–125, pp. 127–128). Legal advocacy groups and their allies contend that their intention is only to defend free speech and persecuted Christians. For Katherine Stewart, however, the goal seems to be to allow their version of Christianity, and their understanding of the Bible, to shape law and government" (p. 215), resulting in "the broader privileging of conservative Christianity in America" (p. 211; see also pp. 234–235). More broadly, the rhetoric of Christian nationalism is a form of jeremiad, a lament about how a people has departed from its founding principles and/or future promise. To this end, "All jeremiads subdivide their respective communities into those deemed faithful to the founders' examples and those apostates who have squandered national promise" (Murphy 2009, p. 120; see pp. 109–124; Hickel and Murphy 2022). The Christian nationalist jeremiad, however, does not rely on exhortation, but seeks to access to the levers of political power to the exclusion of all others.

The views of some observers who are not Christian nationalists coincide with the latter's goals but for different reasons. Some libertarians and others who are politically conservative desire less government in many areas of public life. Legal scholar Michael McConnell, for example, supports the privatization of public education because public education is *not* pluralistic (McConnell 2002, pp. 105–106). Citizens of a liberal, pluralistic society hold a diversity of reasonable but conflicting views about education. Just as government does not prefer some conceptions of the good, religious or nonreligious, over others, it should not espouse any particular educational philosophy (p. 88). "It is time to discard the notion that democratic control over education is *in principle* the form best suited to a liberal, pluralistic society. It is the public school establishment—not educational choice—that is inconsistent with disestablishmentarian liberal values" (p. 89, emphasis original; see also pp. 100–104, pp. 122–133). Why should majoritarian preferences determine educational aims? Whatever one's view of educational disestablishment, Christian nationalists, however, are using it to inculcate Christian principles across the board. Giving one interpretation of religious values a controlling place in the public arena protects neither liberty nor democracy.

Although not Christian nationalists, some public servants have also reinterpreted religious liberty to instantiate their own values. In 2019, for example, former Secretary of State Mike Pompeo, an evangelical Christian, created a Commission on Unalienable Rights "to provide a new vision for human rights policy that would more closely align with the 'nation's founding principles and uphold religious freedom as America's most fundamental value." Supporters deplored the seeming current departure "from our nation's founding principles of natural law and natural rights." When the Commission's report was released in 2020, Pompeo criticized the *New York Times*'s 1619 Project, based on scholarly reexaminations of the legacy of slavery, as "a dark vision of America's birth" and a "disturbed reading of our history" (Verma 2020b). Former agency officials and human rights scholars have criticized the elevation of religious liberty as in conflict with the United States's longstanding policy that all rights are created equal.

Protecting religious freedom over other rights allows these other rights to be upheld only insofar as they coincide with the religious beliefs of those in a position to define and enforce their own interpretations of religious freedom. Various religions, as well as groups and individuals within the same religious community, vary in their interpretations of their own commitments. Some of Pompeo's panel members were religious conservatives opposing abortion and marriage equality. Other nations that follow this lead use religious reasons to deny access to reproductive health services or to persecute LGBT individuals and same-sex couples. Past diplomatic efforts by the United States and others to promote women's rights in Iran and Saudi Arabia and to protest the persecution of the Uighur minority in China may come to naught. A former Obama administration official opined that a hierarchy of rights may bolster repressive governments to say, "We are no different from you. You have your priorities; we have ours. Now butt out" (Verma 2020a; see also Verma 2020b, c).

5 Conclusion

In sum, today's political climate is such that too many religionists, especially Christians, desire a great deal more than equal access. Rosenfeld's comprehensive pluralism might work out differently in some alternative context. Now, however, religious conceptions of the good might well swamp and obliterate nonreligious ones under this rubric. "As a moral tool that imposes what 'the good life' is, conscientious objection [or equal access] framed as a reasonable accommodation might well be the Trojan horse of ultra-conservative religious groups attempting to regain … legal ground" (Bribosia and Rorive 2018, p. 411). Comprehensive pluralism would afford even more public power to conservative religionists as religion is politicized. It represents a conscientious effort to place both religious and secular conscientious beliefs on an equal footing. But it would inevitably accelerate the influence of conservative Christians and Christian nationalists at the expense of the separation of religion and state that is at the core of liberal constitutionalism.

References

Bradley GV (2020) The challenge ahead: reconnecting religion, reason, and truth. In: Breidenbach MD, Anderson O (eds) The Cambridge companion to the first amendment and religious liberty. Cambridge University Press, Cambridge and New York, pp 428–456

Bribosia E, Rorive I (2018) Seeking to square the circle: a sustainable conscientious objection in reproductive health care. In: Mancini S, Rosenfeld M (eds) The conscience wars: rethinking the balance between religion, identity, and equality. Cambridge University Press, New York and Cambridge, pp 392–413

Burwell v. Hobby Lobby Stores 134 S. Ct. 2751 (2014)

Carson v. Makin 576 U.S. ___ (2022)

Chik JT (2020) The philosophical meaning of religious exercise. In: Breidenbach MD, Anderson O (eds) The Cambridge companion to the first amendment and religious liberty. Cambridge University Press, Cambridge and New York, pp 45–73

Church of the Lukumi Babalu Aye v. City of Hialeah. 508 U.S. 520 (1993)

Davis DH (1998) Equal treatment: a Christian separationist perspective. In: Monsma CV, Soper CJ (eds) Equal treatment of religion in a pluralistic society. William B. Eerdmans, Grand Rapids, pp 136–115

DeGirolami MO (2020) The two separations. In: Breidenbach MD, Anderson O (eds) The Cambridge companion to the first amendment and religious liberty. Cambridge University Press, Cambridge and New York, pp 396–427

Eisgruber CL, Sager LG (2007) Religious freedom and the constitution. Harvard University Press, Cambridge

Esbeck CH (1998) Equal treatment: its constitutional status. In: Monsma SV, Soper CJ (eds) Equal treatment of religion in a pluralistic society. William B. Eerdmans, Grand Rapids, pp 101–135

Espinoza v. Montana Department of Revenue. 140 S. Ct. 2246 (2020)

Finnis J (2020) Freedom of religion: special, valuable, and qualified. In: Breidenbach MD, Anderson O (eds) The Cambridge companion to the first amendment and religious liberty. Cambridge University Press, Cambridge and New York, pp 74–97

Gill ER (2019) Free exercise of religion in the liberal polity: conflicting interpretations. Palgrave Macmillan, Cham

Greenawalt K (2012) Coercion and religious exercise. In: Bradley GV (ed) Challenges to religious liberty in the twenty-first century. Cambridge University Press, New York, pp 49–70

Hickel FR Jr, Murphy AR (2022) Making America exceptional again: Donald Trump's traditionalist jeremiad, civil religion, and the politics of resentment. Polit Relig 15(2):247–269

Hosanna-Tabor Evangelical Lutheran Church and School v. EEOC. 565 U.S. 171(2012)

Joppke C (2015) The secular state under siege: religion and politics in Europe and America. Polity Press, Malden

Koppelman A (2013) Defending American religious neutrality. Harvard University Press, Cambridge

Koppelman A (2018) Neutrality and the religion analogy. In: Vallier K, Weber M (eds) Religious exemptions. Oxford University Press, New York, pp 9–20

Lee WC (2022) Comment offered at the 2022 biennial meeting of Amintaphil, Winter Park, FL, October 6–8

Lupu IC, Tuttle RW (2014) Secular government, religious people. William B. Eerdmans, Grand Rapids

Maclure J, Taylor C (2011) Secularism and freedom of conscience. Harvard University Press, Cambridge

McConnell MW (2002) Education disestablishment: why democratic values are ill-served by democratic control of schooling. In: Macedo S, Tamir Y (eds) Moral and political education (nomos 43). New York University Press, New York, pp 87–146

Miller PD (2022) The religion of American greatness: what's wrong with Christian nationalism. InterVarsity Press Academic, Downers Grove

Muñoz VP (2020) Two concepts of religious liberty: the natural rights and moral autonomy approaches to the free exercise of religion. In: Breidenbach MD, Anderson O (eds) The Cambridge companion to the first amendment and religious liberty. Cambridge University Press, Cambridge and New York, pp 276–306

Murphy AR (2009) Prodigal nation: moral decline and divine punishment from New England to 9/11. Oxford University Press, New York

Nussbaum MC (2008) Liberty of conscience: in defense of America's tradition of religious equality. Basic Books, New York

Pellegrini A (2015) *Everson*'s children. In: Sullivan WF, Hurd ES, Mahmood S, Danchin PG (eds) Politics of religious freedom. University of Chicago Press, Chicago, pp 253–261

Robinson Z (2020) The first amendment religion clauses in the United States supreme court. In: Breidenbach MD, Anderson O (eds) The Cambridge companion to the first amendment and religious liberty. Cambridge University Press, Cambridge and New York, pp 219–248

Rosenberger v. Rector of the University of Virginia, 115 S. Ct. 2510 (1995)

Rosenblum NL (2000) Introduction: pluralism, integralism, and political theories of religious accommodation. In: Rosenblum NL (ed) Obligations of citizenship and demands of faith: religious accommodation in pluralist democracies. Princeton University Press, Princeton, pp 3–31

Rosenfeld M (2018) The conscience wars in historical and philosophical perspective: the clash between religious absolutes and democratic pluralism. In: Mancini S, Rosenfeld M (eds) The conscience wars: rethinking the balance between religion, identity, and equality. Cambridge University Press, Cambridge and New York, pp 58–101

Smith RM (1998) "Equal" treatment? a liberal separationist view. In: Monsma SV, Soper CJ (eds) Equal treatment of religion in a pluralist society. William B. Eerdmans, Grand Rapids, pp 179–199

Stewart K (2019) The power worshippers: inside the dangerous rise of religious nationalism. Bloomsbury Publishing, New York

Trinity Lutheran Church v. Comer, 137 S. Ct. 2012 (2017)

Verma P (2020a) Pompeo panel threatens human rights, critics say. In: New York Times. June 24, p A18

Verma P (2020b) Pompeo says human rights must reflect religion's role. In: New York Times. July 17, p A19

Verma P (2020c) Allies skeptical of U.S. push to redefine human rights. In: New York Times. September 23, p A9

West Virginia Board of Education v. Barnette, 319 U.S. 624 (1943)

Widmar v. Vincent, 454 U.S. 263 (1981)

Emily R. Gill is Caterpillar Professor of Political Science Emerita at Bradley University, where she taught for 43 years, retiring in 2015. Her four books include *Becoming Free: Autonomy and Diversity in the Liberal Polity* (Kansas 2001); *Moral Argument, Religion, and Same-Sex Marriage: Advancing the Public Good*, co-edited with Gordon A. Babst and Jason Pierceson (Lexington 2009); *An Argument for Same-Sex Marriage: Religious Freedom, Sexual Freedom, and Public Expressions of Civic Equality* (Georgetown 2012); and *Free Exercise of Religion in the Liberal Polity: Conflicting Interpretations* (Palgrave Macmillan, 2019). She is a normative political theorist with interests in religion and politics, LGBT rights, and diversity in general.